31 Days Before Your
CCNA Security
Exam

A Day-By-Day Review Guide for the
IINS 210-260 Certification Exam

Patrick Gargano

Cisco Press • 800 East 96th Street • Indianapolis, Indiana 46240 USA

31 Days Before Your CCNA Security Exam

Patrick Gargano

Copyright © 2016 Cisco Systems, Inc.

Published by:
Cisco Press
800 East 96th Street
Indianapolis, IN 46240 USA

Printed in the United States of America

Library of Congress Control Number: 2016936752

ISBN-13: 978-1-58720-578-1

ISBN-10: 1-58720-578-5

Warning and Disclaimer

This book is designed to provide information about exam topics for the Cisco Certified Network Associate Security (CCNA Security) certification exam. Every effort has been made to make this book as complete and as accurate as possible, but no warranty or fitness is implied.

The information is provided on an "as is" basis. The authors, Cisco Press, and Cisco Systems, Inc. shall have neither liability nor responsibility to any person or entity with respect to any loss or damages arising from the information contained in this book or from the use of the discs or programs that may accompany it.

The opinions expressed in this book belong to the author and are not necessarily those of Cisco Systems, Inc.

Trademark Acknowledgments

All terms mentioned in this book that are known to be trademarks or service marks have been appropriately capitalized. Cisco Press or Cisco Systems, Inc., cannot attest to the accuracy of this information. Use of a term in this book should not be regarded as affecting the validity of any trademark or service mark.

Special Sales

For information about buying this title in bulk quantities, or for special sales opportunities (which may include electronic versions; custom cover designs; and content particular to your business, training goals, marketing focus, or branding interests), please contact our corporate sales department at corpsales@pearsoned.com or (800) 382-3419.

For government sales inquiries, please contact governmentsales@pearsoned.com.

For questions about sales outside the U.S., please contact intlcs@pearson.com.

Feedback Information

At Cisco Press, our goal is to create in-depth technical books of the highest quality and value. Each book is crafted with care and precision, undergoing rigorous development that involves the unique expertise of members from the professional technical community.

Readers' feedback is a natural continuation of this process. If you have any comments regarding how we could improve the quality of this book, or otherwise alter it to better suit your needs, you can contact us through email at feedback@ciscopress.com. Please make sure to include the book title and ISBN in your message.

We greatly appreciate your assistance.

Business Operation Manager, Cisco Press	Jan Cornelssen
Executive Editor	Mary Beth Ray
Managing Editor	Sandra Schroeder
Development Editor	Ellie Bru
Senior Project Editor	Tonya Simpson
Copy Editor	Bill McManus
Technical Editor	John Stuppi
Editorial Assistant	Vanessa Evans
Cover Designer	Chuti Prasertsith
Composition	Bumpy Design
Indexer	Ken Johnson
Proofreader	The Wordsmithery LLC

Trademark Acknowledgments

All terms mentioned in this book that are known to be trademarks or service marks have been appropriately capitalized. Cisco Press or Cisco Systems, Inc. cannot attest to the accuracy of this information. Use of a term in this book should not be regarded as affecting the validity of any trademark or service mark.

About the Author

Patrick Gargano has been an educator since 1996 and a Cisco Networking Academy Instructor since 2000. He currently heads the Networking Academy program at Collège La Cité in Ottawa, Canada, where he teaches CCNA/CCNP-level courses. Patrick has twice led the Cisco Networking Academy student Dream Team deploying the wired and wireless networks supporting the U.S. Cisco Live conferences. In 2014 he co-authored *CCNP Routing and Switching Portable Command Guide*. Recognitions of his teaching include prizes from Collège La Cité for innovation and excellence and from the Ontario Association of Certified Engineering Technicians and Technologists for excellence in technology education. Previously, Patrick was a Cisco Networking Academy instructor at Cégep de l'Outaouais (Gatineau, Canada) and Louis-Riel High School (Ottawa, Canada) and a Cisco instructor (CCSI) for Fast Lane UK (London). His certifications include CCNA (R&S), CCNA Wireless, CCNA Security, and CCNP (R&S). He holds Bachelor of Education and Bachelor of Arts degrees from the University of Ottawa. Find him on Twitter @PatrickGargano.

About the Technical Reviewer

John Stuppi, CCIE No. 11154 (Security), is a technical leader in the Cisco Security Solutions (CSS) organization at Cisco, where he consults Cisco customers on protecting their network against existing and emerging cybersecurity threats. In this role, John is responsible for providing effective techniques using Cisco product capabilities to provide identification and mitigation solutions for Cisco customers who are concerned with current or expected security threats to their network environments. Current projects include helping customers leverage DNS and NetFlow data to identify and subsequently mitigate network-based threats. John has presented multiple times on various network security topics at Cisco Live, Black Hat, and other customer-facing cybersecurity conferences. In addition, John contributes to the Cisco Security Portal through the publication of white papers, security blog posts, and cyber risk report articles. He is also the co-author of *CCNA Security 210-260 Official Cert Guide* with Omar Santos. Before joining Cisco, John worked as a network engineer for JPMorgan and then as a network security engineer at Time, Inc. John is also a CISSP (No. 25525) and holds an Information Systems Security (INFOSEC) professional certification. In addition, John has a BSEE from Lehigh University and an MBA from Rutgers University. John lives in Ocean Township, New Jersey (a.k.a. the "Jersey Shore") with his wife, two kids, and dog.

Dedications

To my wife Kathryn, who is always happy to explain that when in doubt, "that" is always better than "which," and to our son Samuel who, at age 7, already knows that (not which) Mummy is usually right but Daddy is usually more fun.

To my father, who can't read this.

To my mother, who has devoted everything to our family.

To Albert, who has endured with courage.

Acknowledgments

My first thank-you's have to go to Mary Beth Ray for suggesting that I write this book, and to Scott Empson and Hans Roth for making my first Cisco Press project such a thoroughly enjoyable collaboration that I was happy to accept her offer. Mary Beth is a remarkable executive editor, but then everyone at Cisco Press has been fantastic to work with: Ellie Bru, the development editor, has kept the SS Gargano on an even keel, and Tonya Simpson, the project editor, has ensured that everything is shipshape, while Bill McManus, the copy editor, has kept the good ship from sinking under an avalanche of mixed metaphors and grammatical missteps. I confess that I was a bit intimidated when I found out John Stuppi would be the technical editor, because he co-wrote one of my primary sources, the Cisco Press *CCNA Security 210-260 Official Cert Guide*, but in addition to being a true authority, he was a pleasure to work with. Allan Johnson, who initiated the 31 Days series, was my trusty guide on this, and Troy McMillan, who produced the fantastic material used in the Digital Study Guide version of the book, deserves sincere thanks as well.

Alongside the Cisco Press team, I want to offer my sincere gratitude to my colleagues at La Cité, especially Georges Absi, who has been generous with advice, moral support, and his wife's authentic tabbouleh.

My past, present, and future students at La Cité are the inspiration for this book. I had them in mind with every word that I wrote, and if I've produced something that they'll find useful and easy to understand, then I've met my loftiest goal.

Contents at a Glance

Contents

Command Syntax Conventions

The conventions used to present command syntax in this book are the same conventions used in the IOS Command Reference. The Command Reference describes these conventions as follows:

- **Boldface** indicates commands and keywords that are entered literally as shown. In actual configuration examples and output (not general command syntax), boldface indicates commands that are manually input by the user (such as a show command).

- *Italic* indicates arguments for which you supply actual values.

- Vertical bars (|) separate alternative, mutually exclusive elements.

- Square brackets ([ ]) indicate an optional element.

- Braces ({ }) indicate a required choice.

- Braces within brackets ([{ }]) indicate a required choice within an optional element.

Introduction

If you're reading this Introduction, you've probably already spent a considerable amount of time and energy pursuing your CCNA Security certification. Regardless of how you got to this point in your travels through your networking studies, *31 Days Before Your CCNA Security Exam* most likely represents the last leg of your journey on your way to the destination: to become CCNA Security certified.

However, if you happen to be reading this book at the beginning of your studies, then this book provides you with an excellent overview of the material you must now spend a great deal of time studying and practicing. But, I must warn you: Unless you are extremely well-versed in network security technologies and have considerable experience as a network technician or administrator, this book will not serve you well as the sole resource for CCNA Security exam preparation. I know this first hand. I recently took the CCNA Security exam and was impressed with both the breadth and depth of knowledge required to pass. I have been teaching, writing about, and implementing networks for almost two decades. And yet, there was a moment during the CCNA Security exam where I thought, "Wow, this is really a tough exam!"

You see, Cisco states that for the CCNA Security exam, you must "demonstrates the skills required to develop a security infrastructure, recognize threats and vulnerabilities to networks, and mitigate security threats." You simply cannot just study this content. You must practice it. Although I have a solid understanding of network security concepts and technologies, I also have extensive experience implementing and troubleshooting network security. That's why I was able to successfully pass the exam. There really is no other way to correctly answer the many scenario-based questions a candidate will receive during the exam than to have experienced the same or similar scenario in the real world or a lab simulation.

Now that I've sufficiently challenged you, let me spend some time discussing my recommendations for study resources.

Study Resources

Cisco Press offers an abundance of network security books and resources to serve you well as you learn how to install, troubleshoot, and monitor network devices to maintain the integrity, confidentiality, and availability of data and devices. Most of the resources can be purchased in book form or as eBooks for your tablet reader or mobile device by visiting www.ciscopress.com.

Safari Books Online

All the resources I reference in the book are available with a subscription to Safari Books Online (https://www.safaribooksonline.com). If you don't have an account, you can try it free for ten days.

Primary Resources

First on the list is the *CCNA Security 210-260 Official Cert Guide*, written by Omar Santos and John Stuppi. The authors have done an outstanding job of gathering together and organizing all the material you need to study for the CCNA Security certification exam. It is available in print (ISBN: 9781587205668) and Premium Edition eBook (ISBN: 9780134077895) versions. The print version comes with the Pearson IT Certification Practice Test engine and two practice exams, as well as 90 minutes of video training. The Premium Edition eBook version comes with four practice exams, multiplatform accessibility, and performance tracking.

If you are a Cisco Networking Academy student, you are blessed with access to the online version of the CCNA Security curriculum and the wildly popular Packet Tracer network simulator. The course provides an introduction to the core security concepts and skills needed for the installation, troubleshooting, and monitoring of network devices to maintain the integrity, confidentiality, and availability of data and devices. The course helps students learn how to secure Cisco routers, implement AAA, configure ACLs, mitigate common Layer 2 attacks, implement Cisco IOS firewall features, implement site-to-site VPNs, and implement remote-access VPNs. To learn more about the CCNA Security course and to find an Academy near you, visit http://www.netacad.com. Cisco Press also produces a printed course booklet (ISBN: 9781587133510) and lab manual (ISBN: 9781587133503) to accompany the CCNA Security Networking Academy course.

Supplemental Resources

In addition to the book you hold in your hands and to those mentioned previously, there are three more supplemental resources I would recommend to augment your final 31 days of review and preparation.

Omar Santos, Aaron Woland, and Mason Haris recorded more than 13 hours of video in their *CCNA Security 210-260 Complete Video Course* (ISBN: 9780134499314), which is available free with your Safari Books Online account. You can also purchase it separately from Cisco Press. The authors talk you through the full range of topics on the CCNA Security exam using a variety of presentation styles, including live instructor whiteboarding, real-world demonstrations, animations of network activity, dynamic KeyNote presentations, and doodle videos. They also demonstrate router, switch, and ASA CLI/ASDM configuration and troubleshooting in real lab environments, enabling you to learn both the concepts and the hands-on application.

Cisco Press has recently published the second edition of the very popular *CCNA Security Portable Command Guide* (ISBN: 9781587205750), by Bob Vachon. This book summarizes all the relevant Cisco IOS Software security commands, keywords, command arguments, and associated prompts, and offers tips and examples for applying these commands to real-world security challenges. Bob also includes ASDM screenshots to help when configuring the Cisco ASA.

The second book I would suggest is *Cisco ASA: All-in-One Next-Generation Firewall, IPS, and VPN Services*, Third Edition (ISBN: 9781587143076), written by Jazib Frahim, Omar Santos, and Andrew Ossipov. This is an amazingly detailed resource (1248 pages!) on configuring, monitoring, and troubleshooting the entire Cisco ASA firewall family. True, it goes beyond the CCNA Security exam topics, but if you're a geek like me, you'll enjoy delving more deeply into the ASA with this book.

I occasionally reference other Cisco Press books for more specific topics. The simplest way to access this extra content is with a Safari Books Online subscription.

So, which resources should you buy? That question is largely up to how deep your pockets are or how much you like books. If you're like me, you want it all...online access for mobile and tablet reading, as well as hard copies for intensive study sessions with a pencil in hand. I admit it; my bookcase is a testament to my "geekness." But that's not practical for most students. So if you are on a budget, then choose one of the primary study resources and one of the supplemental resources, such as the *CCNA Security 210-260 Official Cert Guide* and the *CCNA Security Portable*

Command Guide. Whatever you choose, you will be in good hands. Any or all of these authors will serve you well.

Goals and Methods

The main goal of this book is to provide you with a clear and succinct review of the CCNA Security exam objectives. Each day's exam topics are grouped into a common conceptual framework and uses the following format:

- A title for the day that concisely states the overall topic

- A list of one or more CCNA Security IINS 210-260 exam topics to be reviewed

- A Key Topics section to introduce the review material and quickly orient you to the day's focus

- An extensive review section consisting of short paragraphs, lists, tables, examples, and graphics

- A Study Resources section to provide you a quick reference for locating more in-depth treatment of the day's topics (as introduced in the previous section)

The book counts down starting with Day 31 and continues through exam day to provide post-test information. You will also find a calendar and checklist inside the book that you can tear out and use during your exam preparation.

Use the calendar to enter each actual date beside the countdown day and the exact day, time, and location of your CCNA Security exam. The calendar provides a visual for the time that you can dedicate to each CCNA Security exam topic.

The checklist highlights important tasks and deadlines leading up to your exam. Use it to help map out your studies.

Who Should Read This Book?

The audience for this book is anyone finishing their preparation for taking the CCNA Security IINS 210-260 exam. A secondary audience is anyone who needs a refresher review of CCNA Security exam topics, perhaps before attempting to recertify.

Getting to Know the CCNA Security IINS 210-260 Exam

Cisco launched the newest version of the CCNA Security exam, numbered 210-260, on September 1, 2015. The exam tests the candidate's knowledge of secure network infrastructure, core security concepts, managing secure access, VPN encryption, firewalls, intrusion prevention, web and email content security, and endpoint security. It also validates skills for installation, troubleshooting, and monitoring of a secure network to maintain integrity, confidentiality, and availability of data and devices. As a prerequisite, Cisco states that a candidate must be CCENT or CCNA Routing and Switching certified before attempting the exam.

Currently for the CCNA Security exam, you are allowed 90 minutes to answer 60 to 70 questions. Most recently, a passing score is 860 on a scale of 300 to 1000, but the passing score often rises as the exam matures. If you've never taken a certification exam before with Pearson VUE, there is a 2 minute 45 second video titled What to Expect in a Pearson VUE Test Center that nicely summarizes the experience: https://home.pearsonvue.com/test-taker/security.aspx. You can also search for it on YouTube.

When you get to the testing center and check in, the proctor verifies your identity, gives you some general instructions, and then takes you into a quiet room containing a PC. When you're at the PC, you have a few things to do before the timer starts on your exam. For instance, you can take the tutorial to get accustomed to the PC and the testing engine. Every time I sit for an exam, I go through the tutorial even though I know how the test engine works. It helps me settle my nerves and get focused. Anyone who has user-level skills in getting around a PC should have no problems with the testing environment.

What Topics Are Covered on the CCNA Security

Table I-1 summarizes the seven domains of the CCNA Security exam.

Table I-1   CCNA Security IINS 210-260 Exam Domains and Weightings

Domain	% of Examination
1.0 Security Concepts	12%
2.0 Secure Access	14%
3.0 VPN	17%
4.0 Secure Routing and Switching	18%
5.0 Cisco Firewall Technologies	18%
6.0 IPS	9%
7.0 Content and Endpoint Security	12%
Total	100%

Registering for the CCNA Security IINS 210-260 Exam

If you are starting 31 Days Before Your CCNA Security Exam today, register for the exam right now. In my testing experience, there is no better motivator than a scheduled test date staring me in the face. I'm willing to bet it's the same for you. Don't worry about unforeseen circumstances. You can cancel your exam registration for a full refund up to 24 hours before taking the exam. So if you're ready, then you should gather the following information and register right now!

- Legal name
- Social Security or passport number
- Company name
- Valid email address
- Method of payment

You can schedule your exam at any time by visiting www.pearsonvue.com/cisco/. I recommend you schedule it now for 31 days from now. The process and available test times will vary based on the local testing center you choose.

Digital Study Guide

Cisco Press offers this book in an online digital format that includes enhancements such as video, activities, and Check Your Understanding questions—plus Packet Tracer activities and a full-length exam.

> *31 Days Before Your CCNA Security Certification Exam Digital Study Guide* is available for a discount for anyone who purchases this book. There are details about redeeming this offer in the back of the book. If you are reading this in eBook format, please see the instructions below to access the companion website to get the discount offer.

- **Read** the complete text of the book on any web browser that supports HTML5, including mobile.

- **Watch** unique embedded videos (totaling more than 5 hours of video instruction) that demonstrate tasks, explain important topics, and visually describe key CCNA Security exam objectives.

- **Reinforce** key concepts with more than 31 dynamic and interactive hands-on exercises, and see the results with the click of a button. Also included are 7 Packet Tracer activities.

To get your copy of Packet Tracer software please go to the companion website for instructions. To access this companion website, follow these steps:

1. Go to www.ciscopress.com/register and log in or create a new account.

2. Enter the ISBN: 9781587205781.

3. Answer the challenge question as proof of purchase.

4. Click on the Access Bonus Content link in the Registered Products section of your account page, to be taken to the page where your downloadable content is available.

Test your understanding of the material at the end of each day with more than 300 fully interactive online quiz questions, PLUS a full-length final quiz of 60 questions that mimic the type you will see in the CCNA Security certification exam.

Throughout this book there are references to the Digital Study Guide enhancements that look like this:

Video: Data Encapsulation Summary

Refer to the Digital Study Guide to view this video.

Activity: Identify the Encapsulation Layer

Refer to the Digital Study Guide to complete this activity.

Check Your Understanding

Refer to the Digital Study Guide to take a 10-question quiz covering the content of this day.

When you are at these points in the Digital Study Guide you can start the enhancement.

Common Security Principles

CCNA Security 210-260 IINS Exam Topics

- 1.1.a Describe confidentiality, integrity, availability (CIA)
- 1.1.b Describe SIEM technology
- 1.1.c Identify common security terms
- 1.1.d Identify common network security zones

Key Topics

Today's review focuses on the basic principles, concepts, and terminology of network security. First we will look at the three basic elements of network security and then examine some basic security terminology and the common security zones found in networks today.

Confidentiality, Integrity, and Availability (CIA)

The basic elements of network security are as follows:

- **Confidentiality:** Providing confidentiality of data guarantees that only authorized users can view sensitive information.

- **Integrity:** Providing integrity of data guarantees that only authorized subjects can change sensitive information. Integrity might also guarantee the authenticity of data.

- **Availability:** Providing system and data availability guarantees uninterrupted access by authorized users to important computing resources and data.

Video: CIA

Refer to the Digital Study Guide to view this video.

SIEM

Security Information Event Management (SIEM) is a technology used in enterprise organizations to provide real-time reporting and long-term analysis of security events. SIEM provides user information (name, location), device information (manufacturer, model, OS version), and posture information (compliance, antivirus version, OS patches) for network security staff to quickly and accurately assess the significance of any security event. SIEM tools can aggregate data from many sources (routers, servers, firewalls), correlate the data into meaningful bundles, retain historical data for compliance and analysis, and provide real-time alerts when an attack is detected.

Common Network Security Terms

Table 31-1 lists some of the more common terms encountered in network security.

Table 31-1   Common Network Security Terms

Term	Explanation
Asset	An asset is an item that is to be protected and can include property, people, and information or data that have value to the company.
Vulnerability	A vulnerability is a weakness in a system or its design that can be exploited by a threat.
Threat	A threat is any potential danger to assets. Threats are often realized via an attack or exploit that takes advantage of an existing vulnerability.
Risk	Risk is the potential for unauthorized access to compromise, destroy, or cause damage to an asset. It is also the likelihood that a particular threat using a specific attack will exploit a particular vulnerability of an asset.
Countermeasure	A countermeasure is a safeguard that mitigates a potential risk. A countermeasure mitigates risk by either eliminating or reducing a vulnerability.

 Activity: Identify Common Network Security Terms

Refer to the Digital Study Guide to complete this activity.

Security Zones

Before discussing the concept of security zones, it is important to understand the role of the firewall in network security. A firewall is a system that enforces an access control policy between two or more security zones. Although there are different types of firewalls, every firewall should have the following properties:

- It must be resistant to attack.

- All traffic between networks must flow through it.

- It must have traffic-filtering capabilities.

Firewalls commonly control access between the security zones that are based on packet source and destination IP address and port. Although firewalls can be placed in various locations within a network (including on endpoints), they are typically placed at the Internet edge, where they provide vital security.

The placement of the firewall allows for the creation of two basic security zones, as Figure 31-1 illustrates.

Figure 31-1   Security Zones

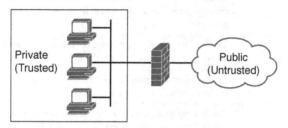

The public, untrusted network is commonly referred to as the "outside" security zone. This zone is fully outside the control of the organization. The private, trusted network is commonly referred to as the "inside" security zone. It is a zone in which systems owned by an organization reside and must be protected from systems that do not belong to the organization. Besides the inside and outside interfaces, it is typical to have at least one interface that is somewhere in between. This interface is often associated with a third zone called the demilitarized zone (DMZ), as shown in Figure 31-2. This zone usually contains a relatively small number of systems whose services are made available to systems residing in the outside zone. The DMZ devices, such as web servers, are owned and controlled by the organization, but they are accessed by systems outside of the organization's control.

Figure 31-2   DMZ

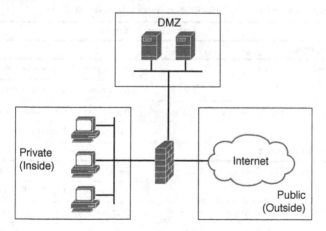

Typically, the traffic flow between these three zones will be as described in Table 31-2.

Table 31-2   Security Zone Filtering Policies

From	To	Filtering Policy
Inside	Outside DMZ	Traffic is inspected as it travels toward the public (outside) or DMZ network. This traffic is permitted with little or no restriction. Inspected traffic returning from the DMZ or public network to the private network is permitted.
Outside	Inside	Traffic originating from the public (outside) network and traveling to the private (inside) network is blocked.
DMZ	Inside	Traffic originating from the DMZ network and traveling to the private (inside) network is usually blocked.
Outside	DMZ	Traffic originating from the public (outside) network and traveling toward the DMZ is selectively permitted and inspected. This type of traffic is typically email, DNS, HTTP, or HTTPS traffic. Return traffic from the DMZ to the public network is dynamically permitted.
DMZ	Outside	Traffic originating from the DMZ network and traveling to the public (outside) network is selectively permitted based on service requirements.

Video: Security Zone Filtering Policies

Refer to the Digital Study Guide to view this video.

Study Resources

For today's exam topics, refer to the following resources for more study.

Resource	Location	Topic
Primary Resources		
CCNA Security Official Cert Guide	1	Networking Security Concepts
	15	Implementing Cisco IOS Zone-Based Firewalls
CCNA Security (Networking Academy Curriculum)	1	Modern Network Security Threats
	4	Implementing Firewall Technologies
Supplemental Resources		
CCNA Security Complete Video Course	1	Networking Security Concepts
	10	Implementing Cisco IOS Zone-Based Firewalls
CCNA Security Portable Command Guide	1	Networking Security Concepts
	12	Configuring Zone-Based Firewalls

Check Your Understanding

Refer to the Digital Study Guide to take a ten-question quiz covering the content of this day.

Common Security Threats

CCNA Security 210-260 IINS Exam Topics

- 1.2.a Identify common network attacks
- 1.2.b Describe social engineering
- 1.2.c Identify malware
- 1.2.d Classify the vectors of data loss/exfiltration

Key Topics

Today's review focuses on common network attacks. More specifically, we will look at social engineering and malware as two major sources of network attacks. We will also discuss the sources of potential data loss for organizations.

Network Attacks

It is important to understand the different types of network attacks used by hackers. To mitigate these attacks, it is useful to first categorize the various types of attacks. The most common categories of network attacks are reconnaissance attacks, access attacks, and denial of service (DoS)/distributed denial of service (DDoS) attacks.

Reconnaissance Attacks

A *reconnaissance attack* is an attempt to learn more about the intended victim before attempting a more intrusive attack. Hackers use reconnaissance (or recon) attacks to do unauthorized discovery and mapping of systems, services, or vulnerabilities. Tools such as information queries via the *WHOIS* service, ping sweeps, port scans, vulnerability scanners, and exploitation tools are common techniques used by hackers when performing reconnaissance attacks.

 Video: Examples of Reconnaissance Attacks
Refer to the Digital Study Guide to view this video.

Access Attacks

After gathering the necessary information during the reconnaissance phase of the attack, the hacker will usually attempt to access the network. *Access attacks* exploit known vulnerabilities in authentication services, FTP services, and web services to gain entry to web accounts, confidential databases, and other sensitive information. The hacker's main objectives may be to retrieve protected information, gain access to secure areas of the network, or escalate its access privileges. There are six common types of access attacks:

- **Password attack:** A hacker attempts to discover critical system passwords using various methods, such as social engineering, dictionary attacks, brute-force attacks, or network sniffing.

- **Trust exploitation:** A hacker uses unauthorized privileges to gain access to a system, possibly compromising the target. For example, if a DMZ device has access to the inside network, an attacker could leverage that by gaining access to the DMZ device and using that location to launch his attacks from there to the inside network.

- **Port redirection:** A hacker uses a compromised system as a base for attacks against other targets.

- **Man-in-the-middle attack:** An attacker places himself in line between two legitimate devices that are communicating, with the intent to perform reconnaissance or to manipulate the data as it moves between them. This can happen at Layer 2 or Layer 3. The main purpose is eavesdropping, so the attacker can see all the traffic.

- **Buffer overflow attack:** An attacker exploits a buffer overflow vulnerability, which is a programming flaw. If a service accepts input and expects the input to be within a certain size but does not verify the size of input upon reception, it may be vulnerable to a buffer overflow attack. This means that an attacker can provide input that is larger than expected, and the service will accept the input and write it to memory, filling up the associated buffer and also overwriting adjacent memory. This overwrite may corrupt the system and cause it to crash, resulting in a DoS. In the worst cases, the attacker can inject malicious code, leading to a system compromise.

- **IP, MAC, DHCP spoofing:** An attacker injects traffic that appears to be sourced from a system other than the attacker's system itself. To perform MAC or IP spoofing, the attacker uses MAC or source IP addresses that are different than their real addresses. DHCP spoofing can be done with either the DHCP server or the DHCP client. To perform DHCP server spoofing, the attacker enables on a network a rogue DHCP server that will then respond to client requests with attacker-defined parameters. From the client side, an attacker can spoof many DHCP client requests, specifying a unique MAC address per request in the hope of exhausting the DHCP server's IP address pool.

Video: Examples of Access Attacks

Refer to the Digital Study Guide to view this video.

DoS and DDoS Attacks

DoS attacks attempt to consume all of the resources of a critical computer or network in order to make it unavailable for valid use. A DoS attack typically results in some sort of interruption of service to users, devices, or applications. Malicious hosts can also coordinate to flood a victim with an abundance of attack packets, so that the attack takes place simultaneously from potentially thousands of sources. This type of attack is called a *DDoS attack*. DDoS attacks typically emanate from networks of compromised systems, known as *botnets*. DDoS attacks can also use reflection and amplification to augment their impact on the victim. A *reflection attack* is a type of DoS attack in which the attacker sends a flood of protocol request packets to various IP hosts. These reflectors respond by sending response packets to a specific target, thus flooding it. In an *amplification attack*, a small forged packet elicits a large reply from the reflectors. Examples of DoS attacks are

- **Ping of death:** An attacker sends a malformed or otherwise malicious ping to a network computer—in this case, a packet larger than the maximum packet size of 65,535 bytes—which then causes legacy systems to hang or crash.

- **Smurf attack:** A hacker sends numerous ICMP echo-request packets to the broadcast address of a large network. These packets contain the victim's address as the source IP address. Every host that belongs to the large network responds by sending ICMP echo-reply packets to the victim.

- **TCP SYN flood attack:** An attacker exploits the TCP three-way handshake design by sending multiple TCP SYN packets with random source addresses to a victim host, forcing the host to respond and wait for an ACK packet that never arrives, thus leaving the victim with a large number of half-open TCP connections.

 Video: Examples of DoS Attacks

Refer to the Digital Study Guide to view this video.

Social Engineering

Social engineering is an access attack that attempts to manipulate individuals into performing actions or divulging confidential information. Social engineering often relies on people's willingness to be helpful. This attack also preys on people's weaknesses. The following are a few of the more common types of social engineering attacks.

Types

- **Phishing:** This type of attack usually presents as an email message with a link that looks like a valid trusted resource to a user. When the user clicks the link, the user is prompted to disclose confidential information such as usernames/passwords, account numbers, or Social Security number.

- **Spear phishing:** This is a targeted phishing attack that presents as an email message tailored for a specific individual or organization.

- **Whaling:** Like spear phishing, whaling uses the concept of targeted emails; however, it increases the profile of the target. The target of a whaling attack is often one or more of the top executives of an organization.

- **Pharming:** Whereas phishing entices the victim to a malicious website, pharming lures victims by compromising domain name services. When victims attempt to visit a legitimate website, the compromised name service instead provides the IP address of a malicious website.

- **Pretexting:** A hacker calls an individual and lies to them in an attempt to gain access to privileged data.

- **Vishing:** Vishing uses the same concept as phishing, except that it uses voice and the phone system as its medium instead of email.

- **Smishing:** Smishing uses the same concept as phishing, except that it uses SMS texting as the medium instead of email.

- **Spam:** Hackers may use spam email to trick a user into clicking an infected link or downloading an infected file.

- **Tailgating:** A hacker quickly follows an authorized person into a secure location.

- **Baiting:** A hacker leaves a malware-infected physical device, such as a USB flash drive, in a public location such as a corporate washroom. The finder of the device loads it onto their computer, unintentionally installing the malware.

- **Something for something:** A hacker requests personal information from a party in exchange for something like a free gift.

- **Malvertising:** A hacker injects malicious or malware-laden advertisements into legitimate online advertising networks and web pages.

Defenses

Here are some of the security techniques and procedures that can be put into place to mitigate social engineering attacks:

- **Password management:** Guidelines such as the number and type of characters that each password must include and how often a password must be changed.

- **Two-factor authentication:** Combining something the user has and something the user knows to authenticate their access to the network.

- **Antivirus/antiphishing defenses:** Both network- and host-based filtering services deployed throughout.

- **Change management:** A well-documented change-management process describing how and when network changes can be made.

- **Information classification and handling:** A policy that clearly sets out what information is considered sensitive and how to handle or destroy it.

Activity: Identify Network Attack Types

Refer to the Digital Study Guide to complete this activity.

Malware

Malware is malicious software that comes in several forms, including the following:

- **Virus:** Malicious code that is attached to executable files, which are often legitimate programs. Most viruses require end-user activation and can lay dormant for an extended period and then activate at a specific time or date.

- **Trojan horse:** Malware that carries out malicious operations under the guise of a desired function. A Trojan horse comes with malicious code hidden inside of it. This malicious code exploits the privileges of the user that runs it and often creates a back door into the infected system. Often, Trojans are found attached to online games.

- **Worm:** Malware that replicates itself by independently exploiting vulnerabilities in networks. Worms usually slow down networks.

- **Ransomware:** Malware that denies access to the infected computer system and then demands a paid ransom for the restriction to be removed.

- **Spyware:** Malware that is used to gather information about a user and send the information to another entity, without the user's consent.

- **Adware:** Malware that typically displays annoying pop-ups to generate revenue for its author.

- **Scareware:** Malware that includes scam software that uses social engineering to shock or induce anxiety by creating the perception of a threat. It is generally directed at an unsuspecting user.

Video: Examples of Malware Attacks

Refer to the Digital Study Guide to view this video.

Data Loss

Data is likely to be an organization's most valuable asset. Data loss or data exfiltration is when data is intentionally or unintentionally lost, stolen, or leaked to the outside world. Common vectors of data loss and exfiltration include the following:

- **Email attachments:** Email attachments often contain sensitive information, such as confidential corporate, customer, and personal data, that could be intercepted as it leaves the corporate network.

- **Unencrypted devices:** Smartphones and other personal devices are often protected only with a password. Employees sometimes send sensitive company information to these devices without using encryption.

- **Cloud storage devices:** Saving data to the cloud has many potential benefits. However, sensitive data can be lost if access to the cloud is compromised due to weak security settings.

- **Removable media:** Putting sensitive data on a removable storage device, such as a USB memory stick, may pose more of a threat than putting that data on a smartphone. Such devices are not only easily lost or stolen; they also typically do not have passwords, encryption, or any other protection for the data they contain.

- **Hard copy:** Corporate data should be disposed of thoroughly. For example, confidential data should be shredded when no longer required.

- **Improper access control:** Passwords are the first line of defense. Stolen passwords or weak passwords that have been compromised can provide an attacker easy access to corporate data.

Study Resources

For today's exam topics, refer to the following resources for more study.

Resource	Location	Topic
CCNA Security Official Cert Guide	1	Networking Security Concepts
	2	Common Security Threats
CCNA Security (Networking Academy Curriculum)	1	Modern Network Security Threats
Supplemental Resources		
CCNA Security Complete Video Course	1	Networking Security Concepts
	2	Common Security Threats
CCNA Security Portable Command Guide	1	Networking Security Concepts

Check Your Understanding

Refer to the Digital Study Guide to take a ten-question quiz covering the content of this day.

Cryptographic Technologies

CCNA Security 210-260 IINS Exam Topics

- 1.3.a Describe key exchange
- 1.3.b Describe hash algorithm
- 1.3.c Compare and contrast symmetric and asymmetric encryption
- 1.3.d Describe digital signatures, certificates, and PKI

Key Topics

Today we will review cryptographic technologies and terminology. In particular, we will look at understanding the challenges of secure key management within a network environment. As well, we will review the different types of hashing algorithms in use today for data integrity. We will compare and contrast symmetric and asymmetric encryption algorithms, and finally delve into digital signatures and certificates. We will review PKI tomorrow.

CIA Triad

Before looking at the different cryptographic technologies in use today, it is important to understand the basic premise of cryptography itself. *Cryptography* is the practice and study of techniques to secure communications in the presence of third parties. Historically, cryptography was synonymous with encryption. Its goal was to keep messages private. Today, cryptography includes other responsibilities:

- **Confidentiality:** Uses encryption algorithms to encrypt and hide data
- **Data integrity:** Uses hashing algorithms to ensure that data is unaltered during any operation
- **Authentication:** Ensures that any messages received were actually sent from the perceived origin

Key Exchange and Management

Key management deals with the secure generation, verification, exchange, storage, and destruction of keys. It is extremely important to have secure methods of key management. Key exchange and management are often considered the most difficult part of designing a cryptosystem. Many cryptosystems have failed because of mistakes in their key management, and all modern cryptographic algorithms require key management procedures. The basic components of any key management system include (1) automated and randomized key generation, (2) key strength verification, (3) encrypted key storage, (4) secure key exchange, (5) short key lifetimes, and (6) revocation and destruction of compromised or expired keys.

Hash Algorithms

Hashing is a mechanism that is used for data integrity assurance. Hashing is based on a one-way mathematical function that is relatively easy to compute but significantly difficult to reverse. Figure 29-1 illustrates how hashing is performed. Data of an arbitrary length is input into the hash function, and the result of the hash function is the fixed-length hash, which is known as the "digest" or "fingerprint."

Figure 29-1   Hash Function

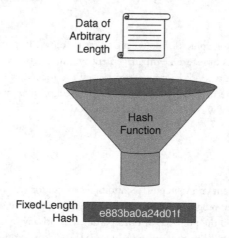

Well-known Hash Functions

Hash functions are helpful when ensuring data is not changed accidentally, such as by a communication error. Although hashing can be used to detect *accidental* changes, it cannot be used to guard against deliberate changes. There is no unique identifying information from the sender in the hashing procedure. Therefore, hashing is vulnerable to man-in-the-middle attacks and does not provide security to transmitted data.

The following are the three most commonly used cryptographic hash functions:

- **Message Digest 5 (MD5):** MD5 is a one-way function that makes it easy to compute a hash from the given input data but makes it very difficult to compute input data given only a hash value. MD5 produces a 128-bit hash and is now considered a legacy algorithm that should be avoided.

- **Secure Hash Algorithm 1 (SHA-1):** SHA-1 takes a message of up to 2^{64} bits in length and produces a 160-bit message digest. The algorithm is slightly slower than MD5, but the larger message digest makes it more secure against brute-force collision and inversion attacks. It is now considered legacy and should be avoided when possible.

- **Secure Hash Algorithm 2 (SHA-2):** SHA-2 algorithms are the secure hash algorithms that the U.S. government requires by law for use in certain applications. The SHA-2 family includes 224-bit, 256-bit, 384-bit, and 512-bit functions. When choosing a hashing algorithm, use SHA-256 or higher, as they are currently the most secure.

CAUTION: Security flaws were discovered in SHA-1 and MD5. Therefore, it is now recommended that these algorithms be avoided.

Authentication Using Hashing

Two systems that have agreed on a secret key can use the key along with a hash function to verify data integrity of communication between them by using a keyed hash. A message authentication code is produced by passing the message data along with the secret key through a hash algorithm. Only the sender and the receiver know the secret key, and the output of the hash function now depends on the message data and the secret key. Figure 29-2 illustrates how the message authentication code is created. Data of an arbitrary length is input into the hash function, together with a secret key. The result is the fixed-length hash that depends on the data and the secret key. This type of authentication is referred to as keyed-hash message authentication code (HMAC) and adds authentication to integrity assurance.

Figure 29-2   HMAC Hashing

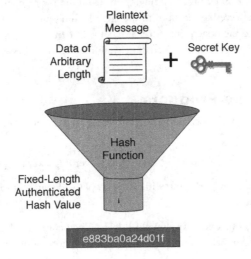

HMAC functions can be used with MD5 (HMAC-MD5) or SHA-1 (HMAC-SHA-1). Figure 29-3 illustrates cryptographic authentication in action. The sender, Alice, wants to ensure that the message is not altered in transit and wants to provide a way for the receiver, Bob, to authenticate the origin of the message.

Figure 29-3   HMAC in Action

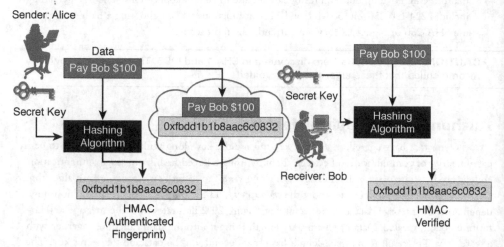

Alice inputs data and the secret key into the hashing algorithm and calculates the fixed-length message authentication code, or fingerprint. This authenticated fingerprint is then attached to the message and sent to Bob. Bob removes the fingerprint from the message and uses the received message with his copy of the secret key as input to the same hashing function. If the fingerprint that is calculated is identical to the fingerprint that was received, then data integrity has been verified. Also, the origin of the message is authenticated, because only Alice possesses a copy of the shared secret key.

Hashing in Cisco Products

Cisco products use hashing for entity authentication, data integrity, and data authenticity purposes such as

- IPsec gateways and clients use hashing algorithms to verify packet integrity and authenticity.

- Cisco IOS routers use keyed hashing with secret keys to add authentication information to routing protocol updates.

- Cisco software images that you can download from Cisco.com have MD5 and SHA-512 based checksums available, so that customers can check the integrity of downloaded images.

Symmetric and Asymmetric Encryption

Before diving into the differences between symmetric and asymmetric encryption algorithms, let's first start by reviewing the basic concepts of encryption itself.

Encryption Overview

Encryption is the process of disguising a message in such a way as to hide its original contents. With encryption, the plaintext readable message is converted to ciphertext, which is the unreadable, "disguised" message. Decryption reverses this process. Encryption is used to guarantee confidentiality so that only authorized entities can read the original message.

Encryption can provide confidentiality at different network layers, such as the following:

- Encrypting application layer data, such as encrypting email messages with Pretty Good Privacy (PGP)

- Encrypting session layer data using a protocol such as Secure Sockets Layer (SSL) or Transport Layer Security (TLS)

- Encrypting network layer data using protocols such as those provided in the IP security (IPsec) protocol suite

- Encrypting data link layer data using proprietary link-encrypting devices

A good cryptographic algorithm is designed in such a way that it resists common cryptographic attacks. Variable key lengths and scalability are also desirable attributes of a good encryption algorithm. A key is a required parameter for encryption algorithms to encrypt and decrypt a message. The key is the link between the plaintext and ciphertext. There are two classes of encryption algorithms, which differ in their use of keys:

- **Symmetric encryption algorithms:** Use the same key to encrypt and decrypt data

- **Asymmetric encryption algorithms:** Use different keys to encrypt and decrypt data

Symmetric Encryption Algorithms

Symmetric, or secret key, encryption is the most commonly used form of cryptography because the shorter key length increases the speed of execution. The typical key-length range of symmetric encryption algorithms is 40 to 256 bits. Figure 29-4 illustrates an example of symmetric encryption in action.

Figure 29-4   Symmetric Encryption Example

In this example, the same key is used to encrypt the data by the sender and decrypt the data by the recipient.

With symmetric encryption, key management can be a challenge. The encryption and decryption keys are the same. The sender and the receiver must exchange the symmetric, secret key using a secure channel before any encryption can occur.

Table 29-1 provides a summary of the types of symmetric encryption algorithms in use today and their respective key lengths.

Table 29-1   Symmetric Encryption Algorithms

Symmetric Encryption Algorithm	Key Length (in bits)
DES	56
3DES	112 and 168
AES	128, 192, and 256
SEAL	160
RC	RC2 (40 and 64)
	RC4 (1 to 256)
	RC5 (0 to 2040)
	RC6 (128, 192, and 256)

DES is considered a legacy algorithm and is vulnerable to brute-force attacks. One way to increase the effectiveness of DES, without changing the well-analyzed algorithm itself, is to use the same algorithm with different keys several times in a row. The technique of applying DES three times in a row to a plaintext block is called *3DES*. Brute-force attacks on 3DES are considered unfeasible today. Because the basic algorithm has been well tested in the field for more than 35 years, it is considered very trustworthy. For several years, it was recognized that DES would eventually reach the end of its usefulness. In 1997, the *AES* initiative was announced. AES was chosen to replace DES and 3DES, because the key length of AES is much stronger than that of DES, and AES runs faster than 3DES on comparable hardware.

 Video: Symmetric Encryption

Refer to the Digital Study Guide to view this video.

Asymmetric Encryption Algorithms

Asymmetric encryption algorithms use a pair of keys to encrypt and decrypt data. Secure messages can be exchanged without having to have a pre-shared key. Because neither party has a shared secret, very long key lengths must be used. These algorithms are resource intensive and slower to execute. Most commonly, an entity with a key pair will share one of the keys (the public key) and keep the other key in complete secrecy (the private key). The private key cannot, in any reasonable amount of time, be calculated from the public key. Data that is encrypted with the private key requires the public key to decrypt. Vice versa, data that is encrypted with the public key requires the private key to decrypt. Asymmetric encryption is also known as public key encryption.

Here is one possible scenario of asymmetric encryption in action. In Figure 29-5, imagine that Bob has generated a public/private key pair. Bob keeps the private key totally secret but publishes the public key so it is available to everyone. Alice has a message that she wants to send to Bob in private. If Alice encrypts the message using Bob's public key, only Bob has the private key that is required to decrypt the message, providing confidentiality.

Figure 29-5   Asymmetric Encryption Example

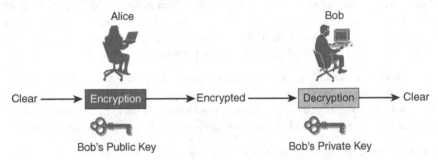

The following table provides a detailed comparison between symmetric and asymmetric encryption algorithms:

Asymmetric Encryption Algorithm	Key Length (in bits)
DH	512, 1024, 2048, 3072, 4096
DSS and DSA	512–1024
RSA	512–2048
ElGamal	512–1024
Elliptical curve techniques	160

Four protocols that use asymmetric encryption algorithms are

- **Internet Key Exchange (IKE):** A fundamental component of IPsec VPNs

- **Secure Sockets Layer (SSL):** Now implemented as IETF standard TLS

- **Secure Shell (SSH):** Provides a secure remote-access connection to network devices

- **Pretty Good Privacy (PGP):** A computer program that provides cryptographic privacy and authentication

 Video: Asymmetric Encryption

Refer to the Digital Study Guide to view this video.

 Video: Comparing Symmetric and Asymmetric Encryption Algorithms

Refer to the Digital Study Guide to view this video.

Activity: Compare Symmetric and Asymmetric Encryption Algorithms

Refer to the Digital Study Guide to complete this activity.

Digital Signatures and RSA Certificates

Digital signatures provide the same functionality as handwritten signatures. Specifically, they are a mathematical technique used to provide three basic security services: authenticates a source, proving that a certain party has seen and signed the data in question; guarantees that the data has not changed from the time it was signed; proves to a third party that the data exchange did take place.

Digital signatures are commonly used in code signing (to verify the integrity of downloaded files) and digital certificates (to verify the identity of an organization or individual). The basic four properties of digital signatures are that (1) the signature is authentic, (2) the signature is not forgeable, (3) the signature is not reusable, and (4) the signer cannot claim later that they did not sign it.

Digital certificates are used to authenticate and verify that a user sending a message is who they claim to be. Figure 29-6 shows how an RSA digital certificate or signature is used. RSA is an asymmetric algorithm that is commonly used for generating and verifying digital signatures. In this scenario, Bob is confirming an order with Alice. The steps are as follows:

1. Bob makes a hash, or fingerprint, of the document, which uniquely identifies the document and all its contents.

2. Bob encrypts the hash with only the private key of the signer (i.e., Bob's private key).

Figure 29-6   Using RSA Digital Signatures

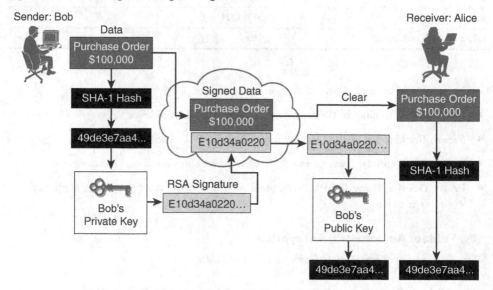

3. The encrypted hash, which is known as the signature, is appended to the document.

4. Alice obtains Bob's public key.

5. Alice decrypts the signature using Bob's public key. This step reveals the hash value initially calculated by Bob.

6. Alice makes a hash of the received document, without its signature, and compares this hash to the decrypted signature hash sent by Bob. If the hashes match, the document is authentic. The match means that the document has been signed by Bob and has not changed since it was signed.

Study Resources

For today's exam topics, refer to the following resources for more study.

Resource	Location	Topic
CCNA Security Official Cert Guide	5	Fundamentals of VPN Technology and Cryptography
CCNA Security (Networking Academy Curriculum)	7	Cryptographic Systems
Supplemental Resources		
CCNA Security Complete Video Course	3	Fundamentals of VPN Technology and Cryptography
CCNA Security Portable Command Guide	14	VPNs and Cryptology
	15	Asymmetric Encryption and PKI

Check Your Understanding

Refer to the Digital Study Guide to take a ten-question quiz covering the content of this day.

PKI and Network Security Architectures

CCNA Security 210-260 IINS Exam Topics

- 1.3.d Describe digital signatures, certificates, and PKI
- 1.4.a Campus area network (CAN)
- 1.4.b Cloud, wide area network (WAN)
- 1.4.c Data center
- 1.4.d Small office/home office (SOHO)
- 1.4.e Network security for a virtual environment

Key Topics

Today we will finish our review of cryptographic technologies from yesterday by looking at how PKI works, its terminology, and its components. We will then examine the different types of network security architectures commonly found today.

Public Key Infrastructure

A public key infrastructure (PKI) is a framework used to securely exchange information between parties. The foundation of a PKI identifies a certificate authority (CA). The CA, which plays the role of a trusted third party, issues digital certificates that authenticate the identity of organizations and users. These certificates are also used to sign messages to ensure that the messages have not been tampered with.

Figure 28-1 is an example of a trusted third-party scenario similar to how the CA operates in a PKI. Bob applies for a passport. In the process, he submits evidence of his identity. His application is approved and a passport is issued. Later, when Bob travels abroad, he presents his passport at an international border crossing. Because his passport is issued by a trusted government, Bob's identity is proven and he is allowed to enter the country.

Here the CA is equivalent to the government body issuing the passport. The passport itself is analogous to a certificate in a PKI.

Figure 28-1   Third-Party Trust Model

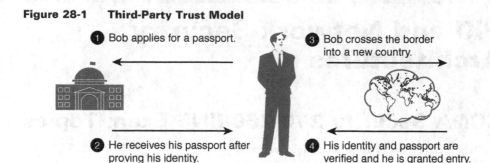

① Bob applies for a passport.

③ Bob crosses the border into a new country.

② He receives his passport after proving his identity.

④ His identity and passport are verified and he is granted entry.

PKI Terminology, Components, and Classes of Certificates

A PKI is the service framework that is needed to support large-scale, public-key-based technologies. A PKI is a set of technical, organizational, and legal components that are needed to establish a system that enables large-scale use of public-key cryptography to provide authenticity, confidentiality, integrity, and nonrepudiation services.

Two very important terms must be defined when talking about a PKI:

- **Certificate authority (CA):** The trusted third party that signs the public keys of entities in a PKI-based system
- **Certificate:** A document that in essence binds together the name of the entity and its public key and that has been signed by the CA

The certificate of a user is always signed by a CA. Moreover, every CA has a certificate, containing its public key, signed by itself. This is called a CA certificate or, more properly, a self-signed CA certificate.

A PKI is more than just a CA and its users. And implementing an enabling technology and building a large PKI involves a huge amount of organizational and legal work. There are five main components of a PKI:

- CAs for key management
- PKI users, such as people, devices, servers, and so on
- Storage and protocols
- Supporting organizational framework, known as practices, and user authentication using local registration authorities (LRAs)
- Supporting legal framework

Many vendors offer CA servers as a managed service or as an end-user product: VeriSign, Entrust Technologies, and GoDaddy are some examples. Organizations may also implement private PKIs using Microsoft Server or Open SSL. CAs, especially those that are outsourced, can issue certificates of a number of classes, which determine how trusted a certificate is. A certificate class is usually a number from 0 through 5; the higher the number, the more trusted the certificate is considered.

PKI Topologies

PKIs also form different topologies of trust. In the simple model, a single CA, which is also known as the root CA, issues all the certificates to the end users, as shown in Figure 28-2.

Figure 28-2   Single-Root PKI Topology

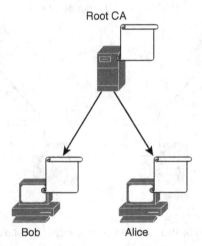

The benefit in such a setup is simplicity, but there are several pitfalls:

- It is difficult to scale this topology to a large environment.

- This topology needs a strictly centralized administration.

- There is a critical vulnerability in using a single-signing private key; if this key is stolen, the whole PKI falls apart because the CA can no longer be trusted as a unique signer.

Going beyond the single-root CA, topologies that are more complex can be devised that involve multiple CAs within the same organization. One such topology is the hierarchical CA system, shown in Figure 28-3. With the hierarchical topology, CAs can issue certificates to end users and to subordinate CAs, which in turn issue their certificates to end users, other CAs, or both.

The main benefits of a hierarchical PKI topology are increased scalability and manageability; trust decisions can now be hierarchically distributed to smaller branches.

Figure 28-3   Hierarchical CA Topology

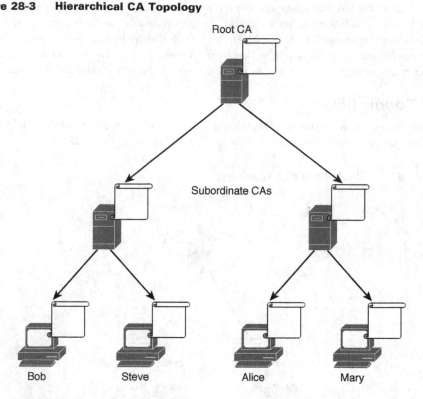

Another approach to hierarchical PKIs is called cross-certifying, as shown in Figure 28-4. In this scenario, multiple flat, single-root CAs establish trust relationships horizontally, by cross-certifying their own CA certificates.

Another entity in the PKI is a registration authority (RA). In a hierarchical CA topology, the RA can accept requests for enrollment in the PKI. This will help reduce the burden on CAs. The RA is responsible for the identification and authentication of subscribers, but does not sign or issue certificates.

PKI Standards

Interoperability between a PKI and its supporting services, such as Lightweight Directory Access Protocol (LDAP) and X.500 directories, is a concern because many CA vendors have proposed and implemented proprietary solutions instead of waiting for standards to develop.

To address this interoperability concern, the IETF formed the PKI X.509 (PKIX) working group, which is dedicated to promoting and standardizing PKI on the Internet. This working group has published the Internet X.509 Public Key Infrastructure Certificate Policy and Certification Practices Framework (RFC 2527).

Figure 28-4   Cross-Certified CA Topology

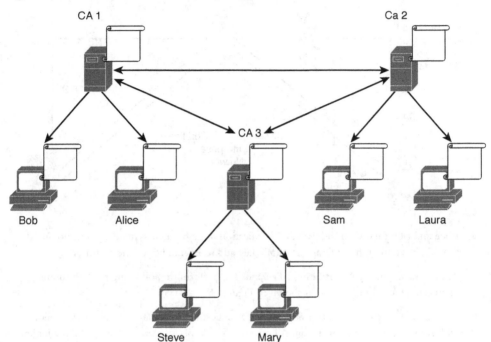

X.509 is a well-known standard that defines basic PKI formats, such as the certificate and certifi-cate revocation list (CRL) format, to enable basic interoperability. Specifically, the X.509 version 3 (X.509v3) standard defines the format of a digital certificate.

Another important set of PKI standards is the Public-Key Cryptography Standards (PKCS), devised and published by RSA Laboratories. PKCS provides basic interoperability of applications that use public-key cryptography.

PKI Operations

One central tenet behind the use of a PKI and trusted third-party protocols is that all participating parties agree to accept the word of a neutral third party. These entities rely on the CA to conduct an in-depth investigation of each entity before credentials are issued. The CA holds a pair of asym-metric keys: one private and one public. In the CA authentication procedure, the first step when contacting the PKI is to securely obtain a copy of the public key of the CA. CA certificates are retrieved in-band over a network, and the authentication is done out-of-band using the telephone. Figure 28-5 shows the process, as described in the following list:

1. Alice and Bob request the CA certificate that contains the CA public key.

2. Upon receipt of the CA certificate, Alice's and Bob's systems verify the validity of the certifi-cate using public-key cryptography.

Figure 28-5 Retrieving a CA Certificate

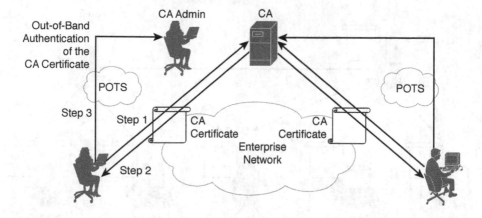

3. Alice and Bob follow up the technical verification done by their systems by telephoning the CA administrator and verifying the public key and serial number of the certificate.

   After retrieving the CA certificate, Alice and Bob perform the following steps to submit certificate requests to the CA, as shown in Figure 28-6.

4. Alice's and Bob's systems forward a certificate request that includes their public keys along with some identifying information. All of this information is encrypted using the public key of the CA.

5. Upon receipt of the certificate requests, the CA administrator telephones Alice and Bob to confirm their submittals and the public keys.

6. The CA administrator issues the certificate by adding some additional data to the certificate request and digitally signing it all.

Figure 28-6 Certificate Enrollment Process

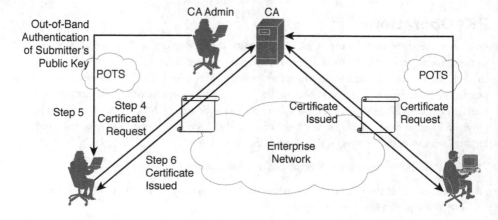

After the parties involved have installed certificates signed by the same CA, they may authenticate each other, as shown in Figure 28-7. This is done when the two parties exchange certificates. The CA's part in this process is finished, so it is not involved in this process, as described in the following list:

1. Bob and Alice exchange certificates. The CA is no longer involved.

2. Each party verifies the digital signature on the certificate by hashing the plaintext portion of the certificate, decrypting the digital signature using the CA public key, and comparing the results. If the results match, the certificate is verified as being signed by a trusted third party, and the verification by the CA that Bob is Bob and Alice is Alice is accepted.

Figure 28-7   Authentication Using Certificates

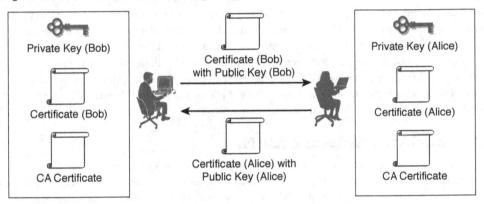

 Activity: Order the Steps in the PKI Process

Refer to the Digital Study Guide to complete this activity.

Enrollment and Revocation

The process of authenticating a CA server, generating a public-private key pair, requesting an identity certificate, and then verifying and implementing the identity certificate can be a several-step process. Cisco, in association with a few other vendors, developed the Simple Certificate Enrollment Protocol (SCEP), which can automate most of the process for requesting and installing an identity certificate.

Digital certificates can be revoked if keys are thought to be compromised, or if the business use of the certificate calls for revocation (for example, VPN access privileges have been terminated). If keys are thought to be compromised, generating new keys forces the creation of a new digital certificate, rendering the old certificate invalid and a candidate for revocation. The two basic ways to check whether certificates have been revoked are as follows:

- **Certificate revocation list (CRL):** This is a list of certificates that, based on their serial numbers, had initially been issued by a CA but have since been revoked and as a result should not be trusted. PKI entities regularly poll the CRL repository to receive the current CRL.

- **Online Certificate Status Protocol (OCSP):** Using this method, a client simply sends a request to find the status of a certificate and gets a response without having to know the complete list of revoked certificates.

 Video: Certificate Authorities and Certificates
   Refer to the Digital Study Guide to view this video.

Network Architectures and Topologies

Enterprise networks are built with routers, switches, and other network devices that keep the applications and services running. Therefore, properly securing these network devices is critical for continued business operation. The network infrastructure not only is often used as a platform for attacks but is also increasingly the direct target of malicious activity. For this reason, the necessary measures must be taken to ensure the security, reliability, and availability of the network infrastructure. In a modular network architecture, security is embedded throughout the network by following a defense-in-depth approach. This ensures the confidentiality, integrity, and availability of data, applications, endpoints, and the network itself. Let's look at some of the more common network modules or topologies in use today.

Campus-Area Network (CAN)

Campus-area networks, also known as local-area networks, have unique security threats that must be addressed. It consists of the enterprise core, campus- or local-area network, the intranet data center, and the enterprise Internet edge. The *core* is the piece of the network infrastructure that glues all the other modules together. The core is a high-speed infrastructure whose objective is to provide a reliable and scalable Layer 2/Layer 3 transport. It routes and switches traffic as fast as possible from one network module to another such as campuses, data center, WAN edge, and Internet edge. The *enterprise campus* is the portion of the infrastructure that provides network access to end users and devices located at the same geographical location. It may span over several floors in a single building, or over multiple buildings covering a larger geographical area. The *intranet data center* houses most of the critical applications and data for the enterprise. The *Internet edge* is the network infrastructure that provides connectivity to the Internet and that acts as the gateway for the enterprise to the rest of the cyberspace. Figure 28-8 depicts a typical CAN.

Figure 28-8   Campus-Area Network Topology

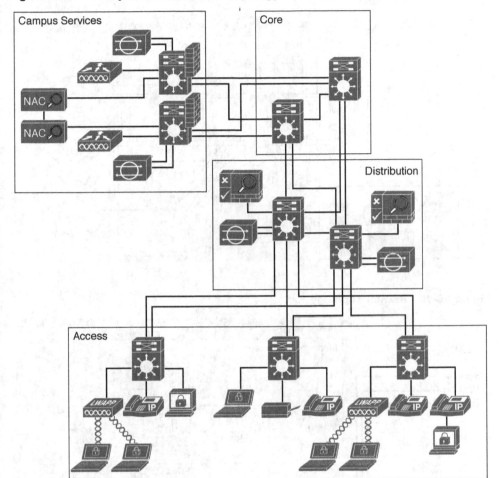

WAN and Branch/SOHO

The enterprise WAN edge, along with the enterprise branch/SOHO, provides users at geographically disperse remote sites with access to the same rich network services as users at the main site.
The availability and overall security of the WAN edge and the branch/SOHO is thus critical to
global business operations and teleworker or partner access. Figures 28-9 and 28-10 depict typical
WAN edge and branch topologies.

Figure 28-9   WAN Topology

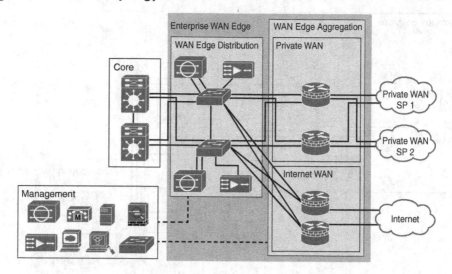

Figure 28-10   Branch Topology

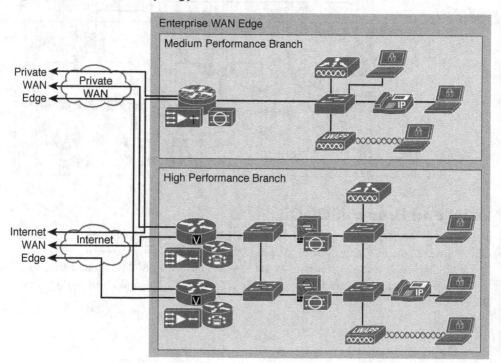

Data Center

Data center networks are typically housed in an offsite facility to store sensitive or proprietary data. These sites are interconnected to corporate sites using VPN technology with Cisco ASA devices and integrated data center switches, such as a high-speed Nexus switches. Implementation of robust data center security capabilities to safeguard sensitive mission-critical applications and data is a cornerstone in the effort to secure enterprise networks. The intranet data center is primarily inward facing and most clients are on the internal enterprise network. The intranet data center is still subject to external threats, but must also be guarded against threat sources inside of the network perimeter. Figure 28-11 depicts an overview of the secure data center topology.

Figure 28-11 Data Center Topology

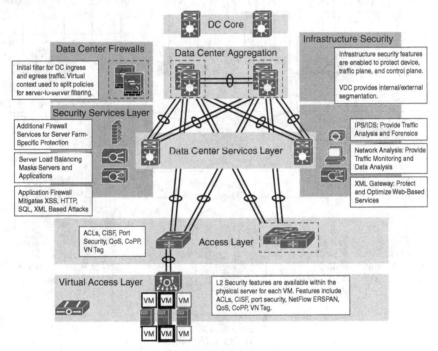

Cloud and Virtual Networks

The cloud is playing an increasing role in enterprise networks. Cloud computing enables organizations to use services such as data storage and cloud-based applications to extend their capacity or capabilities without adding infrastructure. By its very nature, the cloud is outside of the traditional network perimeter, allowing an organization to have a data center that may or may not reside behind the traditional firewall.

Furthermore, virtualization is changing the way data centers are architected. Server virtualization is creating new challenges for security deployments. Visibility into virtual machine (VM) activity and isolation of server traffic becomes more difficult when VM-sourced traffic can reach other VMs within the same server without being sent outside the physical server. Figure 28-12 depicts a virtual firewall appliance that provides trusted access to virtual data center and cloud environments.

Figure 28-12   Virtual Network Topology

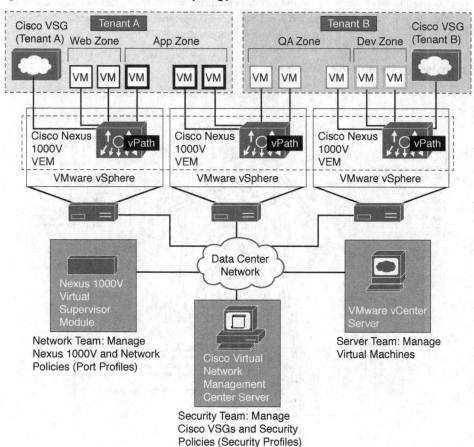

Study Resources

For today's exam topics, refer to the following resources for more study.

Resource	Location	Topic
Primary Resources		
CCNA Security Official Cert Guide	1	Networking Security Concepts
	5	Fundamentals of VPN Technology and Cryptography
CCNA Security (Networking Academy Curriculum)	1	Modern Network Security Threats
	7	Cryptographic Systems
Supplemental Resources		
CCNA Security Complete Video Course	3	Fundamentals of VPN Technology and Cryptography
CCNA Security Portable Command Guide	14	VPNs and Cryptology
	15	Asymmetric Encryption and PKI

Check Your Understanding

Refer to the Digital Study Guide to take a ten-question quiz covering the content of this day.

Secure Management Systems

CCNA Security 210-260 IINS Exam Topics

- 2.1.a Compare in-band and out-of-band
- 2.1.b Configure secure network management
- 2.1.c Configure and verify secure access through SNMPv3 using an ACL
- 2.1.d Configure and verify security for NTP
- 2.1.e Use SCP for file transfer

Key Topics

Today the focus is on secure management. Management plane traffic is generated either by network devices or network management stations using processes and protocols such as Telnet, SSH, and TFTP. The management plane is a very attractive target to hackers. We will look at different management systems, protocols, and tools that can be used to secure the information flow between device and administrator.

In-band and Out-of-band Management

When logging and managing information, the information flow between management hosts and the managed devices can take two paths:

- **In-band:** Information flows across an enterprise production network, the Internet, or both, using regular data channels.

- **Out-of-band (OOB):** Information flows on a dedicated management network on which no production traffic resides.

Figure 27-1 shows more detail for the protected management network, as well as the encrypted connection to the production network.

Figure 27-1   Secure Management Architecture

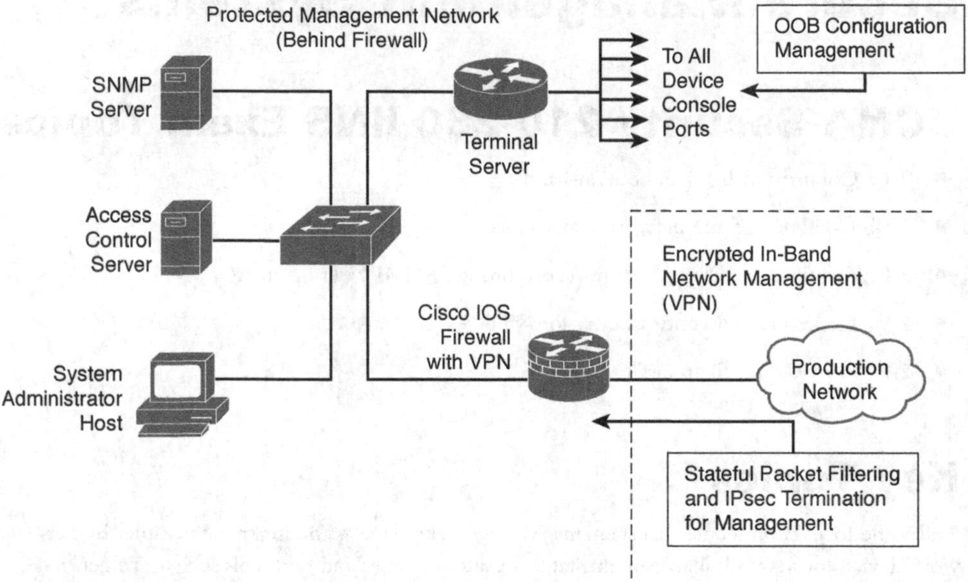

The connection to the production network is provided only for selective Internet access, limited in-band management traffic, and IPsec-protected management traffic from predetermined hosts. In-band management should apply only to devices that need to be managed or monitored. The Cisco IOS firewall is configured to allow syslog information into the management segment, and, in addition, Telnet, SSH, HTTPS, and SNMP, if these services are first initiated by the inside network. Another option is to create secure tunnels, using protocols such as IPsec, for management traffic. OOB management provides large networks the highest level of security and mitigates the risk of passing unsecure management protocols over the production network, whereas in-band management is recommended in smaller networks as a means of achieving a more cost-effective security deployment.

Management Plane Security

When securing the management plane, it is important to consider locking down device access, as well as using secure management protocols.

Access Security

There are multiple router configuration commands that can be used to increase access security, either at the console or via the vty lines. Table 27-1 summarizes some of the more useful options.

NOTE: Type 8 and type 9 were introduced in Cisco IOS 15.3(3)M. Both type 8 and type 9 use SHA encryption, but type 9 is slightly stronger than type 8.

Table 27-1   Access Security Configuration

Command	Explanation
security password min-length *length*	(Global configuration) Ensures that all configured passwords are at least a specified length. The default value is six characters.
service password-encryption	(Global configuration) Encrypts all plaintext passwords using type 7 encryption.
no service password-recovery	(Global configuration) Disables the ROMMON password recovery feature.
enable algorithm-type [md5 | scrypt | sha256] secret *plaintext-password*	(Global configuration) Allows the creation of a type 8 (sha256) or type 9 (scrypt) secret password instead of using the legacy MD5 algorithm.
username *name* **algorithm-type [md5 | scrypt | sha256] secret** *plaintext-password*	(Global configuration) Configures a local database entry using either a type 8 (sha256) or type 9 (scrypt) secret password instead of using the legacy MD5 algorithm.
login local	(Console or vty lines) Configures the use of a local database for console or line authentication.
transport input ssh	(vty lines) Allows only inbound SSH connections instead of Telnet.
login block-for *seconds* **attempts** *tries* **within** *seconds*	(Global configuration) Disables logins after a specific number of failed login attempts within a specific time.
login quiet-mode access-class [*acl-name* | *acl-number*]	(Global configuration) ACL identifies permitted hosts to ensure authorized devices can always connect.
login delay *seconds*	(Global configuration) Specifies a number of seconds the user must wait between unsuccessful login attempts.
login on-success log [every *login*] **login on-failure log [every** *login*]	(Global configuration) Logs successful and unsuccessful login attempts.

SSH/HTTPS

SSH provides a more secure method of accessing a Cisco IOS device's command line than Telnet. This is because SSH uses cryptographic technology for privacy (encryption), origin authentication (public/private key pairs), and data integrity (hash algorithms). The same applies to using HTTPS instead of HTTP for GUI access to the device. Example 27-1 shows the configuration necessary for enabling SSH and HTTPS.

Example 27-1 SSH and HTTPS Configuration

```
Router(config)# hostname R1
R1(config)# ip domain-name mycorp.com
R1(config)# crypto key generate rsa modulus 1024
R1(config)# ip ssh version 2
R1(config)# username Bob algorithm-type scrypt secret Cisco12345
R1(config)# line vty 0 4
R1(config-line)# login local
R1(config-line)# transport input ssh
R1(config-line)# exit
R1(config)# no ip http server
R1(config)# ip http secure-server
R1(config)# ip http authentication local
```

In Example 27-1, user Bob has been configured with a type 9 secret password. The router has been given a hostname and a domain name, both of which are requirements for generating the 1024-bit RSA key. Only SSH version 2 connections will be accepted on the vty lines, and they will be authenticated using the local database. The HTTP server has been disabled, and the HTTPS server has been enabled and configured to use the local database for authentication.

Syslog

The most common method of accessing system messages from networking devices is to use a protocol called syslog, which is described in RFC 5424. Syslog uses User Datagram Protocol (UDP) port 514 to send event notification messages across IP networks to event message collectors. Cisco routers can be configured to send syslog messages to several different facilities, such as

- **Logging buffer:** Messages are stored in router memory (RAM) for a period of time.
- **Console:** Console logging is turned on by default.
- **Terminal lines:** Log messages can be sent to the vty lines for viewing during a Telnet or SSH session.
- **Syslog server:** Log messages can be forwarded to an external device running a syslog daemon.

Syslog defines eight severity levels, 0 through 7. The lower the number, the more severe the issue. Syslog also defines standard names to associate with each of the levels. Table 27-2 lists the eight levels of syslog messages.

Table 27-2   Syslog Severity Levels

Level	Name	Description
0	Emergencies	System is unusable.
1	Alerts	Immediate action needed.
2	Critical	Critical conditions.
3	Errors	Error conditions.
4	Warnings	Warning conditions.
5	Notifications	Normal, but significant conditions.
6	Informational	Informational messages.
7	Debugging	Highly detailed information based on current debugging that is turned on.

Example 27-2 shows a common syslog configuration.

Example 27-2 Syslog Configuration

```
R1(config)# logging host 192.168.1.25
R1(config)# logging source-interface Loopback0
R1(config)# logging trap notifications
R1(config)# no logging console
```

In Example 27-2, R1 has been configured to send syslog to the syslog server at 192.168.1.25. Only messages with a severity level of 5 or lower (i.e., levels 0–5) will be sent to the server. Since syslog messages are being sent to an external server, logging to the console has been disabled to save on CPU resources. Use the **show logging** command to view logging configuration and buffered syslog messages.

 Activity: Match the Syslog Severity Level to Its Keyword

Refer to the Digital Study Guide to complete this activity.

Simple Network Management Protocol (SNMP)

One option for configuration management across the network is SNMP. SNMP was developed to allow administrators to manage devices on an IP network. SNMP consists of three elements relevant to the network management system (NMS):

- **SNMP manager:** An SNMP manager runs a network management application.

- **SNMP agent:** An SNMP agent is a piece of software that runs on a managed device (such as a server, router, or switch).

- **Management Information Base (MIB):** Information about a managed device's resources and activity is defined by a series of objects. The structure of these management objects is defined by a managed device's MIB.

SNMP managers and agents use UDP to exchange information. Specifically, SNMP agents listen to UDP port 161, and SNMP managers listen to UDP port 162.

There are three main mechanisms for SNMP communication between a network management system and a network device:

- **GET:** An SNMP GET message is used to retrieve information from a managed device.

- **SET:** An SNMP SET message is used to set a variable in a managed device or to trigger an action on a managed device.

- **Trap:** An SNMP trap message allows a network device to send unsolicited updates to a network management station or notify the SNMP manager about a significant event.

SNMP has evolved through three versions. SNMP versions 1 and 2 do not provide much security. SNMP operations are only controlled by community strings. Community strings can be read-only or read-write. GET requests will be honored if the NMS provides either a valid read-only or read-write community string. SET requests require the NMS to provide a read-write community string. With SNMP versions 1 and 2, all data is sent in clear text, including the community strings.

SNMPv3 adds a well-developed security model. SNMPv3 authentication verifies the origin and data integrity. That is, SNMPv3 verifies the originator of the message and that the message has not been altered in transit. SNMPv3 also offers privacy via encryption. SNMPv3 offers three modes of operation:

- **noAuthNoPriv:** This security level simply uses the community string or a username for authentication. No cryptographic hash or encryption is supported.

- **authNoPriv:** This security level uses a cryptographic hash to secure authentication credentials, but no encryption for data is supported.

- **authPriv:** This security level uses a cryptographic hash to secure authentication credentials and also uses encryption for data privacy.

Table 27-3 summarizes the differences between SNMPv1, SNMPv2, and SNMPv3.

Table 27-3   SNMP Security Models and Levels

Model	Level	Authentication	Encryption	Result
SNMPv1	noAuthNoPriv	Community string	No	Authenticates with a community string match
SNMPv2	noAuthNoPriv	Community string	No	Authenticates with a community string match

Model	Level	Authentication	Encryption	Result
SNMPv3	noAuthNoPriv	Username	No	Authenticates with a username
	AuthNoPriv	MD5 or SHA	No	Provides HMAC MD5 or HMAC SHA algorithms for authentication
	AuthPriv	MD5 or SHA	DES, 3DES, or AES	Provides HMAC MD5 or HMAC SHA algorithms for authentication; provides DES, 3DES, or AES encryption in addition to authentication

All versions of SNMP utilize the concept of the MIB. The MIB organizes configuration and status data into a tree structure. Objects in the MIB are referenced by their object ID (OID), which specifies the path from the tree root to the object.

The MIB tree for any given device includes branches with variables common to many networking devices and branches with variables specific to that device or vendor. For example, a common branch is "MIB-2," which contains a subsection called "ipRouteTable" under section "IP." This particular subsection, or object, allows the SNMP manager application to obtain the managed device's IPv4 routing table. The OID reference number for this object would be 1.3.6.1.2.1.4.21.

NOTE: See the Cisco SNMP Object Navigator to research other OID values and the objects they refer to.

The steps to configure secure user-based SNMP are as follows:

1. Configure an SNMP engine ID. This is a unique value identifying the managed device, typically a decimal representation of the IP address of the device.

2. Define an SNMP view to define and limit user access to the MIB tree.

3. Define an SNMP group, its version, and its cryptographic policy.

4. Define an SNMP user, assign it to an SNMP group, and specify authentication and encryption information.

5. Define and apply an ACL to the SNMP group and/or SNMP user.

6. Define a host device that will be allowed SNMP access.

Example 27-3 shows how to configure and secure SNMPv3.

Example 27-3 SNMPv3 Configuration

```
R1(config)# ip access-list standard SNMP_FILTER
R1(config-std-acl)# permit host 10.10.10.50
R1(config-std-acl)# exit
R1(config)# snmp-server engineID local 192168100254
R1(config)# snmp-server view myview mib-2 included
```

```
R1(config)# snmp-server view myview cisco included
R1(config)# snmp-server group ADMIN v3 priv write myview access SNMP_FILTER
R1(config)# snmp-server user ALICE Admin v3 auth sha Cisco123 priv aes 128 Cisco456
R1(config)# snmp-server host 10.10.10.50 version 3 priv Alice
```

In Example 27-3, ALICE is configured as an SNMP user in group ADMIN. SNMP is set to version 3 and supports both SHA authentication and AES 128-bit encryption. The entire "MIB-2" and "cisco" trees are viewable by the SNMP manager. An ACL is applied to the ADMIN group that only allows the 10.10.10.50 device access to the SNMP agent running on router R1.

Video: SNMPv3 Configuration and Demonstration

Refer to the Digital Study Guide to view this video.

Network Time Protocol (NTP)

NTP is an automated method to synchronize date and time settings for devices on the network. NTP uses UDP port 123 and is documented in RFC 1305. NTP version 3 introduced cryptographic authentication, which prevents an attacker from being able to send malicious time updates to NTP clients. NTP version 4 is described in RFC 5905. It introduces several new features, including IPv6 support, more precise clock discipline algorithms, and a dynamic server discovery scheme.

When an IOS system is configured to synchronize with an NTP server, it will assume the role of an NTP server itself and take on one stratum level higher than the server to which it references. As such, a hierarchy of NTP can be implemented within your network devices. The top system in the hierarchy can reference a trusted NTP source, or it can be configured to reference its own battery-backed clock and calendar. The stratum number is the number of hops away a device is from an authoritative source such as a private atomic clock or Internet-based public clock. Figure 27-2 shows the configuration for an NTP server (R1) and an NTP client (R2).

Figure 27-2   Using Authentication Keys with NTP

R1
Loopback0
172.16.1.1

R2

```
R1#sh run | section ntp
ntp authentication-key 1 md5 02252D682829 7
ntp authenticate
ntp trusted-key 1
ntp source Loopback0
ntp master
```

```
R2#sh run | section ntp
ntp authentication-key 1 md5 05282F3C0263 7
ntp authenticate
ntp trusted-key 1
ntp server 172.16.1.1 key 1 source Ethernet0/0
```

MD5 authentication has been enabled to allow both the server and the client to mutually authenticate each other using trusted key #1. NTP authentication uses a keyed hash technique. It requires a shared secret to be configured on the client and the server. Notice in the output that the authentication key has been encrypted in the running configuration with the type 7 algorithm used by the **service password-encryption** feature. It may appear that the keys do not match, but that is because the two routers generated different encryption initialization vectors when producing the type 7 values.

To verify the status of an NTP client's synchronization, you could use the commands from the CLI shown in Example 27-4.

Example 27-4 Verifying NTP Client Synchronization

```
R2# show ntp associations
  address          ref clock       st   when   poll reach  delay  offset   disp
*~172.16.1.1       127.127.1.1      8    32     64     1   0.000 -144391 7938.4
 * sys.peer, # selected, + candidate, - outlyer, x falseticker, ~ configured


R2# show ntp associations detail | include 172.16.1.1
172.16.1.1 configured, ipv4, authenticated, our_master, sane, valid, stratum 8


R2# show ntp status
Clock is synchronized, stratum 9, reference is 172.16.1.1
nominal freq is 250.0000 Hz, actual freq is 250.0000 Hz, precision is 2**10
ntp uptime is 155500 (1/100 of seconds), resolution is 4000
reference time is D9B27C36.2E147B60 (14:31:18.180 UTC Sun Sep 27 2015)
clock offset is -14439140.5000 msec, root delay is 1.00 msec
root dispersion is 14447082.51 msec, peer dispersion is 7938.47 msec
loopfilter state is 'CTRL' (Normal Controlled Loop), drift is 0.000000000 s/s
system poll interval is 64, last update was 15 sec ago.
```

Notice in Example 27-4 that R2 is running NTP version 4, and its association with the NTP server (R1) is successfully established and authenticated.

Secure Copy Protocol (SCP)

SCP provides a secure and authenticated method for copying router configuration or router image files to a remote location. SCP relies on SSH and requires that AAA authentication and authorization be configured so that the router can determine whether the user has the correct privilege level.

NOTE: AAA configuration is covered in greater detail on Day 26.

Example 27-5 provides the procedure to configure a Cisco device for SCP server-side functionality.

Example 27-5 SCP Configuration

```
R1(config)# ip domain-name mycorp.com
R1(config)# crypto key generate rsa general-keys modulus 2048
R1(config)# username Alice privilege 15 algorithm-type scrypt secret Cisco123
R1(config)# aaa new-model
R1(config)# aaa authentication login default local
R1(config)# aaa authorization exec default local
R1(config)# ip scp server enable
```

Note the optional use of the stronger SCRYPT algorithm instead of MD5 when configuring the secret password for Alice. R1 is now ready to act as an SCP server and will use SSH connections to accept secure copy transfers from authenticated and authorized users, in this case Alice. Transfers can originate from any SCP client, whether that client is another router, switch, or workstation.

Packet Tracer Activity: Configure NTP, Syslog, and NTP

Refer to the Digital Study Guide to access the PKA file for this activity. You must have Packet Tracer software to run this activity.

Study Resources

For today's exam topics, refer to the following resources for more study.

Resource	Location	Topic
Primary Resources		
CCNA Security Official Cert Guide	11	Securing the Management Plane on Cisco IOS Devices
CCNA Security (Networking Academy Curriculum)	2	Securing Network Devices
Supplemental Resources		
CCNA Security Complete Video Course	15	Securing the Management Plane
CCNA Security Portable Command Guide	6	Securing the Management Plane

Check Your Understanding

Refer to the Digital Study Guide to take a ten-question quiz covering the content of this day.

AAA Concepts

CCNA Security 210-260 IINS Exam Topics

- 2.2.a Describe RADIUS and TACACS+ technologies

- 2.2.d Explain the integration of Active Directory with AAA

- 2.2.e Describe authentication and authorization using ACS and ISE

Key Topics

Today we will look at the concepts and technologies behind authentication, authorization, and accounting (AAA). In particular, we will first review the two main types of AAA deployments (local and server-based). We will then discuss two protocols typically used in AAA (RADIUS and TACACS+), and finally we will examine two Cisco options for implementing AAA: ACS and ISE.

AAA

AAA network security services provide the primary framework to set up access control on a network device. AAA is a way to control who is permitted to access a network (*authenticate*), control what they can do while they are there (*authorize*), and audit what actions they performed while accessing the network (*accounting*). During an authentication process, a user or a system is challenged to identify itself and provide proof of its identity. The proof generally requires providing something that you know (password), something that you have (ID card), or something that you are (biometric).

AAA authentication can be used to authenticate users for administrative access or it can be used to authenticate users for remote network access. Cisco provides two common methods of implementing AAA services:

- **Local AAA authentication:** This method stores usernames and passwords locally in the Cisco router, and users authenticate against the local database.

- **Server-based AAA authentication:** A central AAA server contains the usernames and passwords for all users. The routers access this server using either Remote Authentication Dial-In User Service (RADIUS) or Terminal Access Controller Access Control System (TACACS+) protocols. The Cisco Secure Access Control System (ACS) server is an example of this type of server.

Table 26-1 briefly summarizes the differences between local AAA and server-based AAA.

Table 26-1   Comparing Local and Server-Based AAA

Local AAA	Server-based AAA
Usernames, passwords, and authorization specifications are configured and maintained in the local database of each network device.	User IDs are defined and managed centrally and made available to all network devices.
Simplest way to store AAA data.	Authorization policy is defined centrally and made available to all network devices.
Does not scale very well.	Simplified and centralized maintenance.
Does not support accounting.	Simplified and centralized auditing.
Typically used in small deployments.	Typically used in medium to large enterprise networks.

RADIUS and TACACS+

TACACS+ and RADIUS are both authentication protocols that are used to communicate with AAA servers. Both use the client/server model, as shown in Figure 26-1.

Figure 26-1   AAA Communication Overview

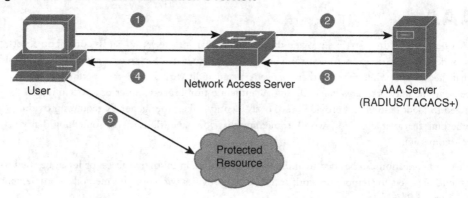

As shown in Step 1 of Figure 26-1, a user or machine sends a request to a networking device such as a router or switch that acts as a network access server (NAS) when running AAA. The NAS then communicates (Steps 2 and 3) with the server to exchange RADIUS or TACACS+ messages. If authentication is successful, the user is granted (Step 4) access to a protected resource (Step 5).

RADIUS

RADIUS is a general-purpose AAA protocol that is used across many technologies, including network access via wireless access points, wired switches, VPN, and administrative access to network devices. It is a fully open standard protocol developed by Livingston Enterprises and is described in RFC 2865 and RDF 2866.

RADIUS is a distributed client/server system that secures networks against unauthorized access. In the Cisco implementation, RADIUS clients run on Cisco devices and send authentication requests to a central RADIUS server that contains all user authentication and network service access information.

A RADIUS server listens on either UDP 1645 (legacy) or 1812 for authentication and authorization and either UDP 1646 (legacy) or 1813 for accounting. Communication between the NAS and RADIUS server is not completely secure; only the password portion of the RADIUS packet header is encrypted.

As illustrated in Figure 26-2, the RADIUS authentication process between the NAS and RADIUS server starts when a client attempts to connect to the network. The NAS prompts the user, requesting a username and password. The user sends his or her credentials to the NAS. The NAS then sends the authentication request (Access-Request) to the RADIUS server. The RADIUS server responds with an Access-Accept message (if the user is successfully authenticated) or an Access-Reject (if the user is not successfully authenticated).

Figure 26-2   RADIUS AAA Authentication

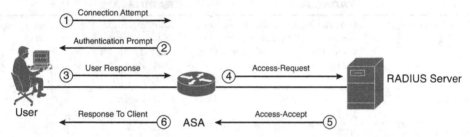

TACACS+

TACACS+ is a Cisco enhancement to the original TACACS protocol. Despite its name, TACACS+ is an entirely new protocol that is incompatible with any previous version of TACACS. TACACS+ is supported by the Cisco family of routers and access servers.

TACACS+ is Cisco proprietary. Under normal operations, it encrypts the entire body of the packet for more secure communications and utilizes TCP port 49. It also allows for greater modularity, by the total separation of all three AAA functions: authentication, authorization, and accounting.

As shown in Figure 26-3, TACACS+ communication between the NAS and the TACACS+ server starts with a connection request. Next, the NAS contacts the TACACS+ server to obtain a username prompt, which is then displayed to the user. The username entered by the user is forwarded to the server. The server prompts the user again, this time for a password. The password is then sent to the server, where it is validated against the database (local or remote).

If a match is found, the TACACS+ server sends an ACCEPT message to the client, and the authorization phase may begin (if configured on the NAS). If a match is not found, however, the server responds with a REJECT message, and any further access is denied.

Figure 26-3   TACACS+ AAA Authentication

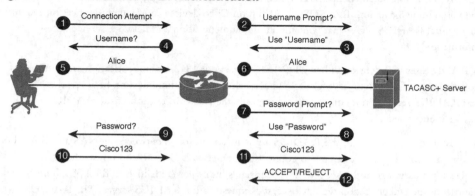

Table 26-2 compares the two protocols.

Table 26-2   TACACS+ Versus RADIUS

	TACACS+	RADIUS
Functionality	Separates AAA functions into distinct elements. Authentication is separate from authorization, and both of those are separate from accounting.	Combines many of the functions of authentication and authorization together. Has detailed accounting capability when accounting is configured for use.
Standard	Cisco proprietary, but very well known.	Open standard, and supported by nearly all vendors' AAA implementations.
L4 protocol	TCP	UDP
Confidentiality	All packets are encrypted between the ACS server and the router (which is the client).	Only the password is encrypted with regard to packets sent back and forth between the ACS server and the router.
Granular command-by-command authorization	This is supported, and the rules about which commands are allowed or disallowed are defined on the ACS server.	No explicit command authorization checking rules can be implemented.
Accounting	Provides accounting support.	Provides accounting support, and generally acknowledged as providing more detailed or extensive accounting capability than TACACS+.

Activity: Identify the AAA Communication Protocol

Refer to the Digital Study Guide to complete this activity.

ACS and ISE

AAA servers facilitate centralized resources for authentication databases, authorization policy configurations, and accounting records. Cisco offers two AAA servers for the enterprise market: Cisco Secure Access Control Server (ACS) and Cisco Identity Services Engine (ISE).

ACS

Cisco Secure ACS is a robust AAA server offering both TACACS+ and RADIUS services in one system. With ACS, an organization can centralize both user network access policies and network device administrative access policies in one server. Most network devices rely on the TACACS+ and RADIUS protocols to communicate with AAA servers. Some network devices have the ability to interact directly with Active Directory (AD) or LDAP for authentication purposes. Although Cisco Secure ACS can be integrated to use the AD service, Microsoft Windows Server can also be configured as an AAA server. Figure 26-4 shows a simple AAA scenario using ACS and an external user identity database (such as AD or LDAP).

Figure 26-4   ACS Authentication with External Database

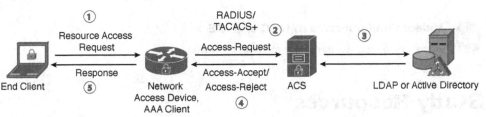

In Figure 26-4, the following sequence of events takes place:

1. The client establishes a connection with the router in an attempt to access a protected resource.

2. The router passes the username and password to the ACS server.

3. The ACS server consults the LDAP or AD server.

4. Based on information that is found in the LDAP or AD server database, the ACS server informs the router that the user is or is not authenticated.

5. The router passes the authentication results on to the client.

ISE

Cisco ISE is a next-generation identity management system that combines ACS with Network Admission Control (NAC) but also includes features such as

- **Profiling:** Determines the type of device from which the user is accessing the network

- **Posture assessment:** Determines the "health" of the device accessing the network

- **Centralized web authentication:** Simplifies the provisioning of guest access

- **AAA:** Offers identity-based network access, logging, compliance, and reporting

Cisco ISE is the main policy component for Cisco TrustSec and is a Cisco technology that protects assets such as data, applications, and mobile devices from unauthorized access. Cisco ISE not only can quickly isolate and contain threats and limit the impact of data breaches, but can also simplify and accelerate safe bring your own device (BYOD) deployments.

The switched, wireless, and routing infrastructure provides the policy enforcement building block. These network devices are instructed by ISE to ensure that only the expected communications is permitted through the network.

ISE utilizes standards-based RADIUS for authentication and authorization functions. User credentials are passed from the NAS to Cisco ISE via a RADIUS Access-Request message. Cisco ISE generally consults an external identity source, such as Microsoft Active Directory or LDAP, for credential verification and for user and group attributes. After the user identity is verified and its account attributes are processed, an appropriate authorization profile can be applied to its session. Cisco ISE conveys the associated authorization policy to the NAS in a RADIUS Access-Accept reply. Both posturing (OS version, patches, antivirus) and profiling (device type) can then be applied and used to determine what resources the user can access.

Video: Fundamentals of NAC and ISE

Refer to the Digital Study Guide to view this video.

Study Resources

For today's exam topics, refer to the following resources for more study.

Resource	Location	Topic
Primary Resources		
CCNA Security Official Cert Guide	3	Implementing AAA in Cisco IOS
	11	Securing the Management Plane on Cisco IOS Devices
CCNA Security (Networking Academy Curriculum)	3	Authentication, Authorization, and Accounting
Supplemental Resources		
CCNA Security Complete Video Course	15	Securing the Management Plane
	18	Implementing AAA Using IOS and ISE
CCNA Security Portable Command Guide	7	Securing Management Access with AAA
Cisco ASA (3rd ed.)	7	Authentication, Authorization, and Accounting (AAA) Services
AAA Identity Management Security	1, 2	Authentication, Authorization, Accounting (AAA)
		Cisco Secure ACS

Check Your Understanding

Refer to the Digital Study Guide to take a ten-question quiz covering the content of this day.

TACACS+ and RADIUS Implementation

CCNA Security 210-260 IINS Exam Topics

- 2.2.b Configure administrative access on a Cisco router using TACACS+

- 2.2.c Verify connectivity on a Cisco router to a TACACS+ server

Key Topics

Today we will look at implementing two sever-based AAA solutions: TACACS+ and RADIUS. First we will review the authentication configuration for both protocols, then move on to authorization, and finish with accounting. The basic steps when deploying server-based AAA are as follows:

1. Enable AAA.

2. Specify the IPv4 and/or IPv6 address of the AAA server (ACS or other).

3. Configure the shared secret key that will be used between the network access server (NAS) and the AAA server.

4. Configure authentication to use either the RADIUS or TACACS+ server.

5. Configure authorization to use either the RADIUS or TACACS+ server.

6. Configure accounting to use either the RADIUS or TACACS+ server.

Server-based AAA Authentication

Unlike local AAA authentication, server-based AAA authentication must identify various TACACS+ and RADIUS servers that the AAA service should consult when authenticating users, as shown in Example 25-1.

Example 25-1 Initial Setup for TACACS+ and RADIUS Servers

```
R1(config)# aaa new-model
R1(config)# tacacs server TACSRV
R1(config-server-tacacs)# address ipv4 172.16.255.100
R1(config-server-tacacs)# single-connection
R1(config-server-tacacs)# key SecretTACACS
R1(config-server-tacacs)# exit
R1(config)# radius server RADSRV
```

```
R1(config-radius-server)# address ipv4 172.16.255.101 auth-port 1812 acct-port 1813
R1(config-radius-server)# key SecretRADIUS
R1(config-radius-server)# exit
```

In Example 25-1, we are enabling AAA globally and then configuring the parameters for two AAA servers: a TACACS+ server at address 172.16.255.100 and a RADIUS server at address 172.16.255.101. Since TACACS+ uses TCP, we are using the **single-connection** command to maintain a single TCP connection for the duration of the session. The RADIUS server is using the standard UDP port numbers instead of the legacy Cisco values. Finally, we have defined a shared secret key to use for each protocol.

When the AAA security servers have been identified, the servers must be included in the method list of the **aaa authentication login** command. The general syntax for the command is

aaa authentication login { **default** | *list-name* } *method1* [*method2* ...]

When configuring login authentication, you can either use the default list name or create a custom list. If **default** is used, this list automatically applies to all login attempts (console, vty, aux, and http sessions). If **default** is not used, the list will need to be applied to each line manually. Finally, you must select the method(s) of authentication. If multiple methods are configured, the first option will act as the primary option and the subsequent methods will act as failover options in the order they are specified. The device will use failover methods only when it fails to get a response from the current method. If an authentication failure is received, the device will not fail over to the next method.

Table 25-1 briefly summarizes some of the authentication methods available.

Table 25-1   AAA Authentication Methods

Authentication Method Keyword	Description
enable	Uses the enable password for authentication.
group *group-name*	Uses a subset of RADIUS or TACACS+ servers for authentication as defined by the **aaa group server radius** or **aaa group server tacacs+** command.
group radius	Uses the list of all RADIUS servers for authentication.
group tacacs+	Uses the list of all TACACS+ servers for authentication.
local	Uses the local username database for authentication.
local-case	Uses case-sensitive local username authentication.
none	Uses no authentication.

In Example 25-2, we define three authentication lists: default, NOAUTH, and SRVAUTH. Each list uses specific authentication methods. For redundancy, a local user has been configured on R1 in case both the TACACS+ and RADIUS servers are unavailable. The default list is then applied to HTTP authentication attempts, while the NOAUTH list is applied to the console line, and the SRVAUTH list is applied to the vty lines. Notice that only SSH connections are permitted on the vty lines.

Example 25-2 Server-based AAA Authentication

```
R1(config)# username ADMIN privilege 15 algorithm-type scrypt secret ADMINPass
R1(config)# aaa authentication login default group tacacs+ group radius local-case
R1(config)# aaa authentication login NOAUTH none
R1(config)# aaa authentication login SRVAUTH group tacacs+ group radius local-case
R1(config)# ip http authentication aaa login-authentication default
R1(config)# line con 0
R1(config)# login authentication NOAUTH
R1(config)# exit
R1(config)# line vty 0 4
R1(config)# transport input ssh
R1(config)# login authentication SRVAUTH
```

 Activity: Match the AAA Method to Its Description

Refer to the Digital Study Guide to complete this activity.

Server-based AAA Authorization

Now that authentication has been enabled, we need to look at controlling what actions and commands a user is allowed to perform. When AAA authorization is not enabled, all users are allowed full access. After authorization is started, the default changes to allow no access. This means that the administrator must create a user with full access rights before authorization is enabled. Failure to do so immediately locks the administrator out of the system the moment the **aaa authorization** command is entered.

NOTE: To avoid accidently locking out the administrator, authorization is not implemented on **line con 0** by default. To enable authorization for the console, use the **aaa authorization console** global-configuration command.

Configuring authorization on Cisco IOS also involves creating method lists. The authorization method lists are similar to authentication method lists and the generic syntax for them is as follows:

```
aaa authorization {commands level | exec | network} {default | list-name}
    method1 [ method2 ... ]
```

Example 25-3 continues to build on Examples 25-1 and 25-2 by adding authorization for access to the EXEC shell (in other words, the CLI) and authorization for access to privilege level 15 and global configuration commands. Both authorization lists are then applied to the vty lines.

Example 25-3 AAA Authorization

```
R1(config)# aaa authorization exec SRVEXEC group tacacs+ group radius local
R1(config)# aaa authorization commands 15 SRVCMD group tacacs+ group radius local
R1(config)# aaa authorization config-commands
R1(config)# line vty 0 4
R1(config-line)# authorization exec SRVEXEC
R1(config-line)# authorization commands 15 SRVCMD
```

Server-based AAA Accounting

Restricting access to a network device alone is not enough for complete security of the device. Restrictions should be followed by regular monitoring. IOS provides the accounting feature to help monitor administrative sessions and commands entered in the session. Cisco Secure ACS can serve as a central repository for accounting information. Each session that is established through ACS can be fully accounted for and stored on the server. In this case, a TACACS+ or RADIUS server can keep accounting records of administrative access sessions and of individual commands.

Similar to authentication and authorization, accounting also requires creating method lists. The general syntax is as follows:

```
aaa accounting {system | network | exec | connection | commands level}
   {default | list-name} {start-stop | stop-only | none} [method1 [method2...]]
```

An important consideration when enabling accounting is selecting the record type, or trigger. The trigger specifies what actions cause accounting records to be updated. Possible triggers are listed in Table 25-2.

Table 25-2   Accounting Record Types

Record Type	Purpose
start-stop	Sends a "start" accounting notice at the beginning of a process and a "stop" accounting notice at the end of a process.
stop-only	Sends a "stop" accounting record for all cases including authentication failures.
none	Disables accounting services on a line or interface.

Example 25-4 continues to build on Example 25-3 by adding the command that will cause an accounting record to be sent at the start of an administrative access session to the device's EXEC process, and another accounting record to be sent at the end of the session. Also, a second command is added that causes an accounting record to be sent for every privilege level 15 command and every configuration mode command that is entered by the user. Both accounting lists are then applied to the vty lines.

Example 25-4 AAA Accounting

```
R1(config)# aaa accounting exec ACCEXEC start-stop group tacacs+ group radius
R1(config)# aaa accounting commands 15 ACCCMDS stop-only group tacacs+ groups
   radius
R1(config)# line vty 0 4
R1(config-line)# accounting exec ACCEXEC
R1(config-line)# accounting commands 15 ACCCMDS
```

This type of accounting is very detailed and includes data such as a device's identity, the user's identity, the IP address from which the user is connected, and the date and time stamps that are associated with the activity.

Server-based AAA Verification and Troubleshooting

When AAA is enabled, it is often necessary to monitor authentication traffic and troubleshoot configurations. The **debug aaa authentication** command is a useful AAA troubleshooting command because it provides a high-level view of login activity. Example 25-5 shows the output for a successful TACACS+ login attempt.

Example 25-5 Verifying AAA TACACS+ Authentication

```
R1# debug aaa authentication
14:01:17: AAA/AUTHEN (567936829): Method=TACACS+
14:01:17: TAC+: send AUTHEN/CONT packet
14:01:17: TAC+ (567936829): received authen response status = PASS
14:01:17: AAA/AUTHEN (567936829): status = PASS
```

The first line of the debug output confirms that the TACACS+ method is being used, and the "PASS" status message in the third and fourth lines shows that authentication was successful.

Example 25-6 shows a failed RADIUS authentication attempt.

Example 25-6 Verifying AAA RADIUS Authentication

```
R1# debug aaa authentication
14:02:55: AAA/AUTHEN (164826761): Method=RADIUS
14:02:55: AAA/AUTHEN (164826761): status = GETPASS
14:03:01: AAA/AUTHEN/CONT (164826761): continue_login
14:03:01: AAA/AUTHEN (164826761): status = GETPASS
14:03:01: AAA/AUTHEN (164826761): Method=RADIUS
14:03:04: AAA/AUTHEN (164826761): status = FAIL
```

Again, the first line of the output confirms that the RADIUS method is being used, and the "FAIL" status message shows that authentication was unsuccessful.

For a more granular view of either the TACACS+ or RADIUS authentication process, use the **debug tacacs** or **debug radius** command.

Example 25-7 shows a successful TACACS+ login attempt, whereas Example 25-8 shows a failed TACACS+ login attempt. The result is confirmed in the penultimate line in each example.

Example 25-7 Verifying Successful TACACS+ Authentication

```
R1# debug tacacs
14:00:09: TAC+: Opening TCP/IP connection to 192.168.60.15 using source 10.116.0.79
14:00:09: TAC+: Sending TCP/IP packet number 383258052-1 to 192.168.60.15
  (AUTHEN/START)
14:00:09: TAC+: Receiving TCP/IP packet number 383258052-2 from 192.168.60.15
14:00:09: TAC+ (383258052): received authen response status = GETUSER
14:00:10: TAC+: send AUTHEN/CONT packet
14:00:10: TAC+: Sending TCP/IP packet number 383258052-3 to 192.168.60.15
  (AUTHEN/CONT)
14:00:10: TAC+: Receiving TCP/IP packet number 383258052-4 from 192.168.60.15
14:00:10: TAC+ (383258052): received authen response status = GETPASS
14:00:14: TAC+: send AUTHEN/CONT packet
14:00:14: TAC+: Sending TCP/IP packet number 383258052-5 to 192.168.60.15
  (AUTHEN/CONT)
14:00:14: TAC+: Receiving TCP/IP packet number 383258052-6 from 192.168.60.15
14:00:14: TAC+ (383258052): received authen response status = PASS
14:00:14: TAC+: Closing TCP/IP connection to 192.168.60.15
```

Example 25-8 Verifying Unsuccessful TACACS+ Authentication

```
R1# debug tacacs
13:53:35: TAC+: Opening TCP/IP connection to 192.168.60.15 using source 192.48.0.79
13:53:35: TAC+: Sending TCP/IP packet number 416942312-1 to 192.168.60.15
  (AUTHEN/START)
13:53:35: TAC+: Receiving TCP/IP packet number 416942312-2 from 192.168.60.15
13:53:35: TAC+ (416942312): received authen response status = GETUSER
13:53:37: TAC+: send AUTHEN/CONT packet
13:53:37: TAC+: Sending TCP/IP packet number 416942312-3 to 192.168.60.15
  (AUTHEN/CONT)
13:53:37: TAC+: Receiving TCP/IP packet number 416942312-4 from 192.168.60.15
13:53:37: TAC+ (416942312): received authen response status = GETPASS
13:53:38: TAC+: send AUTHEN/CONT packet
13:53:38: TAC+: Sending TCP/IP packet number 416942312-5 to 192.168.60.15 (
  AUTHEN/CONT)
13:53:38: TAC+: Receiving TCP/IP packet number 416942312-6 from 192.168.60.15
13:53:38: TAC+ (416942312): received authen response status = FAIL
13:53:40: TAC+: Closing TCP/IP connection to 192.168.60.15
```

Example 25-9 shows a successful RADIUS login attempt, whereas Example 25-10 shows an unsuccessful RADIUS login attempt.

Example 25-9 Verifying Successful RADIUS Authentication

```
R1# debug radius
13:59:02: Radius: IPC Send 0.0.0.0:1645, Access-Request, id 0xB, len 56
13:59:02:          Attribute 4 6 AC150E5A
13:59:02:          Attribute 5 6 0000000A
13:59:02:          Attribute 1 6 62696C6C
13:59:02:          Attribute 2 18 0531FEA3
13:59:04: Radius: Received from 171.69.1.152:1645, Access-Accept, id 0xB, len 26
```

Example 25-10   Verifying Unsuccessful RADIUS Authentication

```
R1# debug radius
13:57:56: Radius: IPC Send 0.0.0.0:1645, Access-Request, id 0xA, len 57
13:57:56:          Attribute 4 6 AC150E5A
13:57:56:          Attribute 5 6 0000000A
13:57:56:          Attribute 1 7 62696C6C
13:57:56:          Attribute 2 18 49C28F6C
13:57:59: Radius: Received from 171.69.1.152:1645, Access-Reject, id 0xA, len 20
```

In both cases, the last line in the output confirms the result.

It is also possible to verify authorization and accounting with the **debug aaa authorization** and **debug aaa accounting** commands, as shown in Example 25-11 and Example 25-12.

Example 25-11   Verifying AAA Authorization

```
R1# debug aaa authorization
2:23:21: AAA/AUTHOR (0): user='manager'
2:23:21: AAA/AUTHOR (0): send AV service=shell
2:23:21: AAA/AUTHOR (0): send AV cmd*
2:23:21: AAA/AUTHOR (342885561): Method=TACACS+
2:23:21: AAA/AUTHOR/TAC+ (342885561): user=manager
2:23:21: AAA/AUTHOR/TAC+ (342885561): send AV service=shell
2:23:21: AAA/AUTHOR/TAC+ (342885561): send AV cmd*
2:23:21: AAA/AUTHOR (342885561): Post authorization status = FAIL
```

In Example 25-11, the user "manager" is attempting to access the EXEC shell. The TACACS+ method is being used to verify if this access is permitted. The last line confirms that the user's authorization has failed.

Example 25-12 Verifying AAA Accounting

```
R1# debug aaa accounting
16:49:21: AAA/ACCT: EXEC acct start, line 10
16:49:32: AAA/ACCT: Connect start, line 10, glare
16:49:47: AAA/ACCT: Connection acct stop:
task_id=70 service=exec port=10 protocol=telnet address=172.31.3.78 cmd=glare
  bytes_in=308  bytes_out=76 paks_in=45 paks_out=54 elapsed_time=14
```

The accounting information confirms that a Telnet session was initiated from the EXEC shell to a destination IP address of 172.31.3.78.

Finally, to quickly verify if authentication is working between the AAA clients (NAS) and the AAA server (ACS), the **test aaa group** command can be used, as shown in Example 25-13.

Example 25-13 Testing AAA Between the NAS and AAA Server

```
R1# test aaa group tacacs+ ADMIN ADMINPass legacy
Attempting authentication test to server-group tacacs+ using tacacs+
User was successfully authenticated.
```

In this example, the ADMIN user's credentials are successfully verified against the TACACS+ group of servers.

Video: Configuring AAA Using a RADIUS Server

Refer to the Digital Study Guide to view this video.

Video: Configuring AAA Using a TACACS+ Server

Refer to the Digital Study Guide to view this video.

Study Resources

For today's exam topics, refer to the following resources for more study.

Resource	Location	Topic
Primary Resources		
CCNA Security Official Cert Guide	3	Implementing AAA in Cisco IOS
CCNA Security (Networking Academy Curriculum)	3	Authentication, Authorization, and Accounting

Resource	Location	Topic
Supplemental Resources		
CCNA Security Complete Video Course	15	Securing the Management Plane
	18	Implementing AAA Using IOS and ISE
CCNA Security Portable Command Guide	7	Securing Management Access with AAA
Cisco ASA (3rd ed.)	7	Authentication, Authorization, and Accounting (AAA) Services
AAA Identity Management Security	6	Administrative AAA on IOS
CCNP Routing and Switching Portable Command Guide	14	Campus Network Security

Check Your Understanding

Refer to the Digital Study Guide to take a ten-question quiz covering the content of this day.

802.1X

CCNA Security 210-260 IINS Exam Topics

- 2.3.a Identify the functions of 802.1X components

Key Topics

Today we will look at port-based authentication control, commonly known as 802.1X. First we will review the terminology and concepts related to 802.1X, including a brief discussion of EAP over LAN (EAPOL). We will then look at some configuration examples of this type of access control.

802.1X

Cisco switches can support port-based authentication, a combination of AAA authentication and port security. This feature is based on the IEEE 802.1X standard.

Terminology and Concepts

The IEEE 802.1X standard defines a client/server-based access control and authentication protocol that prevents unauthorized clients from connecting to a LAN through switch ports unless they are properly authenticated. As part of the authentication process, the authentication server authenticates each client connected to a switch port before any services offered by the switch or the LAN are made available.

Figure 24-1 illustrates the authentication process that occurs with 802.1X. In this scenario, (1) the supplicant or client initiates an EAPOL exchange with the authenticator (e.g., switch), (2) a RADIUS authentication request is sent to the RADIUS server by the authenticator on behalf of the supplicant, (3) the RADIUS server responds with either an Accept or Reject message, and (4) the authenticator informs the supplicant of the result. If the authentication was successful, (5) the supplicant is granted access to the protected resource (e.g., the network).

Until the client is authenticated, 802.1X access control allows only EAPOL, Cisco Discovery Protocol (CDP), and Spanning Tree Protocol (STP) traffic to pass through the port to which the client is connected. After authentication is successful, normal traffic can pass through the respective port.

If a client that does not support 802.1X authentication connects to an unauthorized 802.1X port, the authenticator requests the client's identity. In this situation, the client does not respond to the request, the port remains in the unauthorized state, and the client is not granted access to the network.

Figure 24-1   IEEE 802.1X Port-based Authentication

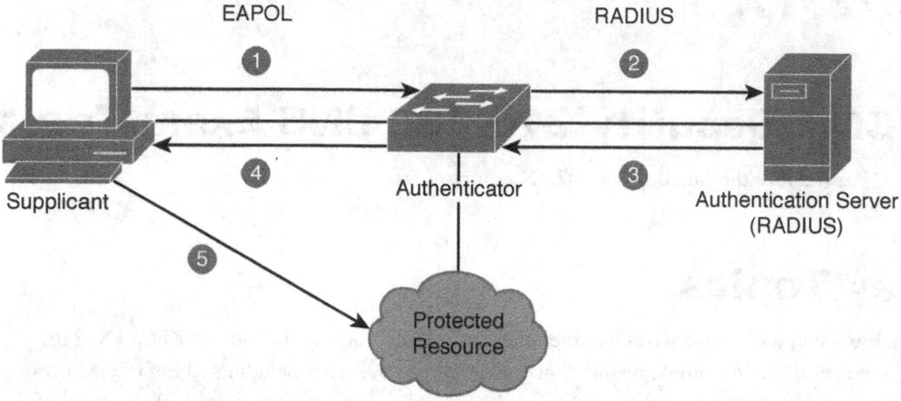

By contrast, when an 802.1X-enabled supplicant connects to a port that is not running the 802.1X standard, the supplicant initiates the authentication process by sending the EAPOL-Start frame. When no response is received, the supplicant sends the request for a fixed number of times. Because no response is received, the supplicant begins sending frames as if the port were in the authorized state.

With 802.1X port-based authentication, the devices in the network have specific roles:

- **Supplicant:** Usually a workstation or laptop with 802.1X-compliant client software. The supplicant may start the authentication process by requesting access to the LAN.

- **Authenticator:** Usually an edge switch or wireless access point (AP). The authenticator controls the physical access to the network based on the authentication status of the client. The switch acts as an intermediary (proxy) between the client and the authentication server, requesting identity information from the client, verifying that information with the authentication server, and relaying a response to the client.

- **Authentication server:** A server that performs the actual authentication of the client. The authentication server validates the identity of the client and notifies the authenticator whether the client is authorized to access LAN and switch services. Because the authenticator acts as a proxy, the authentication service is transparent to the client. Currently, a RADIUS server with EAP extensions is the only supported authentication server.

Figure 24-2 shows in detail the exchange of messages between the supplicant, the authenticator, and the authentication server.

Both the authenticator and the supplicant can initiate authentication. The authenticator initiates authentication when the link state changes from down to up, or periodically as long as the port remains up and unauthenticated. The authenticator sends an EAP-Request/Identity frame to the supplicant to request its identity. Upon receipt of the frame, the supplicant responds with an EAP-Response/Identity frame.

Figure 24-2   802.1X End-to-End Message Exchange

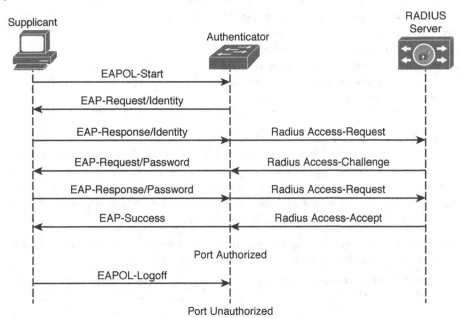

When the supplicant supplies its identity, the authenticator begins its role as the intermediary, passing EAP frames between the supplicant and the authentication server until authentication succeeds
or fails. When a supplicant is successfully authenticated, the port transitions to the authorized state,
allowing all traffic for the supplicant to flow normally.

When a supplicant logs off, it sends an EAPOL-Logoff message, causing the switch port to change
back to the unauthorized state. In addition, if the link state of a port changes from up to down, the
port returns to the unauthorized state.

The 802.1X framework not only provides authentication but also provides authorization of clients
that seek network access. The authorization features can include, for example, VLAN assignment,
ACL assignment, or time-based access.

Configuration and Verification

Example 24-1 shows the steps required to enable 802.1X on a Cisco switch, allowing it to act as an
authenticator for clients.

Example 24-1 802.1X Configuration Example

```
S1(config)# aaa new-model
S1(config)# radius server RADSRV
S1(config-radius-server)# address ipv4 172.16.255.101 auth-port 1812 acct-port 1813
S1(config-radius-server)# key SecretRADIUS
```

```
S1(config-radius-server)# exit
S1(config)# aaa authentication dot1x default group radius
S1(config)# dot1x system-auth-control
S1(config)# interface gigabitethernet 1/0/1
S1(config-if)# switchport mode access
S1(config-if)# authentication port-control auto
S1(config-if)# dot1x pae authenticator
```

In this example, AAA is enabled globally and a RADIUS server, RADSRV, is configured. An 802.1X authentication method list is created, and 802.1X authentication is enabled globally on the switch. Finally, port-based authentication is activated on the switch interface. Notice that the interface has been manually configured as a Layer 2 static-access port. 802.1X is not supported on trunk ports, dynamic ports, or EtherChannel ports. Also, the switch interface has been set to act only as an authenticator and ignore messages meant for a supplicant.

It is important to understand that the **authentication port-control** command offers three options to control port authorization. The basic syntax for the command is

```
S1(config-if)# authentication port-control {auto | force-authorized |
   force-unauthorized}
```

Table 24-1 explains the different command options.

Table 24-1   authentication port-control Command Options

Parameter	Description
force-authorized	Disables 802.1X authentication and causes the port to change to the authorized state without any authentication exchange required. The port sends and receives normal traffic without 802.1X-based authentication of the client. This is the default setting.
force-unauthorized	Causes the port to remain in the unauthorized state, ignoring all attempts by the client to authenticate. The switch cannot provide authentication services to the client through the port.
auto	Enables 802.1X authentication and causes the port to begin in the unauthorized state, allowing only EAPOL frames to be sent and received through the port. The authentication process begins when the link state of the port changes from down to up or when an EAPOL-Start frame is received.

To verify 802.1X functionality, use the **show dot1x** command. The general syntax is

```
R1# show dot1x [ all [summary] | interface interface-name | details | statistics ]
```

The following is sample output from the **show dot1x** command using both the **interface** and **details** keywords. The client is successfully authenticated in this example.

```
S1# show dot1x interface gigabitethernet 1/0/1 details
Dot1x Info for GigabitEthernet1/0/1
----------------------------------------
PAE                       = AUTHENTICATOR
PortControl               = AUTO
ControlDirection          = Both
HostMode                  = MULTI_HOST
QuietPeriod               = 60
ServerTimeout             = 0
SuppTimeout               = 30
ReAuthMax                 = 2
MaxReq                    = 1
TxPeriod                  = 30
Dot1x Authenticator Client List
-------------------------------
Supplicant                = 0123.abcd.6789
Session ID                = 0B346280000000000000006E5
    Auth SM State         = AUTHENTICATED
    Auth BEND SM State    = IDLE
```

Video: Configuring and Verifying 802.1X

Refer to the Digital Study Guide to view this video.

Activity: Match the 802.1X Terminology to Its Description

Refer to the Digital Study Guide to complete this activity.

Study Resources

For today's exam topics, refer to the following resources for more study.

Resource	Location	Topic
Primary Resources		
CCNA Security (Networking Academy Curriculum)	3	Authentication, Authorization, and Accounting
Supplemental Resources		
AAA Identity Management Security	8	IOS Switches / 802.1X
CCNP Security SISAS 300-208 Official Cert Guide	4	EAP Over LAN

Check Your Understanding

Refer to the Digital Study Guide to take a ten-question quiz covering the content of this day.

BYOD

CCNA Security 210-260 IINS Exam Topics

- 2.4.a Describe the BYOD architecture framework
- 2.4.b Describe the function of mobile device management (MDM)

Key Topics

Today we will look at the trend called bring your own device (BYOD). BYOD was initially centered on allowing employees, partners, and guests to connect to the corporate networks and be able to perform a limited number of basic functions such as access to the Internet, access to corporate email, calendar, and contacts, and so on. As more and more personal devices have become prevalent in the enterprise, workers are using these devices to access enterprise resources and applications to do their daily jobs. With employees using personal devices for mission-critical job functions, mobile device management (MDM) and functions associated with MDM are becoming increasingly important. Functions such as ensuring that a device can be locked and remotely wiped in case it gets lost or stolen or when the employee is terminated are becoming a necessity.

BYOD Architecture

Today enterprises have diverse wired LAN and wireless LAN (WLAN) infrastructure implementations. In the past, the focus has been on ensuring that the wired enterprise infrastructure is robust and secure. Communication within the premises is based on a trust model, protected by firewalls at the perimeter and other security tools. In contrast, the enterprise wireless infrastructure was built for convenience as an overlay, at least until the BYOD phenomenon emerged. With BYOD, users will have three or more mobile/WLAN devices (laptop, tablet, phone) connecting to this infrastructure. The devices themselves could be user owned or corporate owned. The WLAN needs to become as robust, secure, scalable, and predictable as the wired network to support BYOD. The main topics to consider for a successful BYOD deployment are

- **Mobile device security:** The devices used to access the corporate network are safe and are not jail-broken or rooted. They should not have threatening malware, spam, or applications that can compromise the corporate network or data. The user can be identified and allowed the appropriate network access according to company policy. Secure access is ensured for data loss prevention. Devices can also be remotely locked or wiped.

- **Mobility:** Investing in WLAN capacity, performance, and intelligent value-add features is a necessity.

- **Collaboration:** Enterprises are expanding their mobility initiatives to include deploying and supporting a variety of mobile devices, mobile applications, and collaboration services. In addition, there is emerging demand for video, streaming, and web-conferencing applications to facilitate employee collaboration and communication capabilities over these mobile devices.

- **Network intelligence:** For BYOD, this means application visibility (seeing what applications are running on the network), application performance (throughput, response time, latency), application optimization across the WAN, and application control (quality of service [QoS] metrics, service-level agreement [SLA] requirements, filtering).

A comprehensive BYOD solution must provide for wired, Wi-Fi, remote, and mobile access to the network, must be supported across many device types and brands, and must be capable of enforcing the various policies across the spectrum of businesses and industries. In addition, as devices move from one context to another—for example, from the corporate Wi-Fi network to a public 3G/4G mobile network, to a public hotspot, and to a branch or home office—the BYOD solution must be able to provide secure access while keeping the experience seamless for the user. Figure 23-1 shows the high-level solution architecture and major components of the Cisco BYOD solution.

Figure 23-1   High-Level BYOD Solution Architecture

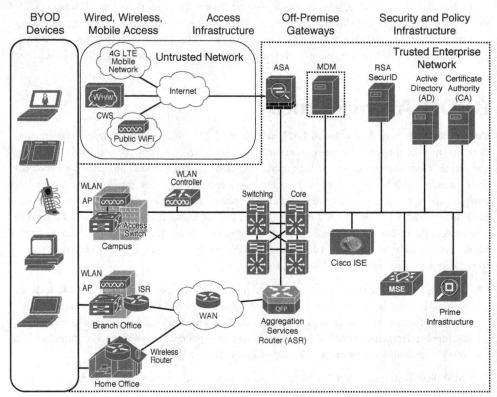

Some of the more important components of this architectural infrastructure are

- BYOD devices

- Wireless access points

- WLAN controllers

- Converged access switches

- Cisco Mobility Services Engine (MSE)

- Cisco Identity Services Engine (ISE)

- Cisco Adaptive Security Appliance (ASA)

- Cisco AnyConnect Client

- Cisco Integrated Services Router (ISR)

- Cisco Aggregation Services Router (ASR)

- Cisco Prime Infrastructure (PI)

- Cisco Cloud Web Security (CWS)

- RSA SecurID

- Microsoft Active Directory (AD)

- Certificate authority (CA)

NOTE: For a detailed explanation of each of these components, see the Cisco Unified Access (UA) and Bring Your Own Device (BYOD) CVD (Cisco Validated Design) at http:// www.cisco.com/c/en/us/td/docs/solutions/Enterprise/Borderless_Networks/Unified_Access/ BYOD_Design_Guide.html.

 Video: Cisco ISE for BYOD Mobility

Refer to the Digital Study Guide to view this video.

BYOD Management

Many enterprises use *mobile device management* (MDM), which is designed to help an enterprise rapidly and securely deploy mobile devices, tablets, and applications with policy, compliance, configuration, and application management. MDM is about enabling, facilitating, monitoring, and securing users, devices, content, and applications. MDM-supported and managed devices include not only handheld devices, such as smartphones and tablets, but increasingly laptop and desktop computing devices as well. MDM offers functions such as

- PIN enforcement

- Strong password enforcement

- Jailbreak/root detection

- Data encryption

- Remote data wipe

- Data loss prevention (DLP)

- Secure application tunnels

There exists two major deployment models for MDM: on-premises and cloud-based. In an *on-premises* model, MDM software is installed on servers in the corporate DMZ or data center, which are supported and maintained by the enterprise IT staff. In a *cloud-based* model, MDM software is hosted, supported, and maintained by a provider at a remote network operations center (NOC); customers subscribe on a monthly or yearly basis and are granted access to all MDM hardware/software via the Internet.

Before deploying an MDM solution, a business must decide which model is best for it. Several factors are involved in this decision, including

- **Cost:** Cloud-based MDM solutions often are more cost-effective than on-premises.

- **Control:** On-premises MDM models offer enterprises the greatest degree of control.

- **Security:** On-premises MDM models are often perceived as being more secure than cloud-based models.

- **Intellectual property:** Most MDM solutions support secure isolation of corporate data on the devices they manage.

- **Regulatory compliance:** Regulatory compliance can dictate where and how financial, healthcare, and government (and other) organizations can store their data.

- **Scalability:** Cloud-based models offer better scalability than on-premises models.

- **Speed of deployment:** Cloud-based solutions are typically faster to deploy.

- **Flexibility:** Cloud-based MDM solutions typically have day-one support for new releases of device hardware and software.

- **Ease of management:** With on-premises models, the IT department must ensure the MDM has all the latest updates; in a cloud-based system, this responsibility rests with the provider.

Figure 23-2 illustrates the network topology for a campus BYOD network utilizing an on-premises MDM deployment model. This model is generally better suited to IT staff that have a higher level of technical expertise or to enterprises that may have stricter security/confidentiality requirements.

Figure 23-3 illustrates the network topology for a branch BYOD network utilizing a cloud-based MDM deployment mode. From a customer's perspective, this model is greatly simplified; however, as a trade-off, the customer relinquishes a degree of control over all its devices (and also some of the data on these devices) to the provider, which may pose security concerns.

Figure 23-2   On-Premises MDM Deployment

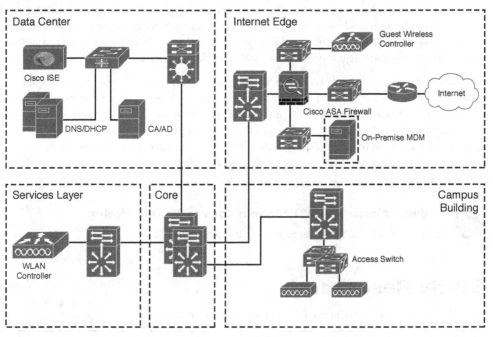

Figure 23-3   Cloud-based MDM Deployment

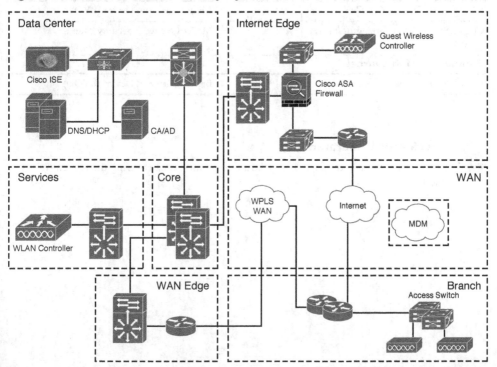

Another important consideration in BYOD management is device onboarding. The idea of device onboarding is that employees can register their own devices. The onboarding process requires the employee to authenticate and includes the provisioning of a device certificate for the onboarded device. Cisco ISE can provide a solution for employee self-service onboarding and registration. ISE authorization policy can integrate with either MDM solutions or simpler BYOD onboarding.

Onboarding for new devices involves certificate enrollment and profile provisioning, and should be easy for end users to perform with minimal intervention by IT, especially for employee-owned devices. Device choice does not mean having to give up security. IT needs to establish the minimum security baseline that any device must meet to access the corporate network. Proper device authentication is critical to ensure that the onboarding of new devices and the access of other devices is secure and protects the entire network infrastructure, but authentication should also be as simple as possible for both the IT personnel and the user.

Activity: Match the BYOD Terminology to Its Description

Refer to the Digital Study Guide to complete this activity.

Study Resources

For today's exam topics, refer to the following resources for more study.

Resource	Location	Topic
Primary Resources		
CCNA Security Official Cert Guide	4	Bring Your Own Device (BYOD)
CCNA Security (Networking Academy Curriculum)	1	Modern Network Security Threats
Supplemental Resources		
CCNA Security Complete Video Course	19	Bring Your Own Device (BYOD)

Check Your Understanding

Refer to the Digital Study Guide to take a ten-question quiz covering the content of this day.

Day 22

IPsec Technologies

CCNA Security 210-260 IINS Exam Topics

- 3.1.a Describe IPsec protocols and delivery modes (IKE, ESP, AH, tunnel mode, transport mode)

Key Topics

Today we will focus on the fundamentals of virtual private network (VPN) technologies, as well as look in detail at the building blocks behind Internet Protocol security (IPsec).

VPNs

A VPN provides security services to traffic traversing a relatively less trustworthy network between two relatively more trusted systems or networks. Most commonly, the less trusted network is the public Internet. A VPN is *virtual* in that it carries information within a private network, but that information is actually transported over a public network. A VPN is also *private* in that the traffic is encrypted to keep the data confidential while it is transported across the public network. There are four main benefits to using VPNs:

- **Cost savings:** Organizations can use VPNs to reduce their connectivity costs.

- **Security:** Advanced encryption and authentication protocols protect data.

- **Scalability:** Organizations can use the Internet to easily interconnect new offices.

- **Compatibility:** VPNs can be implemented across a wide variety of WAN link options.

There are many different types of VPN technologies, some of which offer privacy through isolation, and some of which offer both privacy and security by implementing cryptographic protocols. Table 22-1 summarizes some of these VPN options.

Table 22-1   Types of VPNs

VPN Type	Description
Generic Routing Encapsulation (GRE)	Tunneling protocol developed by Cisco that can encapsulate a wide variety of network layer protocol packet types inside IP tunnels to create virtual point-to-point links between routers. (Private but not secure.)
Multiprotocol Label Switching (MPLS) VPN	Provided by a service provider to allow a company with two or more sites to have logical connectivity between the sites using the service provider network for transport. (Private but not secure.)
Secure Sockets Layer (SSL) VPN	Implements security of TCP sessions over encrypted SSL tunnels, and can be used for remote-access VPNs. (Private and secure.)

VPN Type	Description
IPsec VPN	Implements security of IP packets at Layer 3 of the OSI model, and can be used for site-to-site VPNs and remote-access VPNs. (Private and secure.)
Legacy VPN (X.25, Frame Relay, ATM)	Layer 2 technology commonly used to provide WAN connectivity between organizations. (Private but not secure.)

The CCNA Security exam focuses on three of these types of VPN:

- Site-to-site IPsec VPN

- Remote-access IPsec VPN

- Remote-access SSL VPN

A site-to-site IPsec VPN is an extension of a classic WAN network. Site-to-site VPNs connect entire networks to each other. For example, site-to-site VPNs can connect a branch office network to a company headquarters network. Transport across a site-to-site VPN is transparent to the communicating hosts. The hosts send and receive normal TCP/IP traffic between each other. VPN gateways provide security services at the borders between the trusted and non-trusted networks. Figure 22-1 shows how site-to-site VPNs can be used to securely connect branch offices to a company headquarters network using an insecure Internet connection.

Figure 22-1   Site-to-Site VPNs

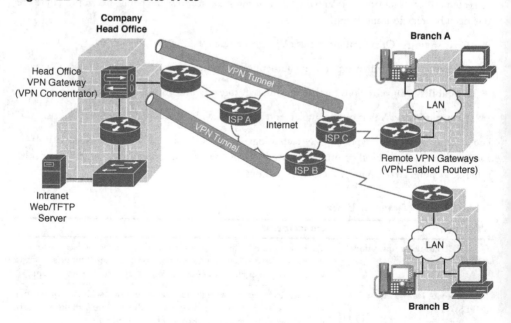

Remote-access VPN technology is an evolution of dialup connections. Remote-access VPNs can support the needs of telecommuters, mobile users, and extranet consumer-to-business traffic, as shown in Figure 22-2. Remote-access VPNs connect individual hosts that must access their company network securely over the Internet. In a remote-access VPN, each host typically has VPN client software. Whenever the host tries to send any traffic, the VPN client software encapsulates and encrypts that traffic before sending it over the Internet to the VPN gateway at the edge of the target network.

Figure 22-2   Remote-Access VPNs

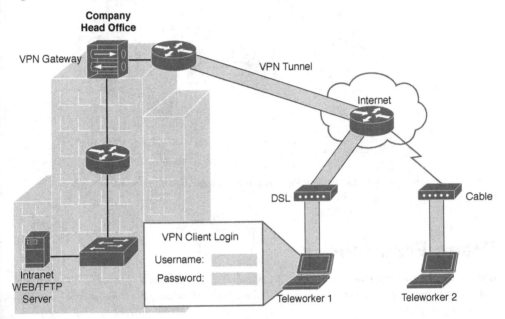

On the other hand, SSL VPNs provide a suite of security services that are similar to the security services provided by IPsec. SSL VPN technology has become popular for the implementation of remote-access VPNs with or without the use of client software. SSL-based VPNs leverage the SSL protocol. SSL was initially developed by Netscape in the 1990s. The Internet Engineering Task Force (IETF) later produced a standards-based more secure alternative called TLS. There are slight differences between SSL and TLS, but the protocols remain similar. The terms are sometimes used interchangeably, but interestingly, the protocols are not interoperable. Cisco SSL VPNs are really using TLS behind the scenes, so both SSL and TLS are mentioned in this chapter.

One of the most popular features of a clientless SSL VPN is the capability to launch a browser and simply connect to the address of the VPN device, as opposed to running a separate VPN client program to establish an IPsec VPN connection.

The most successful application running on top of SSL is HTTP because of the huge popularity of the World Wide Web. All the most popular web browsers in use today support HTTPS (HTTP over SSL/TLS). Figure 22-3 shows two types of SSL VPN connections across the Internet: the noncorporate user connects using a clientless SSL VPN through a web browser, while the employee connects using a client-based SSL VPN. Both clients are authenticated using the AAA server in order to access the internal protected resources.

Figure 22-3   SSL VPNs

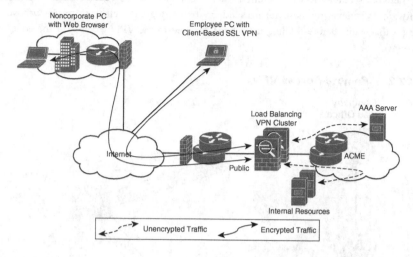

We will cover the concepts, the terminology, and the configuration of these three types of VPN deployments in upcoming review days.

IPsec Framework

IPsec is an open standard that defines how a VPN can be secured across IP networks. IPsec protects and authenticates IP packets between source and destination. IPsec provides these essential security functions:

- **Confidentiality:** IPsec ensures confidentiality by using encryption.

- **Data integrity:** IPsec ensures that data arrives unchanged at the destination, meaning that the data has not been manipulated at any point along the communication path.

- **Origin authentication:** Authentication ensures that the connection is made with the desired communication partner. IPsec uses Internet Key Exchange (IKE) to authenticate users and devices that can carry out communication independently. IKE can use the following methods to authenticate the peer system:

  - Pre-shared keys (PSK)

  - Digital certificates

  - RSA-encrypted nonces

- **Anti-replay protection:** Anti-replay protection verifies that each packet is unique and is not duplicated.

- **Key management:** Allows for an initial safe exchange of dynamically generated keys across a non-trusted network and a periodic rekeying process, limiting the maximum amount of time and data that are protected with any one key.

These security functions define the IPsec framework and spell out the rules for secure communi-nications. IPsec relies on existing algorithms to implement encryption, authentication, and key exchange. Figure 22-4 illustrates some of the standard algorithms that IPsec uses. The framework allows technologies to be replaced over time. When cryptographic technologies become obsolete, it doesn't make the IPsec framework obsolete. Instead, obsolete technologies are replaced with more current versions, keeping the framework in place.

Figure 22-4   IPsec Framework Components

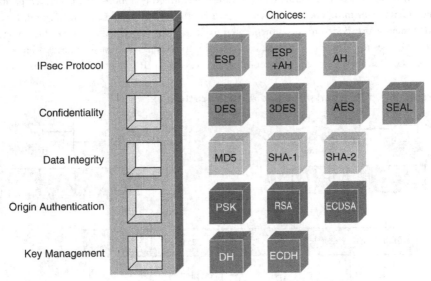

The following subsections will look at each individual line of the IPsec framework in detail.

IPsec Protocols

There are two main IPsec framework protocols: Authentication Header (AH) and Encapsulating Security Payload (ESP).

AH

AH, which is IP protocol 51, is the appropriate protocol to use when confidentiality is not required. In other words, AH does not provide data encryption. AH does, however, provide origin authentication, data integrity, and anti-replay protection for IP packets that are passed between two systems. AH achieves data integrity and origin authentication by applying a keyed one-way hash function to the packet to create a hash, or message digest. The hash is combined with the text and is transmitted. The receiver detects changes in any part of the packet that occur during transit by performing the same one-way hash function on the received packet and comparing the result to the value of the message digest that the sender has supplied. AH supports the HMAC–MD5 and HMAC–SHA-1 algorithms.

ESP

Like AH, ESP provides origin authentication, data integrity, and anti-replay protection; however, unlike AH, it also provides confidentiality. ESP, which is IP protocol 50, provides confidentiality by encrypting IP packets. ESP supports various symmetric encryption algorithms, including DES, 3DES, and AES. The original data is well protected by ESP, because the entire original IP packet is encrypted. When ESP authentication is also used, the encrypted IP packet and the ESP header and trailer are included in the hashing process. When both authentication and encryption are used, encryption is performed first. Authentication is then performed by sending the encrypted payload through a hash algorithm. The hash provides data integrity and data origin authentication. Last, a new IP header is prepended to the authenticated payload. The new IP address is used to route the packet. ESP does not attempt to provide data integrity for this new external IP header. Figure 22-5 illustrates the ESP encryption and authentication process on an IP packet using tunnel mode.

Figure 22-5   ESP Encryption and Authentication

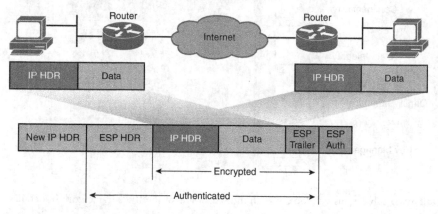

In modern IPsec VPN implementations, the use of ESP is more common than AH.

IPsec Modes of Operations

ESP and AH can be used in two different ways, or *modes*. The encapsulation can be done in tunnel mode or in transport mode.

ESP *transport mode* does not protect the original packet's IP header. Only the original packet's payload is protected. An ESP header is inserted between the original IP header and the protected payload.

ESP *tunnel mode* protects the entire original IP packet. The entire original IP packet, including its IP header, is encrypted and becomes the payload for the new packet. An ESP header is applied for the transport layer header, and this is encapsulated in a new packet with a new IP header. The new IP header specifies the VPN peers as the source and destination IP addresses. The IP addresses specified in the original IP packet are not visible.

The encapsulation performed on an ESP packet with each mode is illustrated in Figure 22-6.

Figure 22-6   ESP with Tunnel Mode and Transport Mode

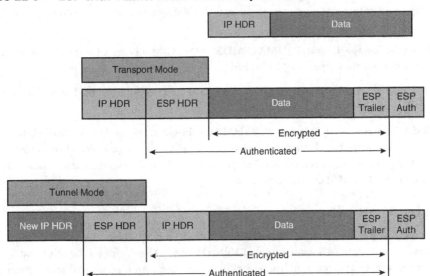

AH can also be implemented in either tunnel mode or transport mode. AH transport mode provides authentication and integrity for the entire packet. It does not encrypt the data, but it is protected from modification. AH tunnel mode encapsulates the IP packet with an AH and a new IP header, and signs the entire packet for integrity and authentication.

Confidentiality

Day 29 provided an in-depth review of the different encryption technologies. The following are some of the encryption algorithms and key lengths that IPsec can use:

- **DES algorithm:** DES uses a 56-bit symmetric key.

- **3DES algorithm:** 3DES is a variant of the 56-bit DES. It uses three independent 56-bit encryption keys per 64-bit block, which provides significantly stronger encryption strength over DES.

- **AES:** AES provides stronger security than DES and is computationally more efficient than 3DES. AES offers three different key lengths: 128 bits, 192 bits, and 256 bits.

- **SEAL:** As a stream cipher, SEAL encrypts data continuously rather than encrypting blocks of data. SEAL uses a 160-bit key.

Data Integrity

VPN data is typically transported over the public Internet. Potentially, this data could be intercepted and modified. To guard against this problem, you can use one of the data-integrity algorithms, which were discussed in our review on Day 29. Remember that a data-integrity algorithm adds a hash to the message, which guarantees the integrity of the original message. If the transmitted hash matches the received hash, the message has not been tampered with. However, if there is no match, the message was altered. A Hashed Message Authentication Code (HMAC) is a data-integrity algorithm that guarantees the integrity of the message. IPsec currently supports three common HMAC algorithms:

- **HMAC-Message Digest 5 (HMAC-MD5):** HMAC-MD5 uses a 128-bit shared-secret key of any size but the output is a 128-bit hash.

- **HMAC-Secure Hash Algorithm 1 (HMAC-SHA-1):** HMAC-SHA-1 uses a secret key of any size but the output is a 160-bit hash.

- **HMAC-Secure Hash Algorithm 2 (HMAC-SHA-2):** The SHA-2 family of HMACs is based on the same base algorithm as SHA-1. The SHA-2 family (the second generation of SHA algorithms) includes the 256-, 384-, and 512-bit hash algorithms, referred to as SHA-256, SHA-384, and SHA-512 respectively.

Origin Authentication

When you are conducting business long distance, it is necessary to know who is at the other end of the phone, email, or fax. The same is true of VPN networks. The device on the other end of the VPN tunnel must be authenticated before the communication path is considered secure. Four peer-authentication methods exist:

- **Pre-shared keys (PSK):** A secret key value is entered into each peer manually and is used to authenticate the peer. This is a shared secret that both parties must exchange ahead of time.

- **RSA signatures:** The exchange of digital certificates authenticates the peers. The local device derives a hash and encrypts it with its private key. The encrypted hash is attached to the message and is forwarded to the remote end, and it acts like a signature. At the remote end, the encrypted hash is decrypted using the public key of the local end. If the decrypted hash matches the recomputed hash, the signature is genuine. (RSA is named after its inventors, Rivest, Shamir, and Adleman.)

- **RSA encrypted nonces:** A nonce is a random number that is generated by the peer. RSA-encrypted nonces use RSA to encrypt the nonce value and other values. This method requires that each peer is aware of the public key of the other peer before negotiation starts.

- **ECDSA signatures:** The ECDSA is the elliptic curve analog of the Digital Signature Algorithm (DSA) signature method. ECDSA signatures are smaller than RSA signatures of similar cryptographic strength. ECDSA operations can be computed more quickly than similar-strength RSA operations.

Key Management

Encryption algorithms require a symmetric, shared secret key to perform encryption and decryption. How do the encrypting and decrypting devices get the shared secret key? The easiest key exchange method is to use a public key exchange method. Public key exchange methods allow shared keys to be dynamically generated between the encrypting and decrypting devices. The method has two variants:

- The Diffie-Hellman (DH) key agreement, mentioned on Day 29, is a public key exchange method. This method provides a way for two peers to establish a shared-secret key, which only they know, even though they are communicating over an insecure channel.

- ECDH is a variant of the DH protocol using elliptic curve cryptography (ECC).

These algorithms are used to establish session keys. They support different prime sizes that are identified by different DH or ECDH groups. DH groups vary in the computational expense that is required for key agreement and the strength against cryptographic attacks. Larger prime sizes provide stronger security, but require additional time to compute. The following is a quick listing of the different DH groups:

- DH1: 768-bit

- DH2: 1024-bit

- DH5: 1536-bit

- DH14: 2048-bit

- DH15: 3072-bit

- DH16: 4096-bit

- DH19: 256-bit ECDH

- DH20: 384-bit ECDH

- DH24: 2048-bit ECDH

Suite B Cryptographic Standard

RFC 4869 defines a set of cryptographic algorithms to adhere to National Security Agency (NSA) standards for classified information. Called *Suite B*, it includes these specified algorithms:

- Encryption that is based on AES using 128- or 256-bit keys

- Hashing (digital fingerprinting) based on SHA-2

- Digital signatures with the ECDSA using curves with 256- and 384-bit prime moduli

- Key exchange, either pre-shared or dynamic, using the ECDH method

NOTE: For an excellent article on Cisco-recommended cryptographic algorithms and best practices, see http://www.cisco.com/web/about/security/intelligence/nextgen_crypto.html.

IKE

IPsec uses the IKE protocol to negotiate and establish secured site-to-site or remote-access VPN tunnels. IKE is a framework provided by the Internet Security Association and Key Management Protocol (ISAKMP) and parts of two other key management protocols, namely Oakley and Secure

Key Exchange Mechanism (SKEME). An IPsec peer accepting incoming IKE requests listens on UDP port 500.

IKE uses ISAKMP for Phase 1 and Phase 2 of key negotiation. Phase 1 negotiates a security association (a key) between two IKE peers. The key negotiated in Phase 1 enables IKE peers to communicate securely in Phase 2. During Phase 2 negotiation, IKE establishes keys (security associations) for other applications, such as IPsec.

There are two versions of the IKE protocol: IKE version 1 (IKEv1) and IKE version 2 (IKEv2). IKEv2 was created to overcome some of the limitations of IKEv1. IKEv2 enhances the function of performing dynamic key exchange and peer authentication. It also simplifies the key exchange flows and introduces measures to fix vulnerabilities present in IKEv1. Both IKEv1 and IKEv2 protocols operate in two phases. IKEv2 provides a simpler and more efficient exchange. Both IKEv1 and IKEv2 are reviewed in the following sections.

IKEv1 Phase 1

IKEv1 Phase 1 occurs in one of two modes: main mode and aggressive mode. *Main mode* has three two-way exchanges between the initiator and receiver. These exchanges define what encryption and authentication protocols are acceptable, how long keys should remain active, and whether Perfect Forward Secrecy (PFS) should be enforced. Figure 22-7 summarizes these three two-way exchanges.

Figure 22-7   IKE Phase 1 Main Mode

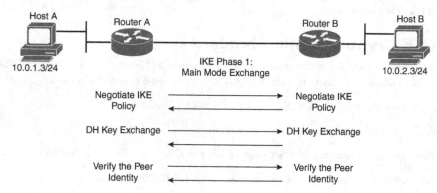

The first step in IKEv1 main mode is to negotiate the security policy that will be used for the ISAKMP SA. There are five parameters, which require agreement from both sides:

- Encryption algorithm

- Hash algorithm

- Diffie-Hellman group number

- Peer authentication method

- SA lifetime

The second exchange in IKEv1 main mode negotiations facilitates Diffie-Hellman key agreement. The Diffie-Hellman method allows two parties to share information over an untrusted network and mutually compute an identical shared secret that cannot be computed by eavesdroppers who intercept the shared information.

After the DH key exchange is complete, shared cryptographic keys are provisioned, but the peer is not yet authenticated. The device on the other end of the VPN tunnel must be authenticated before the communications path is considered secure. The last exchange of IKE Phase 1 authenticates the remote peer.

Aggressive mode, on the other hand, compresses the IKE SA negotiation phases that are described thus far into two exchanges and a total of three messages. In aggressive mode, the initiator passes all data that is required for the SA. The responder sends the proposal, key material, and ID and authenticates the session in the next packet. The initiator replies by authenticating the session. Negotiation is quicker, and the initiator and responder IDs pass in plaintext.

IKEv1 Phase 2

The purpose of IKE Phase 2 is to negotiate the IPsec security parameters that define the IPsec SA that protects the network data traversing the VPN. IKE Phase 2 only offers one mode, called *quick mode*, to negotiate the IPsec SAs. In Phase 2, IKE negotiates the IPsec transform set and the shared keying material that is used by the transforms. In this phase, the SAs that IPsec uses are unidirectional; therefore, a separate key exchange is required for each data flow. Optionally, Phase 2 can include its own Diffie-Hellman key exchange, using PFS. Figure 22-8 illustrates the IKE Phase 2 exchange.

Figure 22-8   IKEv1 Phase 2

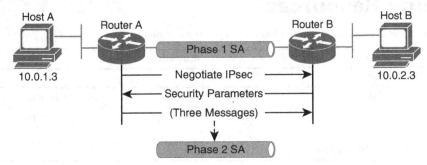

 Video: IKEv1 Phase 1 and IKEv1 Phase 2

Refer to the Digital Study Guide to view this video.

IKEv2

IKE Version 2, a next-generation key management protocol that is based on RFC 7296, is an enhancement of the IKE protocol. IKEv2 offers less overhead, has support for NAT Traversal, has less delay when creating SAs, has faster rekeying times, is less susceptible to DoS attacks, and offers support for EAP between VPN peers. IKEv2, illustrated in Figure 22-9, uses fewer messages to accomplish the same (and more) objectives as IKEv1.

Figure 22-9   IKEv2

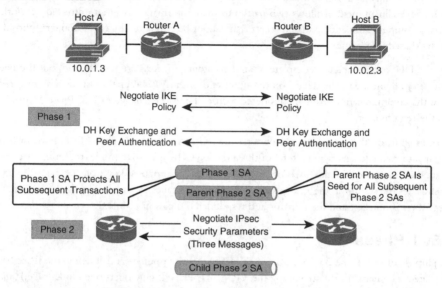

 Activity: Identify the IPsec Terminology

Refer to the Digital Study Guide to complete this activity.

Study Resources

For today's exam topics, refer to the following resources for more study.

Resource	Location	Topic
Primary Resources		
CCNA Security Official Cert Guide	6	Fundamentals of IP Security
CCNA Security (Networking Academy Curriculum)	8	Implementing Virtual Private Networks
Supplemental Resources		
CCNA Security Complete Video Course	4	Fundamentals of IP Security
CCNA Security Portable Command Guide	16	IPsec VPNs
Implementing Cisco IOS Network Security (IINS 640-554) Foundation Learning Guide, Second Edition	13	IPsec Fundamentals

 Check Your Understanding

Refer to the Digital Study Guide to take a ten-question quiz covering the content of this day.

Clientless Remote-Access VPN

CCNA Security 210-260 IINS Exam Topics

- 3.2.a Implement basic clientless SSL VPN using ASDM
- 3.2.b Verify clientless connection

Key Concepts

Today we will be looking at the concepts, the configuration, and the verification of clientless remote-access SSL VPNs. Secure Sockets Layer (SSL) Virtual Private Network (VPN) is the rapidly evolving VPN technology that complements the existing IPsec remote-access deployments. The actual data encryption and decryption occur at the application layer, usually by a browser in the clientless SSL VPN tunnels. Consequently, it is not necessary to install additional software or hardware clients to enable SSL VPN in a network. Furthermore, it is possible to provide full network access to remote users by leveraging the full-tunnel mode functionality of the SSL VPN tunnels.

Clientless SSL VPN Concepts

Transport Layer Security (TLS) and its predecessor, SSL, are cryptographic protocols that provide secure communications on the Internet for such things as web browsing, email, Internet faxing, instant messaging, and other data transfers. TLS is a standards-based alternative to SSL, and the terms are sometimes used interchangeably. Figure 21-1 shows how SSL is used to encrypt and authenticate the session layer and above. As such, it encrypts more than just HTTP (called HTTPS); it can also encrypt FTP (thus FTPS), POP (for POPS), LDAP (for LDAPS), wireless security (EAP-TLS), and others. Cryptographically, SSL and TLS rely on public key infrastructure (PKI) and digital certificates for authenticating the VPN endpoints.

The SSL and TLS protocols support the use of a variety of different cryptographic algorithms, or ciphers, for use in operations such as authenticating the server and client to each other (RSA), transmitting certificates (RSA), and establishing session keys (RSA, DH). Symmetric algorithms are used for bulk encryption (3DES, AES), asymmetric algorithms are used for authentication and the exchange of keys (RSA, DH), and hashing is used as part of the authentication process (MD5, SHA).

Figure 21-2 gives a simplified explanation of the key steps in establishing an SSL/TLS session.

Figure 21-1   SSL/TLS Encapsulation

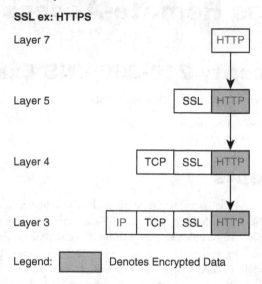

Figure 21-2   SSL VPN Tunnel Establishment

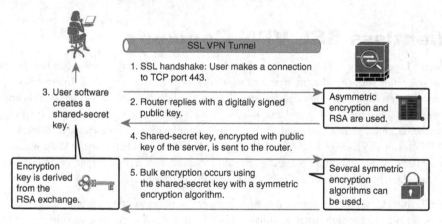

Cisco ASA supports all three flavors of SSL VPN. They include the following modes:

- **Clientless:** The remote client needs only an SSL-enabled browser to access resources on the private network of the security appliances. SSL clients can access internal resources such as HTTP, HTTPS, or even Windows file shares over the SSL tunnel.

- **Thin client:** The remote client needs to install a small Java-based applet to establish a secure connection to the TCP-based internal resources. SSL clients can access TCP-based internal resources such as HTTP, HTTPS, SSH, and Telnet servers.

- **Full tunnel:** The remote client needs to install an SSL VPN client first to give full access to the internal private network over an SSL tunnel. Using the full-tunnel client mode, remote machines send all IP unicast traffic such as TCP-, UDP-, or even ICMP-based traffic. SSL clients can access internal resources such as HTTP, HTTPS, DNS, SSH, and Telnet servers. Most customers prefer using the full-tunnel mode option because a VPN client can be automatically pushed to a user after a successful authentication. We will look at this type of client-based remote-access SSL VPN configuration on Day 20.

Clientless SSL VPN Configuration

The following is the procedure for configuring a clientless SSL VPN using Cisco ASDM on the Cisco ASA. The basic steps to follow when configuring the ASA to support clientless SSL VPNs are

1. Launch the Clientless SSL VPN Wizard from ASDM.

2. Configure the SSL VPN URL and interface.

3. Configure user authentication.

4. Configure user group policy.

5. Configure bookmarks.

Figure 21-3 shows the reference topology used in the following configuration example. The objective here is to allow Internet-based HR employees HTTPS access to the mail server in the corporate DMZ.

Figure 21-3   Clientless SSL VPN Reference Topology

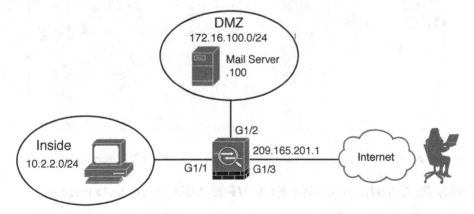

Task 1: Launch Clientless SSL VPN Wizard from ASDM

To open the Clientless SSL VPN Wizard from the ASDM menu bar, choose **Wizards** > **VPN Wizards** > **Clientless SSL VPN Wizard**, as shown in Figure 21-4.

Figure 21-4   Launching the Clientless SSL VPN Wizard from ASDM on Cisco ASA

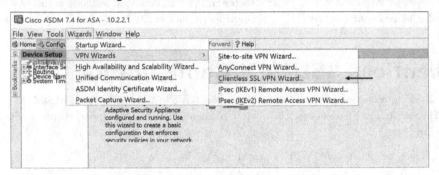

This brings up the welcome page for the SSL VPN Wizard, as shown in Figure 21-5.

Figure 21-5   SSL VPN Wizard Welcome Page

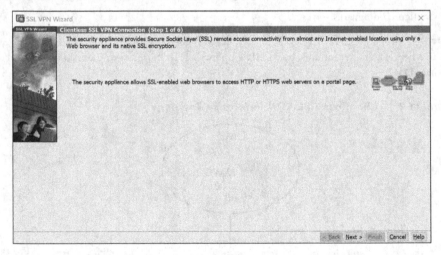

When you click **Next** to continue, you are presented with the SSL VPN Interface page.

Task 2: Configure the SSL VPN URL and Interface

There are four items to configure on the SSL VPN Interface page, as shown in Figure 21-6:

1. Enter a name for the connection profile to be associated with the users who are using clientless SSL VPNs.

2. Choose an interface to be used for the clientless SSL VPN (normally an outside interface on the ASA).

3. Optionally, select a third-party certificate that has been installed on the ASA for use in connecting SSL VPN clients. If no certificates were installed, the ASA will use a self-signed certificate.

4. Configure the URL that users can access to associate them with the correct group. In our scenario, we are allowing HR staff access to specific corporate services.

Figure 21-6   SSL VPN Interface Configuration

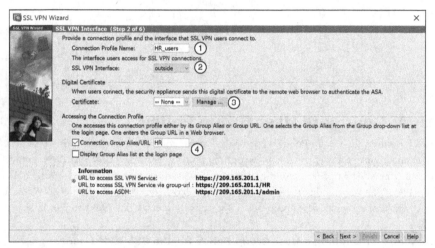

NOTE: The SSL VPN Interface screen in the SSL VPN Wizard provides several links in the Information section. These links identify the URLs that need to be used for the SSL VPN service access (login) and for Cisco ASDM access (to access the Cisco ASDM software download for administrators).

Clicking **Next** brings you to the User Authentication page.

Task 3: Configure User Authentication

User authentication may be managed by external authentication servers (such as RADIUS) or it may be managed locally by using the ASA local user database, as shown in Figure 21-7. To add a new user, enter the username and password and then click **Add**. In our scenario, a user has already been created (Alice) and we are adding a second user (Bob). Click **Next** to continue.

Figure 21-7   Authenticating Users for SSL VPN

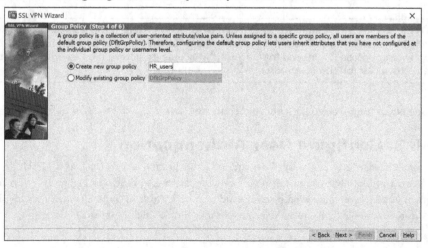

Task 4: Configure User Group Policy

Figure 21-8 shows the Group Policy wizard page, where you may select an existing user group policy to modify or you may add a new user group policy for the clientless SSL VPN connection. By default, a newly created user group policy inherits its settings from the default group policy, *DfltGrpPolicy*. You may modify these settings after you have completed the SSL VPN Wizard. In our case, we have created a new group policy for our HR users. Click **Next** to continue.

Figure 21-8   Assigning a User Group Policy for the SSL VPN Users

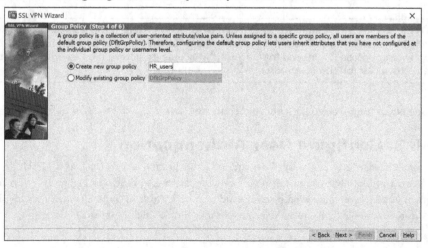

Task 5: Configure Bookmarks

On the Bookmark List page, you are prompted as to whether you want to provide these authenticated SSL VPN users with a convenient list of links/URLs that go to specific services on the corporate network. By default, there are no configured bookmark lists.

To create a bookmark list and add bookmark entries to it, complete the following steps, as shown in Figure 21-9.

Figure 21-9   Configuring Bookmarks

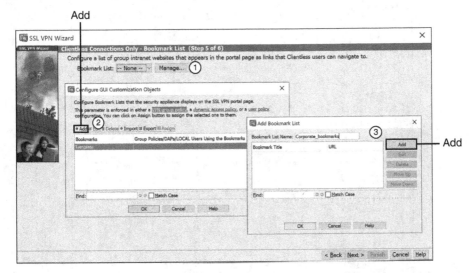

Step 1.   Click **Manage** to add new bookmarks for your VPN users.

Step 2.   In the Configure GUI Customization Objects dialog box, click **Add** to add a bookmark list.

Step 3.   In the Add Bookmark List dialog box, enter the bookmark list name in the corresponding field, in our case "Corporate_bookmarks," and click **Add** again to make the Select Bookmark Type dialog box appear (see Figure 21-10).

Figure 21-10   Step 4—Selecting URL Type

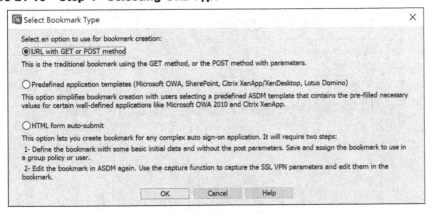

Step 4.   After selecting the type of bookmark, in our case a traditional URL, click **OK** to open the Add Bookmark window (see Figure 21-11).

Figure 21-11   Step 5—Configuring a Bookmark

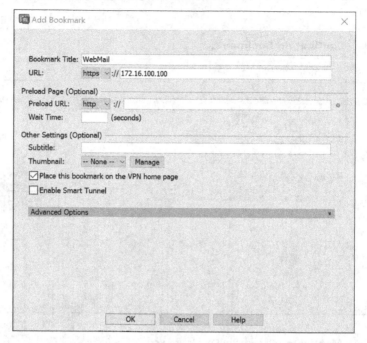

Step 5.   Enter a name for the bookmark in the Bookmark Title field. Next enter the URL value, which could be HTTP, HTTPS, or FTP, and the server destination IP address or hostname to be used with the bookmark entry. As shown in Figure 21-11, in our scenario, we have created a bookmark called "WebMail" that points to the mail server's IP address. Notice that we are using HTTPS. When the details are configured, click **OK** in the Add Bookmark window to return to the Add Bookmark List window.

Step 6.   The newly created bookmark is displayed as shown in Figure 21-12.

Figure 21-12   Step 6— Confirming Bookmark

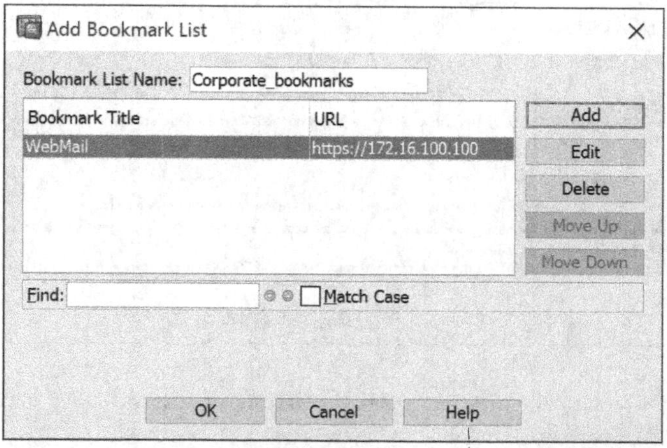

Step 7.   Click **OK** to return to the Configure GUI Customization Objects window as shown in Figure 21-13.

Figure 21-13   Step 7—Confirming Bookmark Template

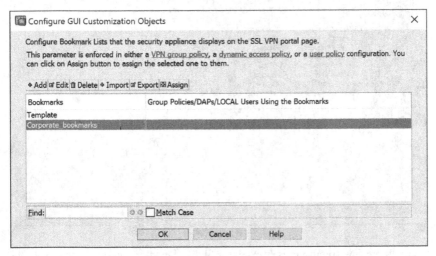

Step 8.   Click **OK** to return to the Bookmark List wizard page as shown in Figure 21-14.

Figure 21-14   Step 8—Bookmark List

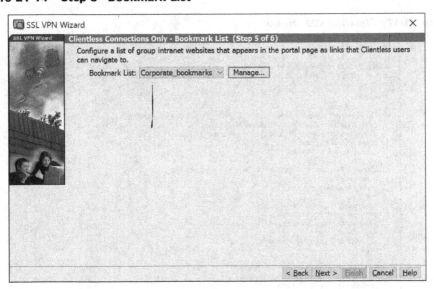

Click **Next** to return to the configuration steps and view a summary before finishing the wizard (see Figure 21-15).

Figure 21-15   Summary of SSL VPN Configuration

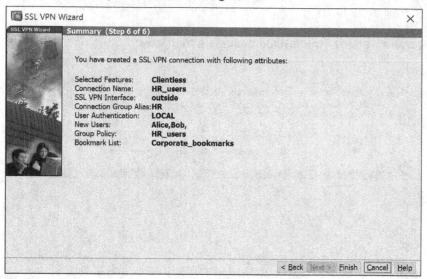

If the option to preview commands is enabled in ASDM, the wizard produces the actual CLI commands that were automatically generated, allowing the administrator an opportunity to save a copy of the clientless SSL VPN configuration before sending the commands to the ASA, as shown in Figure 21-16.

Figure 21-16   Viewing CLI Output

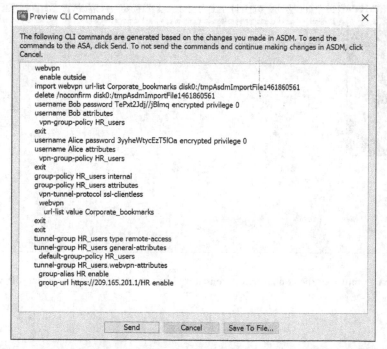

Clientless SSL VPN Verification

Now that the ASA is configured to accept clientless SSL VPN connections, we are ready to test our configuration by logging in to the ASA from a remote host. Open a browser and enter the login URL for the SSL VPN into the address field. Be sure to use secure HTTP (HTTPS) as SSL is required to connect to the ASA. In our example, the ASA login URL is https://209.165.201.1/HR.

The browser will display a security warning since we are using a self-signed certificate. This can be verified by clicking the small lock symbol to the left of the URL and then verifying the details of the certificate, as shown in Figure 21-17 and Figure 21-18.

Figure 21-17   Verifying Secure SSL Connection

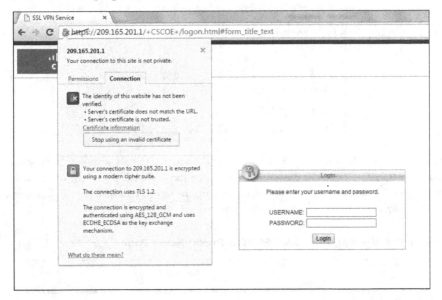

Figure 21-18   Verifying Certificate

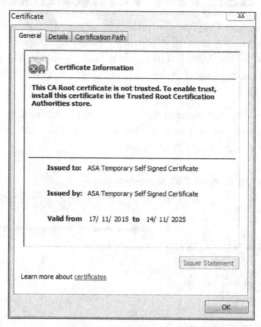

When the user authenticates, the ASA SSL web portal home page displays, listing the various bookmarks previously assigned to the profile, in our case the WebMail bookmark we created with the wizard (see Figure 21-19). From this page, the user can also access other web applications and browse the corporate network if authorization was granted.

Figure 21-19   Viewing the ASA SSL Web Portal Home Page

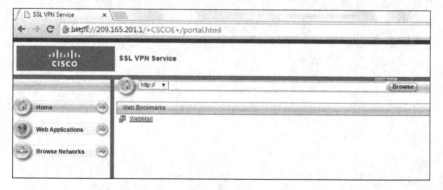

It is possible to verify the status of active SSL VPN connections in ASDM by navigating to **Monitoring > VPN > VPN Statistics > Sessions**, as shown in Figure 21-20. To see the details of a specific client, simply highlight it and click the **Details** button.

Figure 21-20   Viewing SSL VPN Client Details

 Video: Configuring and Testing Clientless SSL VPNs

Refer to the Digital Study Guide to view this video.

 Activity: Order the Steps when Configuring Clientless SSL VPN

Refer to the Digital Study Guide to complete this activity.

Study Resources

For today's exam topics, refer to the following resources for more study.

Resource	Location	Topic
Primary Resources		
CCNA Security Official Cert Guide	8	Implementing SSL VPNs Using Cisco ASA
CCNA Security (Networking Academy Curriculum)	10	Advanced Cisco Adaptive Security Appliance
Supplemental Resources		
CCNA Security Complete Video Course	6	Implementing SSL Remote-Access VPNs Using Cisco ASA
CCNA Security Portable Command Guide	22	Configuring Cisco ASA SSL VPNs
Cisco ASA (3rd ed.)	22	Clientless Remote-Access SSL VPNs

 Check Your Understanding

Refer to the Digital Study Guide to take a ten-question quiz covering the content of this day.

AnyConnect Remote Access VPN

CCNA Security 210-260 IINS Exam Topics

- 3.2.c Implement basic AnyConnect SSL VPN using ASDM
- 3.2.d Verify AnyConnect connection

Key Topics

Today we will focus on configuring and verifying client-based remote-access SSL VPNs using Cisco AnyConnect Secure Mobility Client and the Cisco Adaptive Security Appliance (ASA).

AnyConnect SSL VPN Concepts

A client-based SSL VPN is often called "full-tunnel" because it provides authenticated users with LAN-like, full network access to corporate resources, However, the remote devices require a client application, such as the Cisco AnyConnect Secure Mobility Client, to be preinstalled on the end-user device, or the application can be downloaded as needed by initially establishing a clientless SSL VPN.

Also, this type of solution uses bidirectional authentication: The client authenticates the ASA with a certificate-based authentication method, and the ASA authenticates the user against a local or remote user database, which is based on a username and password.

After authentication, the ASA applies a set of authorization and accounting rules to the user session. When the ASA has established an acceptable VPN environment with the remote user, the remote user can forward raw IP traffic into the SSL/TLS tunnel destined to the enterprise network, as shown in Figure 20-1.

Figure 20-1   Client-based SSL VPN Sample Topology

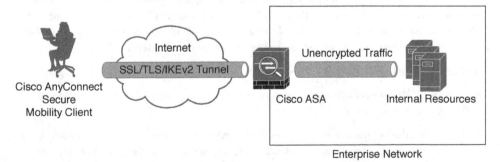

The Cisco AnyConnect Secure Mobility Client creates a virtual network interface to provide this functionality. This virtual adapter requires an IP address, and the most basic method to assign an IP address to the adapter is to create a local pool of IP addresses on the ASA.

The user can use Cisco AnyConnect in the following modes:

- **Standalone mode:** Enables the user to establish a Cisco AnyConnect connection without using a web browser. In standalone mode, a user opens Cisco AnyConnect just like any other application and enters the username and password credentials into the fields of the Cisco AnyConnect GUI.

- **WebLaunch mode:** Enables the user to enter the URL of the Cisco ASA security appliance in the Address or Location field of a browser, using the HTTPS protocol. The user then enters the username and password information in a login window, chooses the group, and clicks Submit. The portal window then appears, allowing the user to launch the client by clicking Start AnyConnect on the main pane. It is also possible to configure the ASA to deploy the AnyConnect package to the user's device.

SSL VPN Server Authentication

As with a clientless SSL VPN, the ASA requires a server identity certificate, which the appliance sends to remote SSL VPN clients to enable them to authenticate the ASA. By default, the security appliance will create a self-signed X.509 certificate on each reboot, resulting in many client warnings when attempting SSL VPN access, as the certificate cannot be verified by any means. This can be avoided by either creating a permanently self-signed certificate or enrolling the ASA with an external certificate authority (CA) within a public key infrastructure (PKI).

SSL VPN Client Authentication

When Cisco AnyConnect SSL VPN users connect to a ASA, the users can choose their connection profile by choosing the desired profile from a drop-down list or connecting to the group URL. If no specific connection profile is chosen, the ASA security appliance will assign the users to the *DefaultWEBVPNGroup* connection profile. By default, this profile is configured to use user authentication, using the local user database on the Cisco ASA security appliance.

SSL VPN Client IP Address Assignment

When clients connect to a full-tunnel SSL VPN, the VPN gateway assigns an IP address to the virtual network interface (adapter) of the client PC. The PC uses this IP address as the source IP address to access resources beyond the VPN gateway. These IP addresses can be from the private IP address space, but they must be routed to the gateway (ASA) in the internal network.

The ASA can assign IP addresses in an SSL VPN full-tunnel solution in several different ways:

- Use an IP address pool that is configured on the ASA, and assign the pool to a default or custom connection profile.

- Use an IP address pool that is configured on the ASA, and assign the pool to a default or custom group policy. This is a good method to use if you want to differentiate between multiple groups of users on the ASA.

- Configure the IP addresses as part of the user account in the local user database, enabling per-user IP addresses. This is a good method to use if you want to assign specific per-user policies on the ASA.

AnyConnect SSL VPN Configuration and Verification

There are three major phases to configuring SSL VPN full-tunnel mode using Cisco ASDM so that remote clients will connect using Cisco AnyConnect:

Phase 1. Configure the ASA for Cisco AnyConnect.

Phase 2. Configure the Cisco AnyConnect VPN Client.

Phase 3. Verify AnyConnect configuration and connection.

For this AnyConnect SSL VPN scenario, we will use the same topology as on Day 21 when we deployed a clientless SSL VPN. We will add one extra element to this topology: an address pool for the VPN AnyConnect client. The ASA will provide IP addresses to connecting clients using the address pool 192.168.1.50 to 192.168.1.100.

In our scenario, we will first initiate a clientless session. From the clientless portal, we will click the AnyConnect option to proceed with the Cisco AnyConnect VPN Client download and installation. We will then start an SSL VPN full-tunnel session using the newly installed AnyConnect client. As on Day 21, we will perform all configuration tasks using the ASDM.

Phase 1: Configure Cisco ASA for Cisco AnyConnect

We will be performing eight tasks to configure the ASA for AnyConnect support using the AnyConnect VPN Wizard, which you access by choosing **Wizards > VPN Wizards > AnyConnect VPN Wizard**, as shown in Figure 20-2.

Figure 20-2   ASDM Client-based VPN Wizard

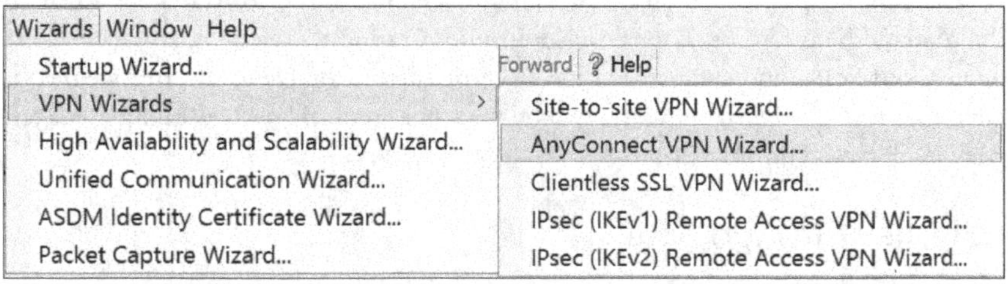

Wizards	Window Help		
Startup Wizard...		Forward	? Help
VPN Wizards	>	Site-to-site VPN Wizard...	
High Availability and Scalability Wizard...		AnyConnect VPN Wizard...	
Unified Communication Wizard...		Clientless SSL VPN Wizard...	
ASDM Identity Certificate Wizard...		IPsec (IKEv1) Remote Access VPN Wizard...	
Packet Capture Wizard...		IPsec (IKEv2) Remote Access VPN Wizard...	

Task 1: Connection Profile Identification

After you click **Next** on the Introduction page of the wizard, the first task is to configure the connection profile identification, used to identify the ASA to the remote-access users, as shown in Figure 20-3.

Figure 20-3   ASDM Connection Profile Identification Window

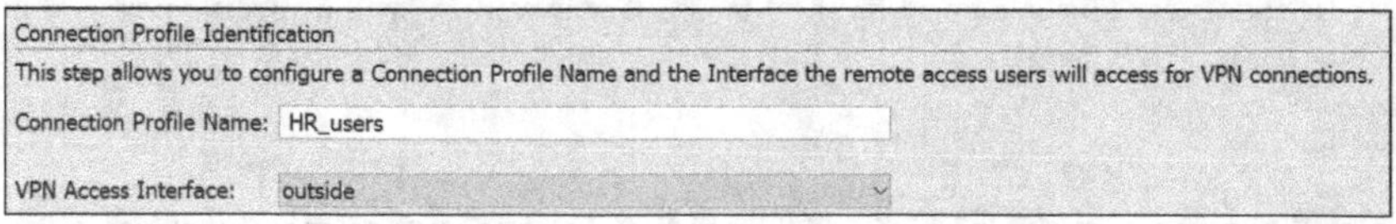

Connection Profile Identification	
This step allows you to configure a Connection Profile Name and the Interface the remote access users will access for VPN connections.	
Connection Profile Name:	HR_users
VPN Access Interface:	outside ⌄

There are two items to configure here. In the Connection Profile Name field, enter a name that remote-access users will access for VPN connections. Connection profiles appear as **tunnel-group** in the CLI. This connection profile name will be displayed in a drop-down list on the initial client-less session. In our example, we are configuring AnyConnect SSL VPN access for our HR users (Connection Profile Name = HR_users). In the VPN Access Interface drop-down menu, choose an interface that remote-access users will access for VPN connections. This is typically the outside interface.

Task 2: VPN Protocols and Device Certificate

After clicking **Next**, the next task is to specify the VPN protocol allowed for this connection profile, as shown in Figure 20-4.

Figure 20-4   ASDM VPN Protocols Window

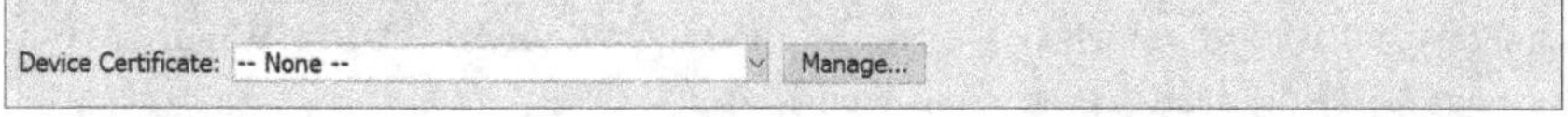

VPN Protocols	
AnyConnect can use either the IPsec or SSL protocol to protect the data traffic. Please select which protocol or protocols you would like this connection profile to support.	
☑ SSL	
☐ IPsec	
Device Certificate	
Device certificate identifies the ASA to the remote access clients. Certain AnyConnect features (Always-On, IPsec/IKEv2) require that valid device certificate be available on the ASA.	
Device Certificate:	-- None -- ⌄ Manage...

The Cisco AnyConnect VPN Client defaults to SSL. You must choose an identity certificate from the Device Certificate drop-down list. This certificate identifies the ASA to remote-access clients. Click the **Manage** button to open the Manage Identity Certificates dialog box, which allows you to create new certificates and manipulate existing certificates. If the Device Certificate field is left at the default, None, a self-signed certificate will be used and users will get a warning message when connecting (as discussed on Day 21).

Task 3: Client Image

ASA can automatically upload the latest Cisco AnyConnect VPN Client package to the client device when it accesses the enterprise network. After clicking **Next**, you will be prompted to add an AnyConnect image file, as shown in Figure 20-5. When you click **Add**, you will be prompted to either browse the ASA's flash memory to select a previously uploaded image or upload a new client image to the ASA.

After confirming the client image file or files, click **Next**.

Figure 20-5   ASDM Client Images Window

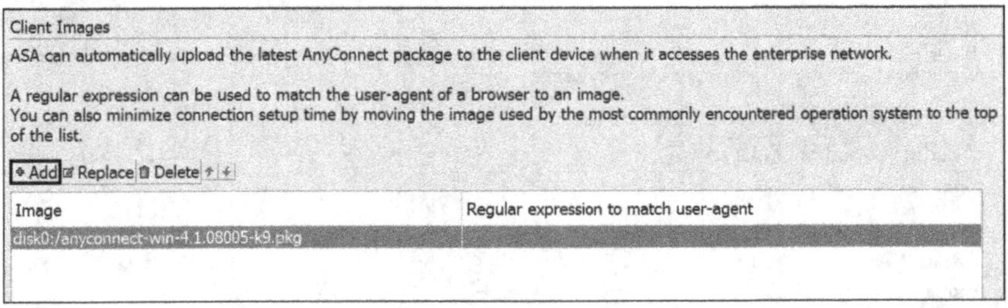

Client Images

ASA can automatically upload the latest AnyConnect package to the client device when it accesses the enterprise network.

A regular expression can be used to match the user-agent of a browser to an image.
You can also minimize connection setup time by moving the image used by the most commonly encountered operation system to the top of the list.

◆ Add ☑ Replace ⎙ Delete ↑ ↓

Image	Regular expression to match user-agent
disk0:/anyconnect-win-4.1.08005-k9.pkg	

Task 4: Authentication Methods

User authentication may be managed either by external authentication servers (such as RADIUS) or locally using the ASA local user database. As shown in Figure 20-6, the keyword LOCAL (in uppercase on the ASA) is the keyword from an AAA perspective on the ASA that represents the local database (in the running configuration). In this example, we have already configured one user, Bob, and are adding a second user, Alice. This will allow them both access to the corporate network via the AnyConnect SSL VPN. Click **Next** to continue the wizard.

Figure 20-6   ASDM Authentication Methods Window

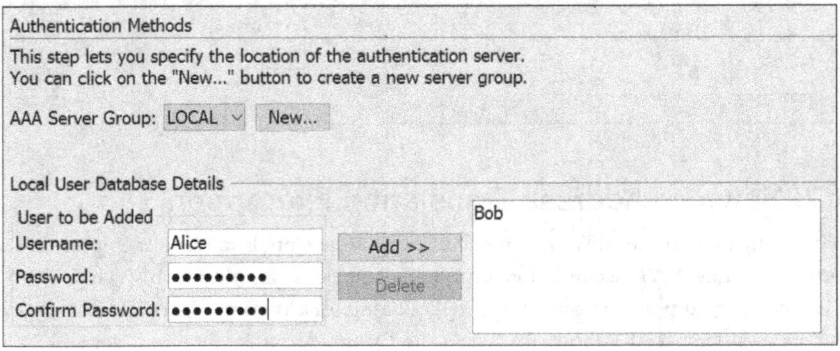

Authentication Methods

This step lets you specify the location of the authentication server.
You can click on the "New..." button to create a new server group.

AAA Server Group: LOCAL ∨   New...

Local User Database Details

User to be Added		Bob
Username:	Alice	Add >>
Password:	••••••••	Delete
Confirm Password:	••••••••	

Task 5: Client Address Assignment

SSL VPN clients receive new IP addresses when they connect to the ASA. Clientless connections do not require new IP addresses. Address pools define a range of addresses that remote clients can receive. Click **New** to create a new IPv4 or IPv6 address pool, as shown in Figure 20-7. You must then specify a pool name, a starting address, an ending address, and a subnet mask. Click **Next** after applying the newly configured address pool. In our example, we are configuring a pool of 51 IPv4 addresses, from 10.2.2.100 to 10.2.2.150.

Figure 20-7   ASDM Client Address Assignment Window

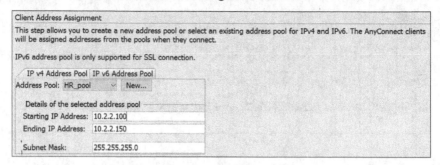

Task 6: Network Name Resolution Servers

The next step, shown in Figure 20-8, lets you specify which DNS entries should be handed out to your clients, and a domain name that will primarily play a part in name resolution. Click **Next** to continue after configuring the appropriate DNS information.

Figure 20-8   ASDM Network Name Resolution Servers Window

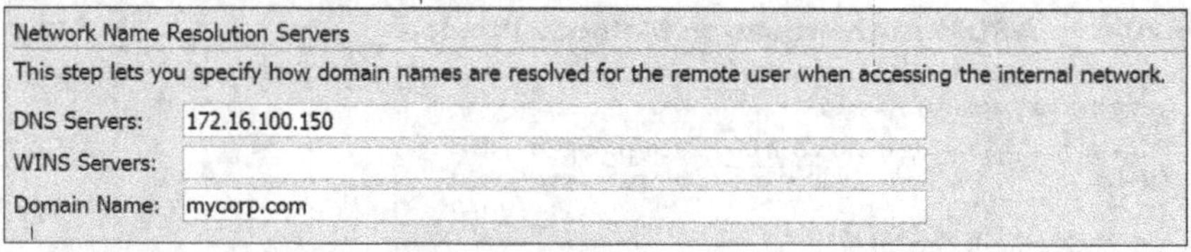

Network Name Resolution Servers
This step lets you specify how domain names are resolved for the remote user when accessing the internal network.

DNS Servers: 172.16.100.150

WINS Servers:

Domain Name: mycorp.com

Task 7: Network Address Translation Exemption

If NAT is configured on the ASA, then the SSL client address pools must be exempt from the NAT process because NAT occurs before encryption functions. In other words, when SSL VPN clients are accessing corporate resources, the replies going back through the ASA must not trigger the NAT process. Figure 20-9 shows that when the Exempt VPN Traffic from Network Address Translation option is checked, two further options must be configured. First, choose the interface connected to the internal network that needs to be exempted from NAT. Second, type the host or subnet IP addresses that are to bypass NAT in the Local Network field. You can also click the ... button and select the addresses from the Browse Local Network dialog box. In our example, the **any4** keyword represents all IPv4 local addresses.

Figure 20-9   ASDM NAT Exempt Window

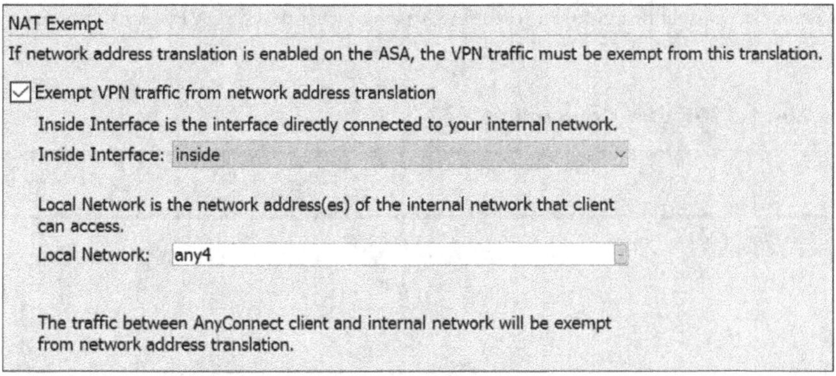

NAT Exempt
If network address translation is enabled on the ASA, the VPN traffic must be exempt from this translation.
☑ Exempt VPN traffic from network address translation
Inside Interface is the interface directly connected to your internal network.
Inside Interface: inside
Local Network is the network address(es) of the internal network that client can access.
Local Network: any4
The traffic between AnyConnect client and internal network will be exempt from network address translation.

Task 8: AnyConnect Client Deployment and Summary

After clicking **Next**, you are presented with the final two wizard pages, which are purely informational.

First, the AnyConnect Client Deployment window explains how you can install the Cisco AnyConnect VPN Client program to a client device using either of two methods. The first method is web launch, which installs automatically when accessing the ASA using a web browser. The second method is predeployment, which manually installs the Cisco AnyConnect VPN Client package.

Second, the Summary window provides a brief overview of your selections from the previous wizard pages, as shown in Figure 20-10.

Figure 20-10   ASDM Wizard Summary Window

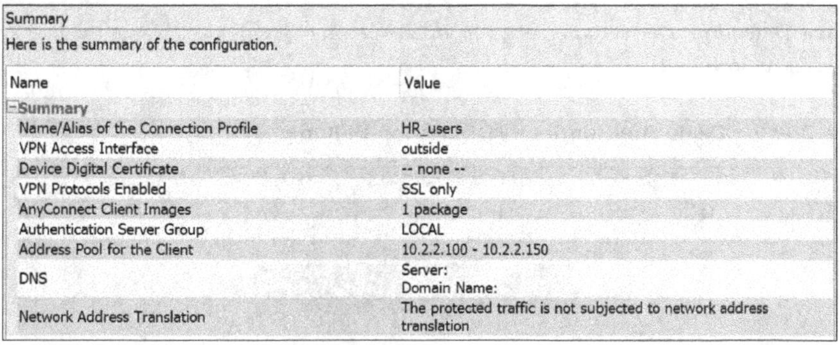

Summary	
Here is the summary of the configuration.	
Name	**Value**
⊟Summary	
Name/Alias of the Connection Profile	HR_users
VPN Access Interface	outside
Device Digital Certificate	-- none --
VPN Protocols Enabled	SSL only
AnyConnect Client Images	1 package
Authentication Server Group	LOCAL
Address Pool for the Client	10.2.2.100 - 10.2.2.150
DNS	Server: Domain Name:
Network Address Translation	The protected traffic is not subjected to network address translation

Click **Finish** to complete the AnyConnect VPN Connection Setup Wizard. If the option was enabled, you will be shown the actual CLI configuration produced by the wizard. You can save this text file before deploying the configuration to the ASA.

Phase 2: Configure the Cisco AnyConnect VPN Client

In our example, we will first connect to the ASA using a clientless SSL VPN, as shown in Figure 20-11.

Figure 20-11   SSL VPN Connection

Once authenticated, the process to upgrade our connection to full client begins with a series of compliance checks for the target system, as shown in Figure 20-12. The following items are checked on the host system:

- **Platform Detection:** The ASA first queries the client system in an attempt to identify the type of client connecting to the security appliance. Based on the platform that is identified, the proper software package may be auto-downloaded.

- **ActiveX:** Detects whether ActiveX is available and authorized on the host system for client download.

- **Java Detection:** Detects whether a supported version of Java is available on the host system for client download.

Figure 20-12   Cisco AnyConnect WebLaunch Window

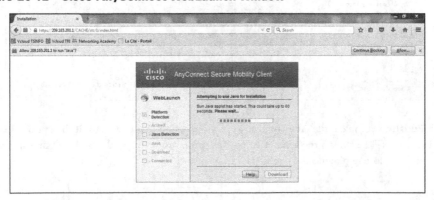

If all the preceding checks succeed, Cisco AnyConnect will be downloaded and installed automatically on your remote system.

Once the client completes the auto-download of the Cisco AnyConnect SSL VPN Client, the web session automatically launches the Cisco AnyConnect SSL VPN Client and attempts to log the user into the network using the same credentials that are supplied when logging into the web portal.

If the ActiveX or Java checks are not successful, the ASA will nevertheless offer you the chance to download manually the Cisco AnyConnect VPN Client located in its flash memory, as shown in Figure 20-13.

Figure 20-13   Cisco AnyConnect VPN Client Manual Installation

After a manual download and install, launch the AnyConnect client, as shown in Figure 20-14. This will initiate a full client SSL VPN with the ASA. In this example, the ASA public IP address is 209.165.201.1. A Security Alert window will appear if the ASA is using a self-signed certificate.

Figure 20-14   Starting Cisco AnyConnect VPN Client

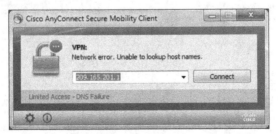

Once authenticated, an icon with a sphere and a lock will appear in the system tray, identifying that the client has successfully connected to the SSL VPN network, as shown in Figure 20-15.

Figure 20-15 AnyConnect Icon in Windows System Tray

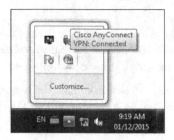

Phase 3: Verify AnyConnect Configuration and Connection

The VPN configuration can be altered, customized, and verified on the AnyConnect Connections Profile page.

To open the Network Client Access window displayed in Figure 20-16, choose **Configuration > Remote Access VPN > Network (Client) Access > AnyConnect Connection Profiles**.

Figure 20-16 ASDM AnyConnect Connection Profiles Page

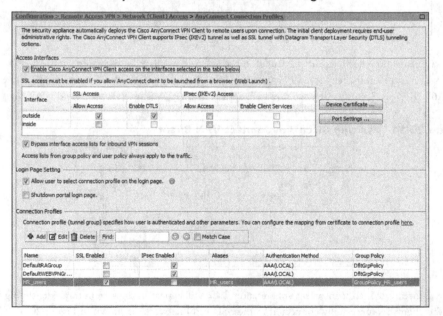

Note that SSL and Data Transport Layer Security (DTLS) is allowed on the outside interface. DTLS is the TLS protocol using UDP for transport instead of TCP. UDP has less overhead than TCP. Also, when encapsulating TCP traffic in tunnels, reliability is provided by the tunneled TCP protocol. If the tunneling protocol also provides reliability, double retransmissions of lost packets may result. Therefore, DTLS is the preferred protocol for SSL VPNs, but the ASA and the client will revert to standard TLS if DTLS is filtered anywhere along the remote-access VPN path.

Scrolling down to the bottom of the page displays the Connection Profiles on the ASA.

To view VPN client information, open the Windows system tray and point to the Cisco AnyConnect Client icon, as previously shown in Figure 20-15. Right-click the icon and choose **Open AnyConnect** to open the Cisco AnyConnect Client window displayed in Figure 20-17. Clicking through the tabs brings up further information such as preferences, statistics, route details, firewall configuration, and message history.

Figure 20-17   Cisco AnyConnect Client Window

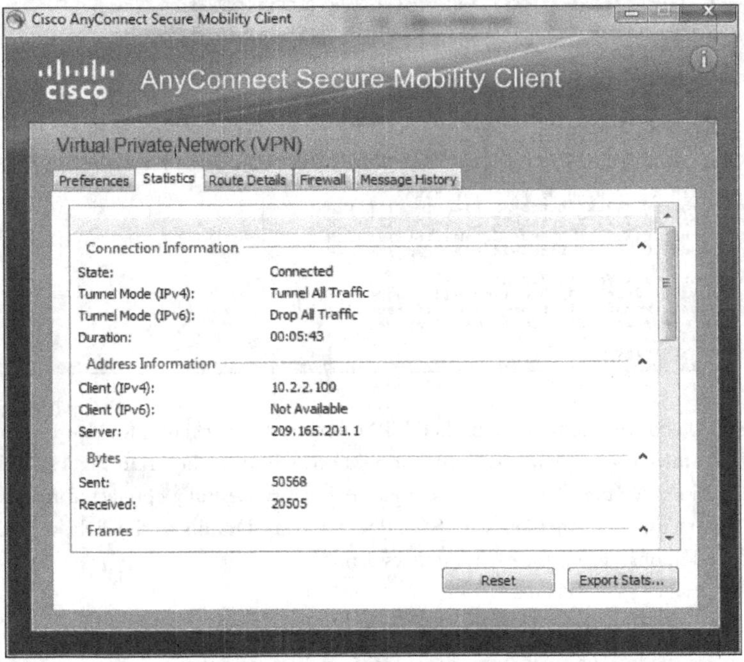

To verify the IP address allocation, open a CMD window and type **ipconfig**, as shown in Figure 20-18. Notice that the host has two IP addresses: one for the VPN connection (Ethernet LAN Connection) and one for the actual network on which the VPN connection is located (Ethernet LAN Connection 2). A ping to a host on the private network confirms that the remote host has access to internal resources.

Figure 20-18 Verifying Connectivity to Internal Network

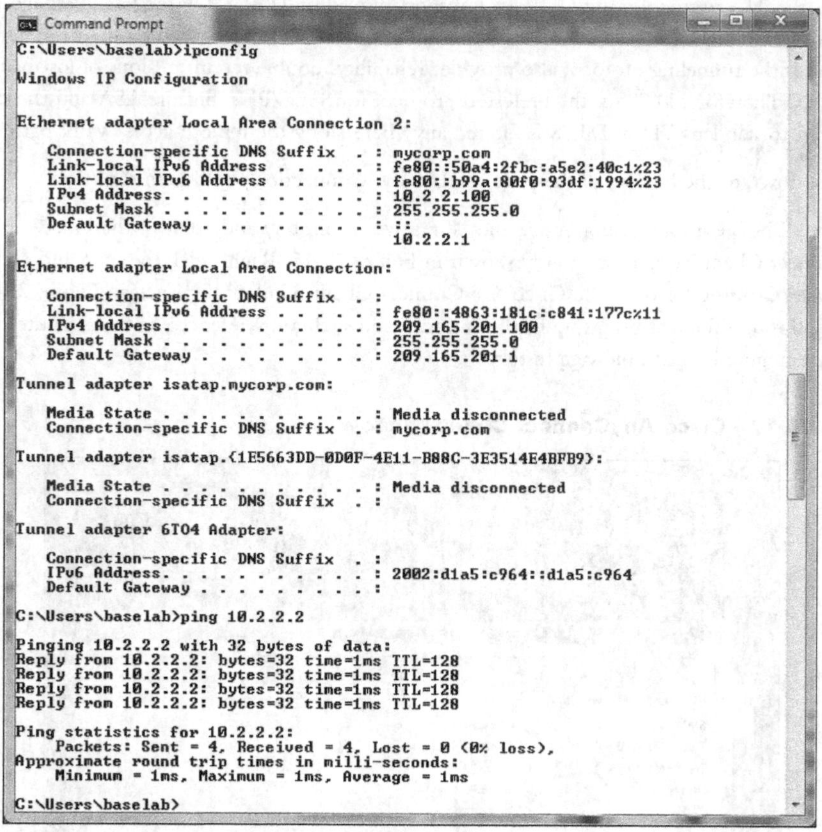
Command Prompt
C:\Users\baselab>ipconfig
Windows IP Configuration
Ethernet adapter Local Area Connection 2:
Connection-specific DNS Suffix . : mycorp.com
Link-local IPv6 Address . . . . . : fe80::50a4:2fbc:a5e2:40c1%23
Link-local IPv6 Address . . . . . : fe80::b99a:80f0:93df:1994%23
IPv4 Address. . . . . : 10.2.2.100
Subnet Mask . . . . : 255.255.255.0
Default Gateway . . . . : ::
10.2.2.1
Ethernet adapter Local Area Connection:
Connection-specific DNS Suffix . :
Link-local IPv6 Address . . . . . : fe80::4863:181c:c841:177c%11
IPv4 Address. . . . . : 209.165.201.100
Subnet Mask . . . . : 255.255.255.0
Default Gateway . . . . : 209.165.201.1
Tunnel adapter isatap.mycorp.com:
Media State . . . . : Media disconnected
Connection-specific DNS Suffix . : mycorp.com
Tunnel adapter isatap.{1E5663DD-0D0F-4E11-B88C-3E3514E4BFB9}:
Media State . . . . : Media disconnected
Connection-specific DNS Suffix . :
Tunnel adapter 6TO4 Adapter:
Connection-specific DNS Suffix . :
IPv6 Address. . . . . : 2002:d1a5:c964::d1a5:c964
Default Gateway . . . . :
C:\Users\baselab>ping 10.2.2.2
Pinging 10.2.2.2 with 32 bytes of data:
Reply from 10.2.2.2: bytes=32 time=1ms TTL=128
Reply from 10.2.2.2: bytes=32 time=1ms TTL=128
Reply from 10.2.2.2: bytes=32 time=1ms TTL=128
Reply from 10.2.2.2: bytes=32 time=1ms TTL=128
Ping statistics for 10.2.2.2:
Packets: Sent = 4, Received = 4, Lost = 0 (0% loss),
Approximate round trip times in milli-seconds:
Minimum = 1ms, Maximum = 1ms, Average = 1ms
C:\Users\baselab>

In Cisco ASDM, you can monitor established VPN sessions by navigating to **Monitoring > VPN > VPN Statistics > Sessions**. From the Sessions window, shown in Figure 20-19, you can view session statistics for the ASA. In our example, Alice is successfully connected to the internal corporate network using an AnyConnect SSL VPN. Clicking **Details** to the right of the bottom pane provides additional details for each VPN session.

Figure 20-19 Monitoring the VPN Sessions Status from ASDM

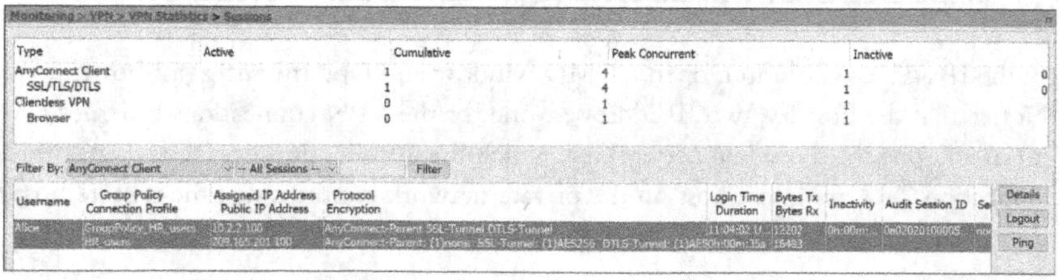
Type
Active
Cumulative
Peak Concurrent
Inactive
AnyConnect Client 1 4 1 0
SSL/TLS/DTLS 1 4 1 0
Clientless VPN 0 1 1
Browser 0 1 1
Filter By: AnyConnect Client
-- All Sessions --
Filter
Username
Group Policy
Connection Profile
Assigned IP Address
Public IP Address
Protocol
Encryption
Login Time
Duration
Bytes Tx
Bytes Rx
Inactivity
Audit Session ID
Details
Logout
Ping

In terms of troubleshooting, if the client is having difficulty establishing an initial connection with the corporate network, use the **debug webvpn svc** command on the ASA and analyze the output. The error messages that appear will usually point out the issue. If the client is successfully connecting but is unable to send traffic over the SSL VPN tunnel, verify the traffic statistics on the client and the ASA. Common traffic issues most often can be related to routing, ACL filtering, or NAT.

Video: Configuring and Verifying AnyConnect SSL VPNs

Refer to the Digital Study Guide to view this video.

Activity: Order the Steps when Configuring AnyConnect SSL VPN

Refer to the Digital Study Guide to complete this activity.

Study Resources

For today's exam topics, refer to the following resources for more study.

Resource	Location	Topic
Primary Resources		
CCNA Security Official Cert Guide	8	Implementing SSL VPNs Using Cisco ASA
CCNA Security (Networking Academy Curriculum)	10	Advanced Cisco Adaptive Security Appliance
Supplemental Resources		
CCNA Security Complete Video Course	6	Implementing SSL Remote-Access VPNs Using Cisco ASA
CCNA Security Portable Command Guide	22	Configuring Cisco ASA SSL VPNs
Cisco ASA (3rd ed.)	23	Client-Based Remote-Access SSL VPNs

Check Your Understanding

Refer to the Digital Study Guide to take a ten-question quiz covering the content of this day.

Site-to-Site VPN

CCNA Security 210-260 IINS Exam Topics

- 3.3.a Implement an IPsec site-to-site VPN with pre-shared key authentication on Cisco routers and ASA firewalls

- 3.3.b Verify an IPsec site-to-site VPN

Key Topics

Today we will review the configuration and verification of site-to-site IPsec VPNs using both a Cisco router and a Cisco ASA. We will first use the CLI to demonstrate the configuration of a site-to-site VPN between two routers. Second, we will use Cisco ASDM to configure a site-to-site VPN between two ASAs.

IPsec Negotiation

IPsec VPN negotiation can be broken down into five steps, as shown in Figure 19-1, including Phase 1 and Phase 2 of Internet Key Exchange (IKE):

Step 1. An ISAKMP tunnel is initiated when Host A sends "interesting" traffic to Host B. Traffic is considered interesting when it travels between the peers and meets the criteria that is defined in the crypto access control list (ACL).

Step 2. IKE Phase 1 begins. The peers negotiate the ISAKMP SA policy. When the peers agree on the policy and are authenticated, a secure tunnel is created.

Step 3. IKE Phase 2 begins. The IPsec peers use the authenticated secure tunnel to negotiate the IPsec SA policy. The negotiation of the shared policy determines how the IPsec tunnel is established.

Step 4. The IPsec tunnel is created and data is transferred between the IPsec peers based on the IPsec SAs.

Step 5. The IPsec tunnel terminates when the IPsec SAs are deleted or when their lifetime expires.

Figure 19-1   Site-to-Site IPsec VPN Negotiations

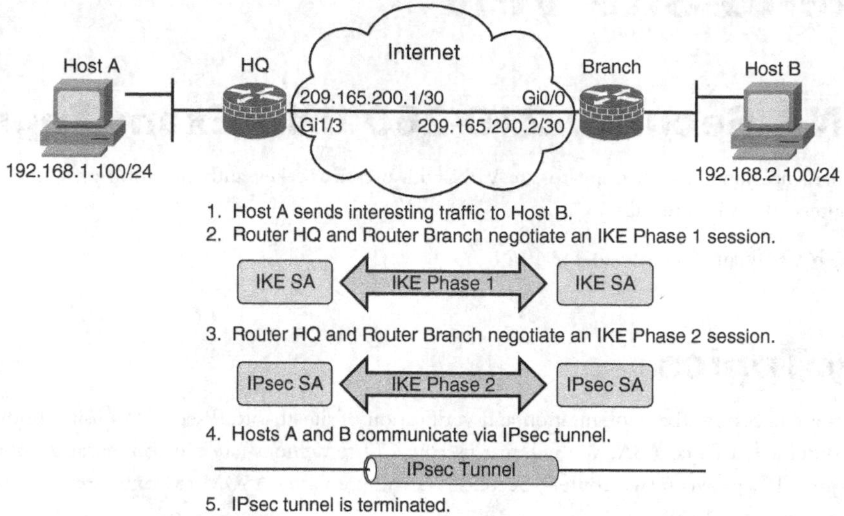

1. Host A sends interesting traffic to Host B.
2. Router HQ and Router Branch negotiate an IKE Phase 1 session.

3. Router HQ and Router Branch negotiate an IKE Phase 2 session.

4. Hosts A and B communicate via IPsec tunnel.

5. IPsec tunnel is terminated.

The basic steps to follow when configuring Cisco IOS CLI-based site-to-site IPsec VPNs are as follows:

Step 1.   Ensure that all ACLs in the IPsec VPN network path are compatible with IPsec.

Step 2.   Configure an ISAKMP policy to determine the ISAKMP parameters that will be used to establish the IKE Phase 1 tunnel.

Step 3.   Define the IPsec transform set. The definition of the transform set defines the parameters that the IPsec tunnel uses and can include the encryption and integrity algorithms.

Step 4.   Create a crypto ACL. The crypto ACL defines which traffic should be sent through the IPsec tunnel and be protected by the IPsec process.

Step 5.   Create and apply a crypto map. The crypto map groups the previously configured parameters together and defines the IPsec peer devices. The crypto map is applied to the outgoing interface of the VPN device.

We will start by building a Cisco CLI IOS-based site-to-site IPsec VPN for the topology shown in Figure 19-1. Afterward, we will review how to configure a Cisco ASA site-to-site IPsec VPN using the ASDM in a similar scenario.

Cisco IOS CLI-based Site-to-Site IPsec VPN

In our example, we want to deploy a site-to-site IPsec VPN between the HQ and Branch routers, allowing corporate traffic behind these routers to travel protected across the Internet.

Configuration

There are five major steps to follow when configuring a Cisco IOS CLI-based site-to-site IPsec VPN.

Step 1: ACL Compatibility

The first step in configuring Cisco IOS ISAKMP is to ensure that existing ACLs on perimeter routers, firewalls, or other devices do not block IPsec traffic. Example 19-1 shows the commands that would be added to the inbound ACL on router HQ Gi0/3. These lines would permit protocol 50 (ESP), protocol 51 (AH), and UDP port 500 (ISAKMP) traffic. They also would permit UDP port 4500 (non500-isakmp). This is used by NAT-T, which is a commonly implemented extension to IKE and has been incorporated into IKEv2. NAT-T facilitates VPN through intermediate devices that perform Port Address Translation (PAT).

Example 19-1   Site-to-Site IPsec VPN ACL

```
access-list 101 permit ahp host 209.165.200.2 host 209.165.200.1
access-list 101 permit esp host 209.165.200.2 host 209.165.200.1
access-list 101 permit udp host 209.165.200.2 host 209.165.200.1 eq isakmp
access-list 101 permit udp host 209.165.200.2 host 209.165.200.1 eq non500-isakmp
```

Step 2: IKE Phase 1—ISAKMP Policy

The second major step in configuring Cisco IOS ISAKMP support is to define a suite of ISAKMP policies. The goal of defining a suite of policies is to define the IKE Phase 1 characteristics.

To configure a new ISAKMP policy, use the **crypto isakmp policy** command. The only argument for the command is to set a priority for the policy (from 1 to 10000). Peers will attempt to negotiate using the policy with the lowest number (highest priority). Peers do not require matching priority numbers.

Within ISAKMP configuration mode, five parameters can be configured, as outlined in Table 19-1.

Table 19-1   ISAKMP Parameters

Parameter	Keyword	Possible Values	Default Value	Description
encryption	des	56-bit DES-CBC	des	Message encryption algorithm
	3des	168-bit Triple DES		
	aes	128-bit AES		
	aes 192	192-bit AES		
	aes 256	256-bit AES		

Table 19-1   **ISAKMP Parameters**   *continued*

Parameter	Keyword	Possible Values	Default Value	Description
hash	sha	SHA-1 (160-bit)	sha	Message integrity (hash) algorithm
	sha256	SHA-2 (256-bit)		
	sha384	SHA-2 (384-bit)		
	sha512	SHA-2 (512-bit)		
	md5	MD5 (HMAC variant)		
authentication	rsa-sig	RSA signatures	rsa-sig	Peer authentication method
	rsa-encr	RSA encrypted nonces		
	pre-share	Pre-shared keys		
group	1	DH-1 768-bit	1	Key exchange parameters (Diffie-Hellman group identifier)
	2	DH-2 1024-bit		
	5	DH-5 1536-bit		
	14	DH-14 and DH-24 2040-bit		
	24			
	15	DH-15 3072-bit		
	16	DH-16 4096-bit		
	19	DH-19, DH-20, and DH-21 use ECDH at 256-, 384-, and 512-bit respectively		
	20			
	21			
lifetime	seconds	60 to 86,400 seconds	86,400 sec. (one day)	ISAKMP-established SA lifetime

For our scenario, let's use some of the stronger options in configuring our ISAKMP policy, as shown in Example 19-2. Both routers would be configured identically at this point. ISAKMP peers negotiate the acceptable ISAKMP policies before they agree upon the SA to use for IPsec. When the ISAKMP negotiation begins in IKE Phase 1 main mode, ISAKMP looks for an ISAKMP policy that is the same on both peers.

Example 19-2 Configuring ISAKMP Policy

```
HQ(config)# crypto isakmp policy 10
HQ(config-isakmp)# authentication pre-share
HQ(config-isakmp)# encryption aes 256
HQ(config-isakmp)# group 15
HQ(config-isakmp)# hash sha256
HQ(config-isakmp)# lifetime 3600
```

> **NOTE:** When determining which ISAKMP functions to use, consult the Cisco "Next Generation Encryption" document at http://www.cisco.com/web/about/security/intelligence/nextgen_crypto.html.

At this point a pre-shared key (PSK) also needs to be configured, which will allow the VPN peers to authenticate each other. To configure this, use the **crypto isakmp key** command in global configuration mode. You must configure this key whenever you specify **authentication pre-share** in an ISAKMP policy. The command syntax is shown in Example 19-3. The administrator can specify either a hostname or an IP address for the peer.

Example 19-3 Configuring PSK

```
HQ(config)# crypto isakmp key VPNpass address 209.165.200.2
Branch(config)# crypto isakmp key VPNpass address 209.165.200.1
```

Notice in this example that both VPN peers are using the same case-sensitive pre-shared key.

Step 3: IKE Phase 2—IPsec Transform Set

The next step is to configure the set of encryption and hashing algorithms that will be used to transform the data sent through the IPsec tunnel. This is called the transform set. During IKE Phase 2 negotiations, the peers agree on the IPsec transform set to be used for protecting interesting traffic.

Transform sets combine these IPsec factors:

- A mechanism for payload authentication: AH HMAC or ESP HMAC transform
- A mechanism for payload encryption: ESP encryption transform
- IPsec mode (transport versus tunnel)

Define a transform set with the **crypto ipsec transform-set** global configuration command, as shown in Example 19-4. The encryption and hashing algorithm that will be transforming the data can then be configured in either order.

Example 19-4 Configuring Transform Sets

```
HQ(config)# crypto ipsec transform-set HQBRANCH esp-aes esp-sha256-hmac
Branch(config)# crypto ipsec transform-set HQBRANCH esp-aes esp-sha256-hmac
```

We are configuring the same transform set on both VPN peers to ensure successful negotiation of IKE Phase 2.

Step 4: Crypto ACLs

To trigger IKE Phase 1, interesting traffic must be detected. In our case, interesting traffic will be defined as any IPv4 communication between the HQ LAN and the Branch LAN.

Interesting traffic is defined by crypto ACLs in site-to-site IPsec VPN configurations. Crypto ACLs perform two functions:

- **Outbound:** For outbound traffic, the ACL defines the flows that IPsec should protect.

- **Inbound:** The same ACL is processed for inbound traffic. The ACL defines traffic that should have been protected with IPsec by the peer. Packets are discarded if they match but arrive unprotected.

The **access-list** command is used to create crypto ACLs. The **permit** keyword specifies that matching packets must be protected in this tunnel, and the **deny** keyword specifies that matching packets are not protected by this tunnel.

Example 19-5 shows the ACL statements for both HQ and Branch routers in our scenario. It is important that the crypto ACLs defined on the peer devices are mirror images of each other. If they are not, IKE Phase 2 negotiation between VPN peers will fail.

Example 19-5 Configuring ACLs

```
HQ(config)# access-list 120 permit ip 192.168.1.0 0.0.0.255 192.168.2.0 0.0.0.255
Branch(config)# access-list 120 permit ip 192.168.2.0 0.0.0.255 192.168.1.0
   0.0.0.255
```

Step 5: IPsec Crypto Map

IPsec policies are defined in crypto maps. Each crypto map must define the following criteria:

- The crypto ACL, which specifies which traffic should be protected by IPsec

- The transform set, which specifies the IPsec protocols and cipher policies that are used to protect the traffic

- The IPsec peer, which specifies where the IPsec-protected traffic is sent

- Optionally specify a lifetime for the IPsec security association

Use the **crypto map** global configuration command to create or modify a crypto map and enter crypto map configuration mode.

In crypto map configuration mode, define the criteria for the crypto map. Use the **match address** command to specify the crypto ACL, the **set transform-set** command to specify the transform set, and the **set peer** command to specify the peer.

To activate a crypto map, use the **crypto map** command in interface configuration mode to apply the crypto map to an interface that is reachable from the VPN peer. Example 19-6 shows the crypto map being defined and applied on Gi0/0 of the HQ router. A similar configuration would be applied to the Branch router. The only difference would be the **set peer** command, which would point to the HQ router's Gi0/0 IP address.

Example 19-6 Configuring Crypto Map

```
HQ(config)# crypto map HQMAP 10 ipsec-isakmp
HQ(config-crypto-map)# match address 120
HQ(config-crypto-map)# set peer 209.165.200.2
HQ(config-crypto-map)# set transform-set HQBRANCH
HQ(config-crypto-map)# set security-association lifetime seconds 3600
HQ(config-crypto-map)# exit
HQ(config)# interface Gi1/3
HQ(config-if)# crypto map HQMAP
```

Verification

You can use the Cisco IOS commands presented in Table 19-2 to verify the VPN configuration.

Table 19-2   IPsec Verification Commands

Command	Description
show crypto isakmp policy	Displays configured IKE policies
show crypto ipsec transform-set	Displays configured IPsec transform sets
show crypto map	Displays configured crypto maps
show crypto ipsec sa	Displays established IPsec tunnels
debug crypto isakmp	Debugs IKE events
debug crypto ipsec	Debugs IPsec events

The **show crypto isakmp policy** command is useful because it reveals the complete ISAKMP (IKE Phase 1) policies, as shown in Example 19-7.

Example 19-7 show crypto isakmp policy Output

```
HQ# show crypto isakmp policy

Global IKE policy
Protection suite of priority 10
        encryption algorithm:   AES - Advanced Encryption Standard (256 bit keys).
        hash algorithm:         Secure Hash Standard 2 (256 bit)
        authentication method:  Pre-Shared Key
        Diffie-Hellman group:   #15 (3072 bit)
        lifetime:               3600 seconds, no volume limit
```

You can use the **show crypto ipsec transform-set** command to show all the configured transform sets, including the default transform set, as shown in Example 19-8.

Example 19-8 show crypto ipsec transform-set Output

```
HQ# show crypto ipsec transform-set
Transform set default: { esp-aes esp-sha-hmac  }
   will negotiate = { Transport,  },


Transform set HQBRANCH: { esp-aes esp-sha256-hmac  }
   will negotiate = { Tunnel,  },
```

Notice that our HQBRANCH transform set will use tunnel mode when establishing our site-to-site IPsec VPN with the Branch router. This is the default behavior. Tunnel mode is used to encrypt and authenticate the IP packets when they are originated by the hosts connected behind the VPN device. In a typical site-to-site IPsec connection, tunnel mode is always used.

To see all the configured crypto maps, use the **show crypto map** command. This command verifies configurations and shows the SA lifetime, as shown in Example 19-9.

Example 19-9 show crypto map Output

```
HQ# show crypto map
Crypto Map IPv4 "HQMAP" 10 ipsec-isakmp
        Peer = 209.165.200.2
        Extended IP access list 120
            access-list 120 permit ip 192.168.1.0 0.0.0.255 192.168.2.0 0.0.0.255
        Current peer: 209.165.200.2
        Security association lifetime: 4608000 kilobytes/3600 seconds
        Responder-Only (Y/N): N
        PFS (Y/N): N
        Mixed-mode : Disabled
        Transform sets={
                HQBRANCH: { esp-aes esp-sha256-hmac  } ,
        }
        Interfaces using crypto map HQMAP:
                GigabitEthernet1/3 (based on Figure 1).
```

The **show crypto isakmp sa** command shows the status and settings of IKE Phase 1 SAs. In Example 19-10, notice the status of the tunnel under the Status column. A state of QM_IDLE is considered normal for an established Phase 1 tunnel.

Example 19-10   show crypto isakmp sa Output

```
HQ# show crypto isakmp sa
IPv4 Crypto ISAKMP SA
dst              src            state        conn-id status
209.165.200.2   209.165.200.1  QM_IDLE           1001 ACTIVE
```

Finally, one of the more useful commands is **show crypto ipsec sa**. When you see that an SA has been established, it indicates that the rest of the configuration is working. To test our site-to-site VPN, we send a ping from Host A to Host B. Example 19-11 shows how the first ping fails, but triggers the VPN configuration with interesting traffic, allowing the other pings to reach their destination encrypted. Make special note of the *pkts encrypt* and *pkts decrypt* values because they indicate that traffic is flowing through the tunnel, in our case the four successful pings.

Example 19-11   show crypto ipsec sa Output

```
HostA# ping 192.168.2.100
Type escape sequence to abort.
Sending 5, 100-byte ICMP Echos to 192.168.2.100, timeout is 2 seconds:
.!!!!
Success rate is 80 percent (4/5), round-trip min/avg/max = 6/7/8 ms


HQ# show crypto ipsec sa
interface: GigabitEthernet0/0
    Crypto map tag: HQMAP, local addr 209.165.200.1

   protected vrf: (none)
   local  ident (addr/mask/prot/port): (192.168.1.0/255.255.255.0/0/0)
   remote ident (addr/mask/prot/port): (192.168.2.0/255.255.255.0/0/0)
   current_peer 209.165.200.2 port 500
     PERMIT, flags={origin_is_acl,}
    #pkts encaps: 4, #pkts encrypt: 4, #pkts digest: 4
    #pkts decaps: 4, #pkts decrypt: 4, #pkts verify: 4
    #pkts compressed: 0, #pkts decompressed: 0
    #pkts not compressed: 0, #pkts compr. failed: 0
    #pkts not decompressed: 0, #pkts decompress failed: 0
    #send errors 0, #recv errors 0

     local crypto endpt.: 209.165.200.1, remote crypto endpt.: 209.165.200.2
     plaintext mtu 1438, path mtu 1500, ip mtu 1500, ip mtu idb GigabitEthernet0/0
     current outbound spi: 0x9056B964(2421602660)
     PFS (Y/N): N, DH group: none

     inbound esp sas:
      spi: 0x9F74FDDE(2675244510)
        transform: esp-aes esp-sha256-hmac ,
        in use settings ={Tunnel, }
        conn id: 1, flow_id: SW:1, sibling_flags 80004040, crypto map: HQMAP
        sa timing: remaining key lifetime (k/sec): (4278426/3551)
        IV size: 16 bytes
        replay detection support: Y
```

```
      ecn bit support: Y status: off
      Status: ACTIVE(ACTIVE)


   inbound ah sas:


   inbound pcp sas:


   outbound esp sas:
    spi: 0x9056B964(2421602660)
      transform: esp-aes esp-sha256-hmac ,
      in use settings ={Tunnel, }
      conn id: 2, flow_id: SW:2, sibling_flags 80004040, crypto map: HQMAP
      sa timing: remaining key lifetime (k/sec): (4278426/3551)
      IV size: 16 bytes
      replay detection support: Y
      ecn bit support: Y status: off
      Status: ACTIVE(ACTIVE)


   outbound ah sas:


   outbound pcp sas:
```

Activity: Order the Steps when Configuring IOS-based Site-to-Site IPsec VPN

Refer to the Digital Study Guide to complete this activity.

Video: Configuring IOS-based Site-to-Site IPsec VPN

Refer to the Digital Study Guide to view this video.

Cisco ASA Site-to-Site IPsec VPN

Like the Cisco ISR routers, the Cisco ASA supports site-to-site IPsec VPN deployments, which can be used to protect traffic between remote and central sites. The scenario for our Cisco ASA site-to-site IPsec VPN is shown in Figure 19-2.

We will once again use an ASDM wizard to help us with the deployment of our site-to-site VPN. Assume that basic connectivity and routing has been established and that PAT has been configured on the ASA outside interfaces. We will use the same configuration steps previously discussed in the Cisco IOS CLI-based site-to-site VPN example, although the ASDM will present them in a more condensed fashion. For this configuration example, we will focus on the HQ ASA, but an almost identical process would need to be implemented on the Branch ASA.

Figure 19-2   Cisco ASA Site-to-Site IPsec VPN Scenario

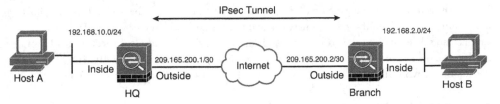

Configuration

There are five major steps to follow when configuring a Cisco ASA site-to-site IPsec VPN.

Step 1: Launch the ASDM Site-to-Site VPN Wizard

From the menu bar, click **Wizards > VPN Wizards > Site-to-Site VPN Wizard**. The VPN Wizard Introduction window is displayed, as shown in Figure 19-3. Click **Next** to start the configuration.

Figure 19-3   Start the Site-to-Site VPN Wizard

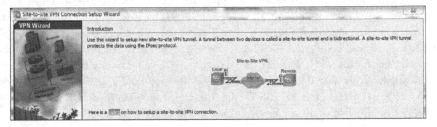

Step 2: Peer Device Identification

This first configuration step prompts you to specify the IP address of the VPN peer and the interface used to reach the peer. In our case, the public IP address of the Branch ASA is 209.165.200.2 and the crypto map will be applied to the HQ ASA's outside interface, as shown in Figure 19-4. Click **Next** to continue.

Figure 19-4   Peer Device Identification

Peer Device Identification
This step lets you identify the peer VPN device by its IP address and the interface used to access the peer.
Peer IP Address: 209.165.200.2
VPN Access Interface: outside

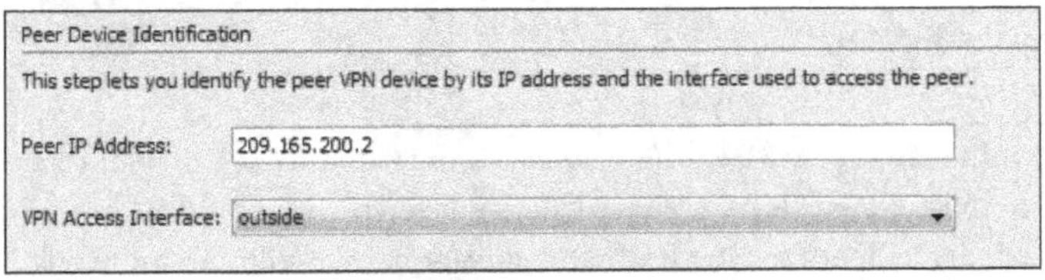

Step 3: Traffic to Protect

We will now define the interesting traffic that will initiate and then use the VPN. This step allows the administrator to identify the local network and remote network. We can manually add an address and subnet mask in the corresponding field, or click the ... button to select from a list of local or remote networks known by the ASA. In our case, the local network is 192.168.1.0/24 and the remote network is 192.168.2.0/24, as shown in Figure 19-5. Click **Next** to continue.

Figure 19-5   Traffic to Protect

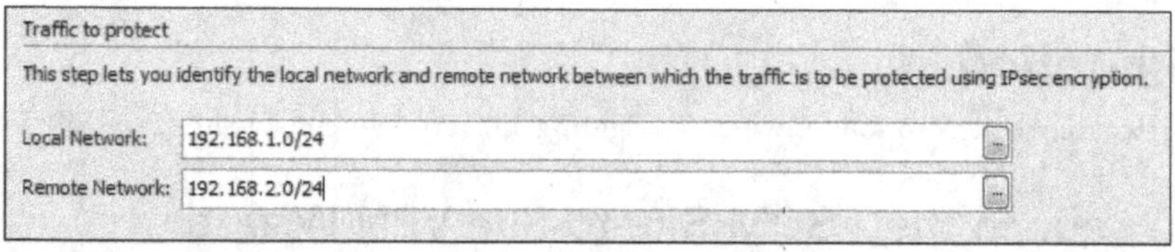

Traffic to protect

This step lets you identify the local network and remote network between which the traffic is to be protected using IPsec encryption.

Local Network: 192.168.1.0/24

Remote Network: 192.168.2.0/24

Step 4: Security

On the Security screen, you can specify the security parameters. You can choose the **Simple Configuration** option to use commonly deployed IKE and ISAKMP security parameters. If you choose this option, you only need to specify the pre-shared key for the connection. Otherwise, you can choose **Customized Configuration** if you want to change the VPN policies. ASDM then permits you to choose the IKE version (1 or 2), local and remote pre-shared keys, IKE policies and IPsec proposals, and Perfect Forward Secrecy (PFS). For our scenario, since we are using ASAs as endpoints for the VPN, we will create a custom configuration using IKEv2. This allows us to use asymmetric pre-shared keys, which is a feature not supported in IKEv1. The PSK for the HQ ASA will be **HQpass**, while the PSK for the Branch ASA will be **Branchpass**. But as shown in Figure 19-6, the passwords do not appear in clear text in the ASDM wizard.

Figure 19-6   Custom Security Configuration

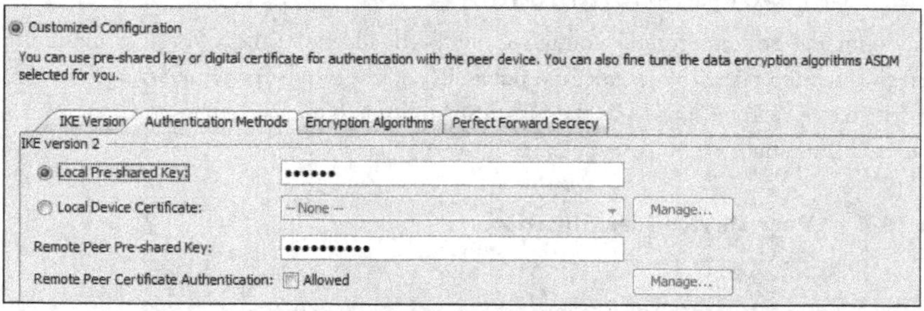

Customized Configuration

You can use pre-shared key or digital certificate for authentication with the peer device. You can also fine tune the data encryption algorithms ASDM selected for you.

IKE Version   Authentication Methods   Encryption Algorithms   Perfect Forward Secrecy

IKE version 2

Local Pre-shared Key: ••••••

Local Device Certificate: -- None --   Manage...

Remote Peer Pre-shared Key: ••••••••••

Remote Peer Certificate Authentication: Allowed   Manage...

PFS is a cryptographic concept where each new key is unrelated to any previous key. In IPsec negotiations, Phase 2 keys are based on Phase 1 keys unless you specify PFS. PFS uses a separate Diffie-Hellman key agreement for each Phase 2 negotiation. We will select a strong encryption level of group 19 (256-bit ECDH) for this feature.

Click **Next** to continue when done.

Step 5: NAT Exempt

Determine whether NAT should be exempted in the NAT Exempt window, as shown in Figure 19-7. Typically NAT exemption should be selected in site-to-site VPNs since, in most cases, you do not want to translate (that is, NAT) the IP addresses of your local and remote host devices when their traffic is traversing the VPN tunnel. In our case, we will exempt traffic originating from our inside network.

Figure 19-7   Enabling NAT Exempt

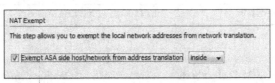

Click **Next** to display the Summary window, which allows the administrator to verify and confirm the configuration built by the wizard, as shown in Figure 19-8.

Figure 19-8   Configuration Summary

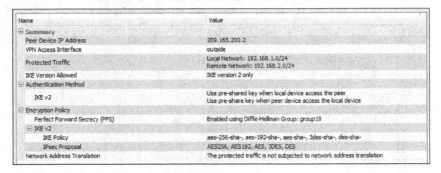

Click **Finish** to apply the configuration to the Cisco ASA. If the option is enabled, you will be presented with a preview of the commands created by the wizard, allowing you to save them to a text file before sending them to the ASA.

Once configured, it is possible to edit the VPN in the ASDM by clicking **Configuration > Site-to-Site > VPN > Connection Profiles**.

Verification

Similar to Cisco IOS devices, the Cisco ASA has several **show** commands that enable you to verify the configuration and the IKE and IPsec tunnel information. Table 19-3 lists and describes some of the most useful **show** commands for troubleshooting IPsec implementations in the Cisco ASA.

Table 19-3   ASA IPsec Site-to-Site VPN Verification Commands

Command	Description
show crypto isakmp stats	Displays detailed information of both IKEv1 and IKEv2 transactions in the Cisco ASA
show crypto ikev1 | ikev2 stats	Displays detailed information of IKEv1 or IKEv2 transactions in the Cisco ASA
show isakmp sa [detail]	Displays the IKEv1 and IKEv2 (Phase 1) runtime security association (SA) database
show crypto ipsec sa [detail]	Displays the Phase 2 runtime SA database

Example 19-12 displays the output for the **show crypto ipsec sa** and **show isakmp sa detail** commands from the HQ ASA after the site-to-site tunnel was established with the Branch ASA.

Example 19-12   show crypto ipsec sa and show isakmp sa detail Output

```
HQ# show crypto ipsec sa
interface: outside
    Crypto map tag: outside_map, seq num: 1, local addr: 209.165.200.1


      access-list outside_cryptomap extended permit ip 192.168.1.0 255.255.255.0
        192.168.2.0 255.255.255.0
      local ident (addr/mask/prot/port): (192.168.1.0/255.255.255.0/0/0)
      remote ident (addr/mask/prot/port): (192.168.2.0/255.255.255.0/0/0)
      current_peer: 209.165.200.2


      #pkts encaps: 3, #pkts encrypt: 3, #pkts digest: 3
      #pkts decaps: 3, #pkts decrypt: 3, #pkts verify: 3
      #pkts compressed: 0, #pkts decompressed: 0
      #pkts not compressed: 3, #pkts comp failed: 0, #pkts decomp failed: 0
      #pre-frag successes: 0, #pre-frag failures: 0, #fragments created: 0
      #PMTUs sent: 0, #PMTUs rcvd: 0, #decapsulated frgs needing reassembly: 0
      #TFC rcvd: 0, #TFC sent: 0
      #Valid ICMP Errors rcvd: 0, #Invalid ICMP Errors rcvd: 0
      #send errors: 0, #recv errors: 0


      local crypto endpt.: 209.165.200.1/500, remote crypto endpt.:
        209.165.200.2/500
      path mtu 1500, ipsec overhead 74(44), media mtu 1500
      PMTU time remaining (sec): 0, DF policy: copy-df
      ICMP error validation: disabled, TFC packets: disabled
      current outbound spi: 71E05519
      current inbound spi : 9D8B4B5C
```

```
  inbound esp sas:
    spi: 0x9D8B4B5C (2643151708)
        transform: esp-aes-256 esp-sha-hmac no compression
        in use settings ={L2L, Tunnel, PFS Group 19, IKEv2, }
        slot: 0, conn_id: 12288, crypto-map: outside_map
        sa timing: remaining key lifetime (kB/sec): (3916799/28749)
        IV size: 16 bytes
        replay detection support: Y
        Anti replay bitmap:
         0x00000000 0x0000000F
  outbound esp sas:
    spi: 0x71E05519 (1910527257)
        transform: esp-aes-256 esp-sha-hmac no compression
        in use settings ={L2L, Tunnel, PFS Group 19, IKEv2, }
        slot: 0, conn_id: 12288, crypto-map: outside_map
        sa timing: remaining key lifetime (kB/sec): (4147199/28749)
        IV size: 16 bytes
        replay detection support: Y
        Anti replay bitmap:
         0x00000000 0x00000001

HQ# show isakmp sa detail

There are no IKEv1 SAs

IKEv2 SAs:

Session-id:3, Status:UP-ACTIVE, IKE count:1, CHILD count:1

Tunnel-id                 Local              Remote        Status        Role
 66613695      209.165.200.1/500    209.165.200.2/500     READY     INITIATOR
     Encr: AES-CBC, keysize: 256, Hash: SHA96, DH Grp:5, Auth sign: PSK,
       Auth verify: PSK
     Life/Active Time: 86400/84 sec
     Session-id: 3
     Status Description: Negotiation done
     Local spi: E7B7854D154236B5        Remote spi: 4669317B9D61D6A5
     Local id: 209.165.200.1
     Remote id: 209.165.200.2
     Local req mess id: 5              Remote req mess id: 3
     Local next mess id: 5            Remote next mess id: 3
     Local req queued: 5              Remote req queued: 3
     Local window: 1                  Remote window: 1
     DPD configured for 10 seconds, retry 2
     NAT-T is not detected
```

```
Child sa: local selector  192.168.1.0/0 - 192.168.1.255/65535
          remote selector 192.168.2.0/0 - 192.168.2.255/65535
          ESP spi in/out: 0x9d8b4b5c/0x71e05519
          AH spi in/out: 0x0/0x0
          CPI in/out: 0x0/0x0
          Encr: AES-CBC, keysize: 256, esp_hmac: SHA96
          ah_hmac: None, comp: IPCOMP_NONE, mode tunnel
```

The same type of verification can be made from the ASDM by clicking **Monitoring > VPN > VPN Statistics > Sessions**, as shown in Figure 19-9. Clicking the **Details** button brings up more granular information about both IKEv2 Phase 1 and Phase 2 parameters.

Figure 19-9   Monitoring the VPN Tunnel

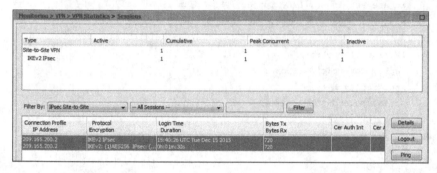

Video: Configuring ASA-based Site-to-Site IPsec VPN

Refer to the Digital Study Guide to view this video.

Packet Tracer Activity: Configure IOS Site-to-Site IPsec VPN

Refer to the Digital Study Guide to access the PKA file for this activity. You must have Packet Tracer software to run this activity.

Study Resources

For today's exam topics, refer to the following resources for more study.

Resource	Location	Topic
Primary Resources		
CCNA Security Official Cert Guide	7	Implementing IPsec Site-to-Site VPNs
CCNA Security (Networking Academy Curriculum)	8	Implementing Virtual Private Networks
	10	Advanced Cisco Adaptive Security Appliance

Resource	Location	Topic
Supplemental Resources		
CCNA Security Complete Video Course	19	Implementing IPsec Site-to-Site VPNs
CCNA Security Portable Command Guide	16	Configuring Site-to-Site VPNs
	21	Configuring Cisco ASA VPNs
Cisco ASA (3rd ed.)	19	Site-to-Site IPsec VPNs

 ## CheckYour Understanding

Refer to the Digital Study Guide to take a ten-question quiz covering the content of this day.

VPN Advanced Topics

CCNA Security 210-260 IINS Exam Topics

- 3.1.b Describe hairpinning, split tunneling, always-on, NAT traversal
- 3.2.e Identify endpoint posture assessment

Key Topics

Today we will review some advanced concepts related to VPN deployment. In particular, we will look at some optional features used in complex remote-access VPN scenarios, as well as discuss the issue of using NAT with VPN tunnel endpoints.

Hairpinning and Client U-Turn

Cisco ASA, by default, does not allow a packet to leave the same interface on which it was originally received. Cisco ASA supports receiving the IPsec traffic from one VPN tunnel and then redirecting it into a different VPN tunnel, if both tunnels terminate on the same interface. This feature is known as IPsec hairpinning. Using this feature, you can implement a true hub-and-spoke scenario, as shown in Figure 18-1.

Figure 18-1   IPsec Hairpinning

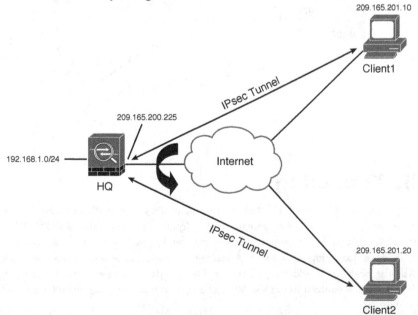

If Client1 needs to send traffic to Client2, it sends all traffic to the hub Cisco ASA (HQ). The hub Cisco ASA, after checking the routing table for the destination address, sends traffic to Client2 over the other VPN tunnel, and vice versa. However, this feature requires both remote VPN devices to be a part of the same crypto map and the crypto map to be applied to the same interface.

You can enable IPsec hairpinning by navigating to **Configuration > Device Setup > Interfaces** and checking the **Enable Traffic Between Two or More Hosts Connected to the Same Interface** check box. Using the CLI, you use the global **same-security-traffic permit intra-interface** command to permit VPN traffic to leave the same physical interface when traffic needs to go over the other VPN tunnel.

Cisco ASA also supports receiving traffic from an IPsec client and then redirecting it to the Internet in clear text, as shown in Figure 18-2. This feature, also known as Client U-turn and enabled with the **same-security-traffic** command mentioned previously, is useful if you

- Are not using split tunneling (discussed in the following section) and all traffic is sent to the ASA

- Want to provide secure Internet access to your IPsec clients

- Do not want return traffic from the Internet that is destined to the VPN clients to enter the inside network of your organization

Figure 18-2   Client U-Turn

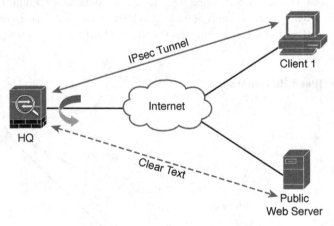

Split Tunneling

After a VPN tunnel is established, the default behavior of the Cisco AnyConnect Secure Mobility Client is to encrypt traffic to all the destination IP addresses. This means that if an SSL VPN user wants to browse to a public web server over the Internet, the packets are encrypted and sent to Cisco ASA. After decrypting them, the ASA searches its routing table and forwards the packet to the appropriate next-hop IP address in clear text. These steps are reversed when traffic returns from the web server and is destined to the SSL VPN client. This process is what we referred to earlier as Client U-turn.

This behavior might not always be desirable, for the following two reasons:

- Traffic destined to the nonsecure networks traverses over the Internet twice: once encrypted (to the ASA) and once in clear text (to the Internet).

- The ASA handles extra VPN traffic destined to the nonsecure subnet (Internet). The ASA analyzes all traffic leaving and coming from the Internet.

With split tunneling, the ASA notifies the Cisco AnyConnect Secure Mobility Client about the secured subnets. The VPN client encrypts only those packets that are destined for the networks behind the ASA. All other traffic is sent normally (in clear text) to the Internet. A split tunnel is not considered to be as secure, because an attacker on the Internet may potentially have access to the remote machine, which in turn has access to the internal network through the VPN. Personal firewall, antivirus, and antimalware software become very important in this scenario.

Split tunneling can be configured under a user policy, user group policy, or default group policy. Choose **Configuration > Remote Access VPN > Network (Client) Access > Group Policies**, select **AnyConnectGroupPolicy**, click **Edit**, and choose **Advanced > Split Tunneling**. From there, specify the networks for which you want to tunnel traffic. Anything not identified as traffic that should be tunneled is simply sent by the user through its natural path not inside the tunnel.

As shown in the ACL Manager dialog box in Figure 18-3, a new ACL called SplitTunnelList has been added with an access control entry (ACE) for 192.168.1.0/24, which is the inside private network behind the ASA. Traffic for all other networks will not be sent inside the VPN tunnel.

Figure 18-3   Configuring Split Tunneling

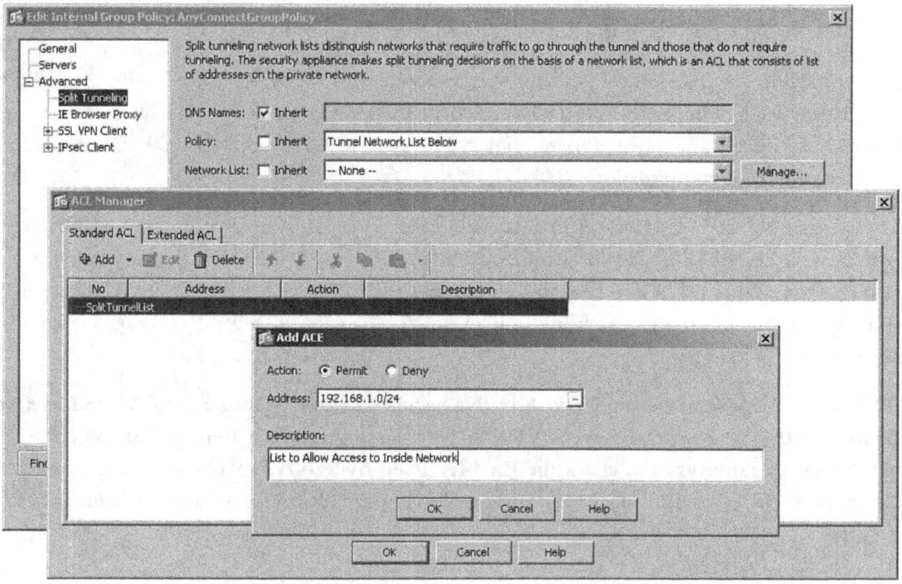

Always-on VPN

It is possible to configure AnyConnect to establish a VPN session automatically after a user logs in to a computer. The VPN session remains open until the user logs out of the computer, or the session timer or idle session timer expires. The group policy assigned to the session specifies these timer values. If AnyConnect loses the connection with the ASA, the ASA and the client retain the resources assigned to the session until one of these timers expires. AnyConnect continually attempts to reestablish the connection to reactivate the session if it is still open; otherwise, it continually attempts to establish a new VPN session. Always-on VPN enforces corporate policies to protect the computer from security threats by preventing access to Internet resources when the computer is not in a trusted network.

NAT Traversal

In many network topologies, the VPN clients reside behind a NAT/PAT device that inspects the Layer 4 port information for address translation. Because IPsec uses ESP (IP protocol 50), which does not have Layer 4 information, the PAT device is usually incapable of translating the encrypted packets going over the VPN tunnel. To remedy this problem, Cisco ASA uses a solution called NAT Traversal (NAT-T).

NAT-T, defined in RFC 3947 ("Negotiation of NAT-Traversal in the IKE"), is a feature that encapsulates the ESP packets into UDP port 4500 packets. NAT-T is dynamically negotiated if the following two conditions are met:

- Both VPN endpoints are NAT-T capable.

- A NAT or PAT device exists between VPN peers.

If both conditions are true, the VPN client tries to connect to the ASA, using UDP port 500 for IKE negotiations. As soon as the VPN peers discover that they are NAT-T capable and that a NAT/PAT device resides between them, they switch over to UDP port 4500 for the rest of tunnel negotiations and data encapsulation.

NAT-T is globally enabled on the ASA by default, with a default keepalive timeout of 20 seconds. In many cases, the NAT/PAT devices time out the UDP port 4500 entries if no active traffic is passing through them. NAT-T keepalives are used so that the ASA can send periodic keepalive messages to prevent the entries from timing out. You can specify a NAT-T keepalive range between 10 and 3600 seconds.

If NAT-T is not enabled, use the Cisco Adaptive Security Device Manager (ASDM) and navigate to **Configuration > Remote Access VPN > Network (Access) Client > Advanced > IPsec > IKE Parameters** and check the **Enable IPsec over NAT-T** check box. Example 18-1 illustrates how NAT-T is globally enabled in the CLI on the HQ ASA, with keepalives sent every 25 seconds.

Example 18-1 Enabling NAT-T Globally Using the CLI

```
HQ(config)# crypto isakmp nat-traversal 25
```

Video: Configuring Advanced Remote-Access VPN Features on Cisco ASA

Refer to the Digital Study Guide to view this video.

Endpoint Posture Assessment

In remote-access VPNs, such as SSL VPNs, it is becoming extremely difficult to correctly identify users' hardware environments. A remote user may establish an SSL VPN tunnel from her corporate-owned workstation in the morning, connect to the corporate resources from an Internet cafe in the afternoon, and then connect to the same corporate resources from home in the evening. Moreover, if you are managing a remote-access solution, it is challenging to map appropriate user authorization attributes based on the connection type. To provide a solution to these issues, Cisco introduced dynamic access policies (DAP).

A DAP is defined as the collection of access-control attributes that is specific to a user's session. These policies are generated dynamically after user authorization attributes have been evaluated, such as the tunnel type to which the user is connecting and the appropriate action, such as how access lists or filters are determined. After a DAP is generated, it is applied to the user's session to allow or deny access to internal resources.

For example, consider a user who connects to the ASA from two different machines and establishes an SSL VPN tunnel. When the user connects from her corporate laptop and is running a compliant and up-to-date firewall, she is given full access to the network via the AnyConnect client. However, if she connects from her home machine, she is given access to only a limited number of servers over the clientless SSL VPN tunnel.

As mentioned earlier, a DAP analyzes the posture assessment result of a host and applies dynamically generated access policies when a user session is established. A DAP supports a number of posture assessment methods to collect endpoint security attributes. They include the following:

- **Cisco Secure Desktop (CSD):** CSD collects the file information, registry key values, running processes information, operating system information, and policy information from an end workstation.

- **Cisco Network Admission Control (NAC):** For NAC deployments, you can use the posture assessment string passed by the Cisco Secure ACS server.

- **Host Scan:** Host Scan is a modular component of CSD. It provides information such as antivirus, antispyware, and personal firewall software information about an end host. After Host Scan gathers this information from the endpoint, it sends it to the ASA, where it can be used to distinguish between corporate-owned, personal, and public computers. The information can also be used in pre-login assessments. This type of assessment can also examine the remote computer for a large collection of antivirus and antispyware applications, associated definitions updates, and firewalls. It can then attempt to initiate remediation by enabling and updating the necessary services.

Activity: Identify Advanced VPN Technologies

Refer to the Digital Study Guide to complete this activity.

Study Resources

For today's exam topics, refer to the following resources for more study.

Resource	Location	Topic
Primary Resources		
CCNA Security Official Cert Guide	8	Implementing SSL VPNs Using Cisco ASA
CCNA Security (Networking Academy Curriculum)	8	Implementing Virtual Private Networks
	10	Advanced Cisco Adaptive Security Appliance
Supplemental Resources		
CCNA Security Complete Video Course	6	Implementing SSL Remote-Access VPNs Using Cisco ASA
CCNA Security Portable Command Guide	22	Configuring Cisco ASA SSL VPNs
Cisco ASA (3rd ed.)	19	Site-to-Site IPsec VPNs

 Check Your Understanding

Refer to the Digital Study Guide to take a ten-question quiz covering the content of this day.

Secure Device Access

CCNA Security 210-260 IINS Exam Topics

- 4.1.a Configure multiple privilege levels

- 4.1.b Configure Cisco IOS role-based CLI access

- 4.1.c Implement Cisco IOS resilient configuration

Key Topics

Today we are reviewing ways to secure network device access. Specifically, we will look at configuring IOS authorization with CLI privilege levels and role-based CLI. Finally, we will discuss how to secure both the startup-configuration and the IOS file stored in flash memory by enabling the Cisco IOS resilient configuration feature.

Cisco IOS Authorization with Privilege Levels

A common method of defining authorization policy for administrative access is to use privilege levels. By default, the Cisco IOS software CLI has two levels of access to commands:

- **User EXEC mode (privilege level 1):** Provides the lowest EXEC mode user privileges at the Router> prompt

- **Privileged EXEC mode (privilege level 15):** Provides the highest EXEC mode user privileges at the Router# prompt

There are 16 privilege levels in total. The higher the privilege level, the more router access a user has. Commands that are available at lower privilege levels are also executable at higher levels. To configure a privilege level with specific commands, use the **privilege** command. Example 17-1 shows the commands necessary to set the privilege level of several commands.

Example 17-1 Configuring Privilege Levels

```
R1(config)# privilege exec level 5 ping
R1(config)# privilege exec level 5 show version
R1(config)# privilege exec level 10 reload
R1(config)# privilege exec level 12 show ip interface brief
R1(config)# enable algorithm-type scrypt secret level 5 PrvLevel5
R1(config)# enable algorithm-type scrypt secret level 10 PrvLevel10
R1(config)# username JRADMIN privilege 12 algorithm-type scrypt secret PrvLevel12
```

In Example 17-1, privilege level 5 has access to the **ping** and **show version** commands, as well as all level 1 commands. Privilege level 10 has access to the **reload** command, as well as all level 5 and level 1 commands. Privilege level 12 has access to the **show ip interface brief** command, as well as all level 10, level 5, and level 1 commands. For level 5 and level 10, a SCRYPT-encrypted secret password has been configured. For level 12 access, a local database entry for JRADMIN has been configured, also using the stronger SCRYPT encryption algorithm.

To access a certain privilege level, use the **enable** [*level*] command. To view the current privilege level, use the **show privilege** command, as shown in Example 17-2.

Example 17-2 Accessing and Verifying Privilege Levels

```
R1> enable 5
Password: <PrvLevel5>
R1# show privilege
Current privilege level is 5
```

Video: Configuring Privilege Levels

Refer to the Digital Study Guide to view this video.

Authorization with Role-Based CLI

In an effort to provide more flexibility than privilege levels allow, Cisco introduced the role-based CLI access feature in Cisco IOS Release 12.3(11)T, often referred to as RBAC. Role-based CLI offers a solution when a hierarchical privilege level system will not suffice. Role-based CLI access enables the network administrator to create different views of router configurations for different users. Each *view* defines the CLI commands that each user can access. These views, also called *parser views* or *CLI views*, can be created with a subset of privilege level 15 commands. One view, named root, is defined by default. The root view is authorized for all commands. To configure any view for the system, the administrator must be in root view. It is also possible to create superviews. A *superview* consists of one or more CLI views. Example 17-3 shows the commands necessary to create a view on a Cisco router.

Example 17-3 Configuring Role-Based CLI

```
R1# configure terminal
Enter configuration commands, one per line.  End with CNTL/Z.
R1(config)# enable secret MySecret
R1(config)# aaa new-model
R1(config)# end
R1# enable view
Password: <MySecret>
R1# show parser view
Current view is 'root'
R1# configure terminal
R1(config)# parser view firstview
```

```
R1(config-view)# secret firstpass
R1(config-view)# commands exec include show version
R1(config-view)# commands exec include all show ip
R1(config-view)# commands exec include configure terminal
R1(config-view)# commands configure include all interface
R1(config-view)# commands configure include all router
R1(config-view)# end
```

Before creating a CLI view, an **enable secret** password must be configured and AAA must be enabled.

Next, the administrator must log in as the root view using the **enable view** command. After entering the **enable secret** password, the new view, in this case called *firstview*, can be created and its own secret password assigned. EXEC and configure commands can then be assigned to the selected view using the **include** and **all** keywords.

Example 17-4 shows how to access and verify a parser view.

Example 17-4 Verifying a Parser View

```
R1# enable view firstview
Password: <firstpass>
R1# show parser view
Current view is 'firstview'
```

As with a privilege level, it is also possible to assign a view to a user in the local AAA database. Example 17-5 shows how to assign firstview to a user.

Example 17-5 Assigning a View to a User

```
R1(config)# username Bob view firstview algorithm-type scrypt secret firstpass
```

Video: Configuring Role-Based CLI

Refer to the Digital Study Guide to view this video.

Cisco IOS Resilient Configuration

The Cisco IOS resilient configuration feature allows for faster recovery if someone maliciously or unintentionally reformats flash memory or erases the startup configuration file in nonvolatile random-access memory (NVRAM). The feature maintains a secure working copy of the router Cisco IOS image file and a copy of the running configuration file. To secure the Cisco IOS image and enable Cisco IOS image resilience, use the **secure boot-image** global configuration mode command. To take a snapshot of the router's running configuration and securely archive it in persistent storage, use the **secure boot-config** global configuration mode command.

To enable and save the primary bootset to a secure archive in persistent storage, follow Example 17-6.

Example 17-6 Cisco IOS Resilient Configuration

```
R1(config)# secure boot-image
*Aug 12 16:34:44.212: %IOS_RESILIENCE-5-IMAGE_RESIL_ACTIVE: Successfully secured
  running image
R1(config)# secure boot-config
*Aug 12 16:35:59.768: %IOS_RESILIENCE-5-CONFIG_RESIL_ACTIVE: Successfully secured
  config archive [flash:.runcfg-20151031-132759.ar]
```

The feature can be verified with the **show secure bootset** command, as shown in Example 17-7.

Example 17-7 Cisco IOS Resilient Configuration Verification

```
R1# show secure bootset
IOS resilience router id FTX1125A28X

IOS image resilience version 12.4 activated at 14:24:44 UTC Wed Feb 3 2016
Secure archive flash:/c2800nm-advipservicesk9-mz.124-25e.bin type is image (elf) []
  file size is 38149592 bytes, run size is 38315276 bytes
  Runnable image, entry point 0x8000F000, run from ram

IOS configuration resilience version 12.4 activated at 14:24:59 UTC Wed Feb 3 2016
Secure archive flash:.runcfg-20160203-142459.ar type is config
configuration archive size 4060 bytes
```

Cisco IOS File Authenticity

If the Cisco IOS on a router is corrupt or compromised, service outages and network attacks may result. Therefore, it is prudent to take security precautions throughout the lifecycle of the IOS images on your Cisco routers. A first step that you can take is to verify that the Cisco IOS image has not been corrupted in any fashion during transit from the Cisco.com download center. Cisco publishes the MD5 digests of the IOS image files available for download. Example 17-8 shows the command to use to verify the IOS MD5 checksum on a Cisco router.

Example 17-8 Verifying Cisco IOS MD5 Checksum

```
Router# verify /md5 flash:c2900-universalk9-mz.SPA.153-3.M5.bin
...................................................................................
.......................................
...................................................................................
.........................................
...................................................................................
.................................
<...Output Omitted...>.............................. MD5 of flash0:c2900-
  universalk9-mz.SPA.153-3.M5.bin Done!
verify /md5 (flash0:c2900-universalk9-mz.SPA.153-3.M5.bin) =
  734abfc00c912969709f3b5be7b44ed2
```

Notice that in Figure 17-1 the MD5 checksum highlighted is a perfect match for the MD5 check-sum previously calculated on the router with the **verify** command.

Figure 17-1   Verifying Cisco IOS MD5 Checksum

A more recent development for IOS validation is the use of digitally signed images. The U.S. Government Federal Information Processing Standard (FIPS) 140-3 will require that software be digitally signed and verified before loading and executing the software. Cisco provides digitally signed IOS images for the Cisco ISR series routers and other network devices. A digitally signed image can be recognized by a three-character string ("SPA") within the filename: c2900-universalk9-mz.**SPA**.153-3.M5.bin.

A running or stored digitally signed image can also be verified using the **show software authenticity** command. Example 17-9 shows that the certificate serial numbers match (54D2516B) for both the IOS stored in flash and the IOS that is currently booted and in use on the Cisco router.

Example 17-9 Verifying Digitally Signed Cisco IOS Software

```
Router# software authenticity file flash:c2900-universalk9-mz.SPA.153-3.M5.bin
File Name                   : flash:c2900-universalk9-mz.SPA.153-3.M5.bin
Image type                  : Production
    Signer Information
        Common Name         : CiscoSystems
        Organization Unit   : C2900
        Organization Name   : CiscoSystems
    Certificate Serial Number : 54D2516B
    Hash Algorithm          : SHA512
    Signature Algorithm     : 2048-bit RSA
    Key Version             : A
```

```
Router# show software authenticity running
SYSTEM IMAGE
------------

Image type                    : Production
   Signer Information
       Common Name            : CiscoSystems
       Organization Unit      : C2900
       Organization Name      : CiscoSystems
   Certificate Serial Number  : 54D2516B
   Hash Algorithm             : SHA512
   Signature Algorithm        : 2048-bit RSA
   Key Version                : A


   Verifier Information
       Verifier Name          : ROMMON 1
       Verifier Version       : System Bootstrap, Version 15.0(1r)M16, RELEASE
           SOFTWARE (fc1)
Technical Support: http://www.cisco.com/techsupport
```

Activity: Order the Steps when Configuring Role-based CLI

Refer to the Digital Study Guide to complete this activity.

Study Resources

For today's exam topics, refer to the following resources for more study.

Resource	Location	Topic
Primary Resources		
CCNA Security Official Cert Guide	11	Securing the Management Plane on Cisco IOS Devices
CCNA Security (Networking Academy Curriculum)	2	Securing Network Devices
Supplemental Resources		
CCNA Security Complete Video Course	15	Securing the Management Plane
CCNA Security Portable Command Guide	6	Securing the Management Plane

Check Your Understanding

Refer to the Digital Study Guide to take a ten-question quiz covering the content of this day.

Secure Routing Protocols

CCNA Security 210-260 IINS Exam Topics

- 4.2.a Implement routing update authentication on OSPF

Key Topics

Today we will look at enabling routing protocol authentication for Open Shortest Path First (OSPF). Because MD5 and SHA-1 are now considered vulnerable to cryptographic attack, it is recommended that SHA-2 be used instead. We will review how to enable both of these options.

Routing Protocol Authentication

Routing protocols are used by routers to communicate with each other, exchanging information that is associated with network connectivity, allowing routers to determine the forwarding path to distant networks. Without configuration of routing, routers are only aware of the networks to which they directly connect. Routing protocols allow the distribution of this data to immediate neighbors, and the data cascades through those neighbors to all the participating routers in the network.

By default, network devices send routing information to and from their routing peers in the clear, making this information visible to all interested parties. Failure to secure the exchange of routing information allows an attacker to introduce false routing information into the network.

The primary method of preventing unauthorized systems from participating in routing protocols is to configure cryptographic authentication on the routing protocols. With this method, a shared secret is configured between peer routers. When a router generates an update, it generates a keyed hash by running the update and the shared secret key through a hash algorithm. A keyed hash is sometimes called a message authentication code (MAC). The router sends the update with the keyed hash appended. The receiving router validates the update by taking the update and the shared secret key to generate a keyed hash. If the computed hash matches what was received with the update, then the receiving router will accept the update. If they do not match, the receiving router will reject the update.

Figure 16-1 shows the topology diagram used in the following configuration examples.

Figure 16-1   Router Authentication Example Topology

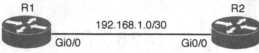

OSPF Area 0

R1   R2

                    192.168.1.0/30

    Gi0/0   Gi0/0

OSPF MD5 Authentication

MD5 authentication for OSPF can be configured either with a key chain or without.

MD5 Authentication with Key Chain

OSPF route authentication is configured on top of a base OSPF configuration. There are two basic components: defining a key chain, and referencing the key chain on the appropriate OSPF interfaces. Example 16-1 shows a key chain configuration.

Example 16-1 Creating an MD5 Key Chain for OSPF

```
R1(config)# key chain OSPF-AUTH-MD5
R1(config-keychain)# key 1
R1(config-keychain-key)# key-string Cisco12345
R1(config-keychain-key)# cryptographic-algorithm md5
```

Send and accept lifetimes may be assigned to keys. By default, the keys are used and accepted forever. By utilizing send and accept lifetimes, key rotation can be simplified, providing a method to change keys on many routers without breaking any router peering relationships during the process. One more thing to be aware of is that the key chain name is only locally significant. Peering routers can use different names for their key chains. The key numbers, however, must match between peering routers.

Once the key chain is defined, it must be applied to the appropriate interfaces. Example 16-2 shows the required configuration command.

Example 16-2 Assigning the Key Chain to an Interface

```
R1(config)# interface Gi0/0
R1(config-if)# ip ospf authentication key-chain OSPF-AUTH-MD5
```

An identical configuration would be applied to the neighbor router, allowing the OSPF relationship to be authenticated. This can be verified with the **show ip ospf interface** command, as shown in Example 16-3. The final two lines of the output confirm the MD5 key chain configuration.

Example 16-3 MD5 Key Chain Configuration Verification

```
R1# sh ip ospf int gi0/0
GigabitEthernet0/0 is up, line protocol is up
  Internet Address 192.168.1.1/30, Area 0, Attached via Network Statement
  Process ID 1, Router ID 192.168.1.1, Network Type BROADCAST, Cost: 1
  Topology-MTID    Cost    Disabled    Shutdown      Topology Name
        0            1        no          no           Base
  Transmit Delay is 1 sec, State BDR, Priority 1
  Designated Router (ID) 192.168.1.2, Interface address 192.168.1.2
  Backup Designated router (ID) 192.168.1.1, Interface address 192.168.1.1
  Flush timer for old DR LSA due in 00:02:45
  Timer intervals configured, Hello 10, Dead 40, Wait 40, Retransmit 5
    oob-resync timeout 40
    Hello due in 00:00:03
  Supports Link-local Signaling (LLS)
  Cisco NSF helper support enabled
  IETF NSF helper support enabled
  Index 1/1, flood queue length 0
  Next 0x0(0)/0x0(0)
  Last flood scan length is 1, maximum is 1
  Last flood scan time is 0 msec, maximum is 0 msec
  Neighbor Count is 1, Adjacent neighbor count is 1
    Adjacent with neighbor 192.168.1.2  (Designated Router)
  Suppress hello for 0 neighbor(s)
  Cryptographic authentication enabled
    Sending SA: Key 1, Algorithm MD5 - key chain OSPF-AUTH-MD5
```

MD5 Authentication Without Key Chain

OSPF also supports configuring MD5 authentication without the use of a key chain, instead allowing the MD5 shared secret key to be configured directly on an interface. Example 16-4 shows the commands required to accomplish this. Again, an identical configuration would be required on the neighbor router.

Example 16-4 Enabling MD5 Authentication on an Interface

```
R1(config)# interface Gi0/0
R1(config-if)# ip ospf authentication message-digest
R1(config-if)# ip ospf message-digest-key 1 md5 Cisco12345
```

The last two lines of output of the **show ip ospf interface** command presented in Example 16-5 confirm that the OSPF adjacency is now using MD5 without the use of a key chain.

Example 16-5 MD5 Interface Configuration Verification

```
R1# sh ip ospf int gi0/0
GigabitEthernet0/0 is up, line protocol is up
  Internet Address 192.168.1.1/30, Area 0, Attached via Network Statement
  Process ID 1, Router ID 192.168.1.1, Network Type BROADCAST, Cost: 1
  Topology-MTID    Cost    Disabled    Shutdown       Topology Name
       0            1       no          no            Base
  Transmit Delay is 1 sec, State BDR, Priority 1
  Designated Router (ID) 192.168.1.2, Interface address 192.168.1.2
  Backup Designated router (ID) 192.168.1.1, Interface address 192.168.1.1
  Timer intervals configured, Hello 10, Dead 40, Wait 40, Retransmit 5
    oob-resync timeout 40
    Hello due in 00:00:00
  Supports Link-local Signaling (LLS)
  Cisco NSF helper support enabled
  IETF NSF helper support enabled
  Index 1/1, flood queue length 0
  Next 0x0(0)/0x0(0)
  Last flood scan length is 1, maximum is 1
  Last flood scan time is 0 msec, maximum is 0 msec
  Neighbor Count is 1, Adjacent neighbor count is 1
    Adjacent with neighbor 192.168.1.2  (Designated Router)
  Suppress hello for 0 neighbor(s)
  Cryptographic authentication enabled
    Youngest key id is 1
```

OSPF SHA Authentication

The OSPF SHA authentication configuration is almost identical to the MD5 key chain in Example 16-5, except we will enable SHA instead of MD5. Using the SHA HMAC algorithm for OSPF authentication is relatively new. Some devices may not support it. More recent Cisco IOS versions offer SHA-1, SHA-256, SHA-384, and SHA-512 options. Example 16-6 shows the commands necessary to enable the SHA-256 algorithm. Both OSPF neighbors would be configured identically.

Example 16-6 Creating a SHA-256 Key Chain for OSPF

```
R1(config)# key chain OSPF-AUTH-SHA
R1(config-keychain)# key 1
R1(config-keychain-key)# key-string Cisco12345
R1(config-keychain-key)# cryptographic-algorithm hmac-sha-256
R1(config-keychain-key)# exit
R1(config)# interface gi0/0
R1(config-if)# ip ospf authentication key-chain OSPF-AUTH-SHA
```

The final two lines of Example 16-7 confirm that the OSPF neighbor adjacency is now using SHA-256 instead of MD5.

Example 16-7 SHA Key Chain Verification

```
R1# sh ip ospf int gi0/0
GigabitEthernet0/0 is up, line protocol is up
  Internet Address 192.168.1.1/30, Area 0, Attached via Network Statement
  Process ID 1, Router ID 192.168.1.1, Network Type BROADCAST, Cost: 1
  Topology-MTID    Cost    Disabled    Shutdown       Topology Name
       0            1        no          no            Base
  Transmit Delay is 1 sec, State BDR, Priority 1
  Designated Router (ID) 192.168.1.2, Interface address 192.168.1.2
  Backup Designated router (ID) 192.168.1.1, Interface address 192.168.1.1
  Timer intervals configured, Hello 10, Dead 40, Wait 40, Retransmit 5
    oob-resync timeout 40
    Hello due in 00:00:07
  Supports Link-local Signaling (LLS)
  Cisco NSF helper support enabled
  IETF NSF helper support enabled
  Index 1/1, flood queue length 0
  Next 0x0(0)/0x0(0)
  Last flood scan length is 1, maximum is 1
  Last flood scan time is 0 msec, maximum is 0 msec
  Neighbor Count is 1, Adjacent neighbor count is 1
    Adjacent with neighbor 192.168.1.2  (Designated Router)
  Suppress hello for 0 neighbor(s)
  Cryptographic authentication enabled
    Sending SA: Key 1, Algorithm HMAC-SHA-256 - key chain OSPF-AUTH-SHA
```

Video: Configuring MD5 Authentication for OSPF with Key Chain

Refer to the Digital Study Guide to view this video.

Activity: Order the Steps when Configuring OSPF SHA Authentication

Refer to the Digital Study Guide to complete this activity.

Packet Tracer Activity: Configure Routing Protocol Authentication

Refer to the Digital Study Guide to access the PKA file for this activity. You must have Packet Tracer software to run this activity.

Study Resources

For today's exam topics, refer to the following resources for more study.

Resource	Location	Topic
Primary Resources		
CCNA Security Official Cert Guide	13	Securing Routing Protocols and the Control Plane
CCNA Security (Networking Academy Curriculum)	2	Securing Network Devices
Supplemental Resources		
CCNA Security Complete Video Course	17	Securing Routing Protocols and the Control Plane
CCNA Security Portable Command Guide	4	Network Foundation Protection

Check Your Understanding

Refer to the Digital Study Guide to take a ten-question quiz covering the content of this day.

Control Plane Security

CCNA Security 210-260 IINS Exam Topics

- 4.3.a Explain the function of control plane policing

Key Topics

Today we will review how the data, control, and management planes interact with each other while still maintaining a clear separation of roles. We will then look at Control Plane Policing (CoPP) and Control Plane Protection (CPPr), which protect the control plane from attacks and from being overwhelmed by high levels of activity from protocols competing for CPU resource utilization.

Functional Planes of the Network

Network devices implement processes that can be broken down into three functional planes: the management plane, the control plane, and the data plane. An understanding of these functional planes is crucial for implementing network security.

The management plane is associated with traffic that is sent to a network device and that is used to configure, monitor, and manage the network device. The management plane encompasses applications and protocols such as SSH, SNMP, and FTP.

The control plane of a network device processes the traffic that maintains the functionality of the network infrastructure. The control plane consists of applications and protocols between network devices. Control plane protocols include Border Gateway Protocol (BGP) and interior gateway protocols, such as Enhanced Interior Gateway Routing Protocol (EIGRP) and Open Shortest Path First (OSPF).

The data plane forwards data through a network device, such as user traffic. The data plane does not include traffic that is sent to the local Cisco IOS device.

Figure 15-1 shows the traffic flow between the three functional planes.

Under normal network operating conditions, the vast majority of packets handled by network devices are data plane packets. These packets are handled by Cisco Express Forwarding (CEF). CEF uses the control plane to pre-populate the CEF Forwarding Information Base (FIB) table in the data plane with the appropriate egress interface for a given packet flow. Subsequent packets that flow between that same source and destination are forwarded by the data plane based on the information contained in the FIB.

Figure 15-1   Functional Planes and Router Processing

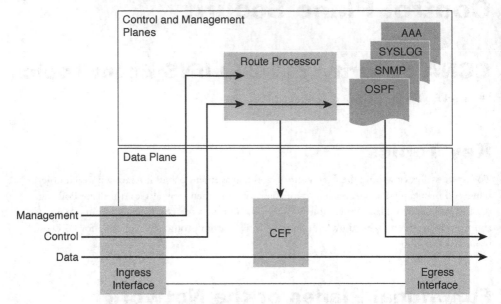

Each plane provides different functionality that needs to be protected. Different types of network devices offer different features to protect aspects of each plane.

We have already reviewed how to secure the management plane of network devices with AAA, SSH, HTTPS, ACLs, and SNMPv3. We will soon be looking at securing the data plane by deploying intrusion protection systems (IPS), firewalls, and Layer 2 security on switches.

In terms of control plane security, Day 16 explains how authentication can be configured on routing protocols to validate routing peers and prevent tampering with routing data shared between routers. Cisco IOS devices also support CoPP and the more refined CPPr. These features facilitate control of traffic that is sent to the route processor to prevent the route processor itself from being overwhelmed and affecting system performance. SNMP traps and syslog messages can be associated with high CPU rates or low memory availability, which can affect control plane functionality. This can provide an early indication of pending failure or network attack.

The importance of protecting the control plane is evidenced by the existence of an RFC on the subject. RFC 6192 discusses the function of the control plane and provides recommendations on methods that should be employed to protect the control plane.

Control Plane Policing

CoPP is a Cisco IOS feature designed to allow administrators to specify controls over traffic that is directed to a device's control plane. The goal is to prevent low-priority or unnecessary traffic from overwhelming system resources, which could lead to issues in system performance. CoPP treats the control plane as a separate entity with its own ingress and egress ports. CoPP facilitates the definition of rules to control traffic traversing the control plane's ingress and egress ports. CoPP not only allows you to specify what traffic is allowed and what traffic is denied on the control plane inter-faces, it also provides for rate limiting of allowed traffic. Therefore, expected traffic that is of lower priority can be allowed, but attacks where floods of lower-priority traffic are sent to the control plane will be mitigated.

CoPP is implemented using the Cisco IOS Modular QoS CLI (MQC), a highly flexible frame-work that allows users to create and attach traffic polices to interfaces. The MQC mechanisms are used by CoPP to define the classification and policing descriptions for its policies. In this way, in addition to the limited permit and deny actions associated with simple ACLs, specific pack-ets may be permitted but rate-limited when using the MQC structure. For example, you may wish to permit certain ICMP packet types, but rate limit them so that the route processor is not adversely impacted.

MQC uses three main concepts: class maps, policy maps, and service policies. Class maps define characteristics that are used to map traffic to classes. Policy maps define actions that should be taken on particular classes of traffic. Finally, to specify where a policy map should be implemented, a service-policy statement is used. When implementing CoPP, control-plane configuration mode is reached using the **control-plane** command in global configuration mode. The service-policy state-ment is then applied in control-plane configuration mode.

Video: Configuring Cisco Control Plane Policing

Refer to the Digital Study Guide to view this video.

Control Plane Protection

CPPr is similar to CoPP but provides a finer granularity on the control plane. Whereas CoPP treats all traffic to the control plane identically, CPPr implements three control plane subinterfaces:

- **Host subinterface:** Receives all control plane IP traffic that is directly destined to one of the router interfaces. Examples of control plane host IP traffic include tunnel termination traffic, management traffic such as SSH or SNMP, and routing protocols. All host traffic terminates on and is processed by the router.

- **Transit subinterface:** Receives all control plane IP traffic that is software switched by the route processor. As a result, packets that are not directly destined to the router itself but are traversing the router are not compatible with Cisco Express Forwarding and would be pro-cessed by the transit subinterface. A tunnel passing through the router is an example of this type of control plane traffic.

- **CEF-exception subinterface:** Receives all traffic that is redirected to the processor as a result of a configured input feature in the CEF packet forwarding path. Examples of this type of traffic are CDP packets, IP packets with a TTL=1, and fragmented packets.

All other traffic not explicitly inspected by CPPr is sent for normal processing by the CEF engine.

Configuration of CPPr is very similar to the configuration of CoPP. It uses the MQC framework, using class maps to categorize traffic, policy maps to define actions to take upon different classes of traffic, and service-policy statements to define where the policy maps are applied. But with CPPr, the service-policy statements are applied under three distinct configuration modes: **control-plane host**, **control-plane transit**, and **control-plane cef-exception**. With CoPP, the service-policy statements are applied in control-plane configuration mode.

Activity: Compare CoPP and CPPr

Refer to the Digital Study Guide to complete this activity.

Study Resources

For today's exam topics, refer to the following resources for more study.

Resource	Location	Topic
Primary Resources		
CCNA Security Official Cert Guide	13	Securing Routing Protocols and the Control Plane
CCNA Security (Networking Academy Curriculum)	2	Securing Network Devices
Supplemental Resources		
CCNA Security Complete Video Course	17	Securing Routing Protocols and the Control Plane
CCNA Security Portable Command Guide	4	Network Foundation Protection

Check Your Understanding

Refer to the Digital Study Guide to take a ten-question quiz covering the content of this day.

Layer 2 Infrastructure Security

CCNA Security 210-260 IINS Exam Topics

- 4.4.a Describe STP attacks

- 4.4.b Describe ARP spoofing

- 4.4.c Describe MAC spoofing

- 4.4.d Describe CAM table (MAC address table) overflows

- 4.4.e Describe CDP/LLDP reconnaissance

- 4.4.f Describe VLAN hopping

- 4.4.g Describe DHCP spoofing

Key Topics

Ethernet is the most commonly deployed data link layer technology. Ethernet alone provides no mechanisms for security. A similar lack of security exists in many technologies that are built on top of Ethernet and dependent on Ethernet, such as transparent bridging and switching, Spanning Tree Protocol (STP), and Address Resolution Protocol (ARP). Features have been designed and implemented within network devices to provide security services for the data link layer. Today we will review a range of Layer 2 attacks. We will then look at implementing mitigation for these attacks on Day 13 and Day 12.

Common Layer 2 Attacks

The first step in mitigating attacks on the Layer 2 infrastructure is to understand the underlying operation of Layer 2 and the threats posed to the Layer 2 infrastructure.

For a thorough review of VLANs, trunks, STP, and Ethernet frame forwarding, see Allan Johnson's *31 Days Before Your CCNA Routing and Switching Exam*. The *CCNA Security 210-260 Official Cert Guide* by Omar Santos and John Stuppi also offers an excellent review of these topics. Wendell Odom's *CCNA Routing and Switching 200-120 Official Cert Guide Library* is another very good source if you are preparing for either the ICND1 exam or ICND2 exam (or both).

STP Attacks

A network attacker can use STP to change the topology of a network so that the attacker's host appears to be a root bridge with a higher priority. The attacker sends out bridge protocol data units (BPDUs) with a better bridge ID and thus becomes the root bridge. As a result, traffic between the two switches in Figure 14-1 passes through the new root bridge, which is actually the attacker system.

Figure 14-1   STP Root Bridge Attack

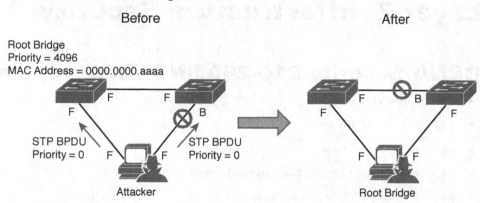

To mitigate STP manipulation attacks, use the Cisco STP stability mechanisms to enhance the overall performance of the switches and to reduce the time that is lost during topology changes.

These are recommended practices for using STP stability mechanisms:

- **PortFast:** PortFast immediately brings an interface configured as an access or trunk port to the forwarding state from a blocking state, bypassing the listening and learning states. Apply to all end-user ports. PortFast should only be configured when there is a host attached to the port, and not another switch.

- **BPDU Guard:** BPDU guard immediately error disables a port that receives a BPDU. Typically used on PortFast-enabled ports. Apply to all end-user ports.

- **Root Guard:** Root guard prevents an inappropriate switch from becoming the root bridge. Root guard limits the switch ports out of which the root bridge may be negotiated. Apply to all ports that should not become root ports.

- **Loop Guard:** Loop guard prevents alternate or root ports from becoming designated ports because of a failure that leads to a unidirectional link. Apply to all ports that are or can become non-designated.

These features enforce the placement of the root bridge in the network and enforce the STP domain borders. We will review the commands necessary to enable these features on Day 13.

Figure 14-2 highlights on which ports these features should be implemented to protect STP.

Figure 14-2   STP Best Practices

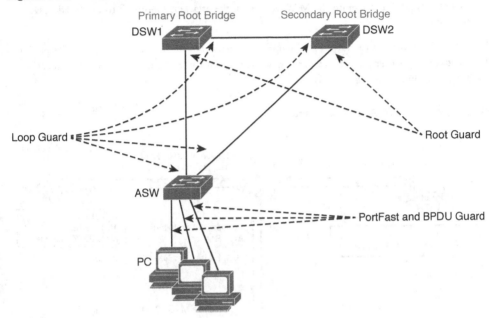

ARP Spoofing

In normal ARP operation, a host sends an ARP request broadcast to determine the MAC address of a destination host with a particular IP address. The device with the requested IP address sends an ARP reply with its MAC address. The originating host caches the ARP response, using it to populate the destination Layer 2 header of frames that are sent to that IP address. By spoofing an ARP message from a legitimate device, an attacking device deceives a victim device, causing it to cache the attacking device's MAC address instead of the legitimate device's IP address. The victim then sends frames that are destined for the legitimate device's IP address to the attacker's MAC address.

An ARP spoofing attack, also known as ARP cache poisoning, can target hosts, switches, and routers that are connected to your Layer 2 network by poisoning the ARP caches of systems that are connected to the subnet, and by intercepting traffic that is intended for other hosts on the subnet.

Figure 14-3 shows an example of ARP cache poisoning. In this scenario, the attacker initiates a man-in-the-middle attack. The attack can be broken down into four steps.

1. PCA sends an ARP request for the MAC address of R1.

2. R1 replies with its MAC and IP addresses. It also updates its ARP cache. PCA binds the MAC address of R1 to R1's IP address in its ARP cache.

3. The attacker sends its ARP reply to PCA, binding its MAC address to the IP of R1. PCA updates its ARP cache with the MAC address of the attacker, binding it to the IP address of R1.

4. The attacker sends its ARP reply to R1, binding its MAC address to the IP of PCA. R1 updates its ARP cache with the MAC address of the attacker, binding it to the IP address of PCA.

The attacker can process the intercepted frames and then forward them to their correct destination. The attacker may either passively capture private data as a man in the middle or actively inject or modify data or hijack network sessions.

Figure 14-3   ARP Spoofing Attack

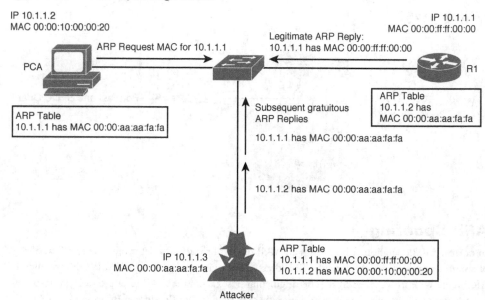

To prevent ARP cache poisoning, a switch must ensure that only valid ARP requests and responses are allowed within a subnet. The Dynamic ARP Inspection (DAI) feature of Cisco switches prevents ARP cache poisoning by intercepting and validating all ARP requests and responses. We will review DAI on Day 13.

MAC Spoofing

MAC spoofing attacks involve the use of a known MAC address of another host to attempt to make the target switch forward frames that are destined for the remote host to the network attacker. By sending a single frame with the source Ethernet address of the other host, the network attacker overwrites the Content Addressable Memory (CAM) table entry so that the switch forwards packets that are destined for the host to the network attacker. Until the host sends traffic, it does not receive any traffic. When the host sends out traffic, the CAM table entry is rewritten once more so that it moves back to the original port. MAC spoofing attacks can be mitigated by configuring port security, which we will review on Day 13.

CAM Table Overflows

The most important point to understanding how CAM overflow attacks work is to know that CAM tables are limited in size. MAC flooding takes advantage of this limitation by bombarding the switch with fake source MAC addresses until the switch CAM table is full. If enough entries are entered into the CAM table, the CAM table fills up to the point that no new entries can be accepted. Note that this attack will not cause legitimate entries that were in the CAM table before the attack to be removed. As long as activity is seen from the legitimate MAC addresses, their spot in the CAM table will be reserved. But if they time out, the attack will quickly consume the freed spot in the CAM table and the legitimate MAC address will not be relearned.

In a CAM table overflow attack, a network attacker uses a tool such as the **macof** program and floods the switch with many invalid source MAC addresses until the CAM table fills up. When that occurs, the switch begins to flood traffic for unknown MAC addresses to all ports because there is no room in the CAM table to learn any legitimate MAC addresses. In essence, the switch acts like a hub. As a result, the attacker can see all the frames that are sent from a victim host to another host without a CAM table entry. CAM table overflow floods traffic only within the local VLAN, so the intruder will see only traffic within the local VLAN to which the attacker is connected. Like MAC address spoofing, the CAM table overflow attack can also be mitigated by configuring port security on the switch.

CDP/LLDP Reconnaissance

Cisco Discovery Protocol and Link-Layer Discovery Protocol (LLDP) enable Cisco IOS network devices to announce themselves to their neighbors. By default, Cisco devices send a CDP announcement out every interface once per minute. If they receive a CDP announcement, they store that information in a table with a hold time of 3 minutes.

The potential problem with CDP and LLDP is that they provide an easy reconnaissance vector to any attacker with an Ethernet connection. When the switch sends a CDP or LLDP announcement out of a port where a workstation is connected, the workstation normally ignores it. However, with a simple tool such as WireShark, an attacker can capture and analyze the CDP or LLDP announcement. Included in the CDP or LLDP data is the model number and operating system version of the switch. An attacker can then use this information to look up published vulnerabilities that are associated with that operating system version and potentially follow up with an exploit of the vulnerability.

An organization's security policy should dictate CDP or LLDP configuration policy. The organization must decide whether the convenience that CDP or LLDP brings is greater than the security risk that comes with it. It is possible to disable these protocols globally with the **no cdp run/no lldp run** commands, or disable them on a per-interface basis with the **no cdp enable/no lldp enable** commands.

VLAN Hopping

In a basic VLAN hopping attack, the attacker takes advantage of the fact that Dynamic Trunking Protocol (DTP) is enabled by default on most switches. The network attacker configures a system to use DTP to negotiate a trunk link to the switch. As a result, the attacker is a member of all the VLANs that are trunked on the switch and can "hop" between VLANs. In other words, the attacker can send and receive traffic on all those VLANs. The best way to prevent a basic VLAN hopping attack is to turn off DTP on all ports, and explicitly configure trunking mode or access mode as appropriate on each port.

The double-tagging (or double-encapsulated) VLAN hopping attack takes advantage of the way that hardware operates on some switches. Some switches perform only one level of 802.1Q decapsulation and allow an attacker, in specific situations, to embed a second 802.1Q tag inside the frame. This tag allows the frame to go to a VLAN that the outer 802.1Q tag did not specify. An important characteristic of the double-encapsulated VLAN hopping attack is that it can work even if DTP is disabled on the attacker's access port.

Figure 14-4 illustrates an example of the VLAN hopping attack using double-tagging to allow access to the victim's VLAN (VLAN 20).

Figure 14-4   VLAN Hopping Attack

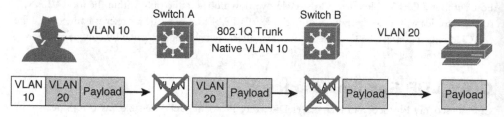

It is important to note that this attack is unidirectional and works only when the attacker and trunk port have the same native VLAN. Thwarting this type of attack is not as easy as stopping basic VLAN hopping attacks. The best approach is to create a VLAN to use as the native VLAN on all trunk ports and explicitly do not use that VLAN for any access ports.

DHCP Spoofing

DHCP is built on a client-server model. The DHCP server hosts allocate network addresses and deliver configuration parameters to dynamically configured hosts. The term "client" refers to a host that is requesting initialization parameters from a DHCP server. DHCP uses a four-message exchange process. First, the client issues a discover broadcast. Second, the server responds with an offer. Third, the client responds to the offer with a request. Finally, the server responds to the request with an acknowledgement that contains the IP configuration information for the client.

Two DHCP-related attacks can be performed at Layer 2: DHCP spoofing attacks and DHCP starvation attacks.

DHCP does not include authentication and is therefore easily vulnerable to spoofing attacks. The simplest attack is DHCP server spoofing. The attacker runs DHCP server software and replies to DHCP requests from legitimate clients. As a rogue DHCP server, the attacker can cause a denial of service (DoS) by providing invalid IP information. The attacker can also perform confidentiality or integrity breaches via a man-in-the-middle attack. The attacker can assign itself as the default gateway or DNS server in the DHCP replies, later intercepting IP communications from the configured hosts to the rest of the network.

A DHCP starvation attack works by sending a flood of DHCP requests with spoofed MAC addresses. If enough requests are sent, the network attacker can exhaust the address space available to the DHCP servers. This flooding would cause a loss of network availability to new DHCP clients as they connect to the network. A DHCP starvation attack may be executed before a DHCP spoofing attack. If the legitimate DHCP server's resources are exhausted, then the rogue DHCP server on the attacker system has no competition when it responds to new DHCP requests from clients on the network.

To mitigate both these attacks, it is possible to enable the DHCP snooping feature on Cisco switches. We will look at how to configure DHCP snooping on Day 13.

Video: Layer 2 Security Threats

Refer to the Digital Study Guide to view this video.

Activity: Match the Switch Attack to Its Description

Refer to the Digital Study Guide to complete this activity.

Study Resources

For today's exam topics, refer to the following resources for more study.

Resource	Location	Topic
Primary Resources		
CCNA Security Official Cert Guide	9	Securing Layer 2 Technologies
CCNA Security (Networking Academy Curriculum)	6	Securing the Local Area Network
Supplemental Resources		
CCNA Security Complete Video Course	13	Securing Layer 2 Technologies
CCNA Security Portable Command Guide	4	Network Foundation Protection

Check Your Understanding

Refer to the Digital Study Guide to take a ten-question quiz covering the content of this day.

Layer 2 Protocols Security

CCNA Security 210-260 IINS Exam Topics

- 4.5.a Implement DHCP snooping

- 4.5.b Implement Dynamic ARP Inspection

- 4.5.c Implement port security

- 4.5.d Describe BPDU guard, root guard, loop guard

- 4.5.e Verify mitigation procedures

Key Topics

Today we will review how to implement mitigation for Layer 2 network attacks. In particular, we will look at securing protocols such as Dynamic Host Control Protocol (DHCP), Address Resolution Protocol (ARP), and Spanning Tree Protocol (STP). We will also discuss how to protect the network against MAC attacks using Layer 2 port security.

DHCP Snooping

DHCP snooping is a Layer 2 security feature that specifically prevents DHCP server spoofing attacks and mitigates DHCP starvation to a degree. DHCP snooping provides DHCP control by filtering untrusted DHCP messages and by building and maintaining a DHCP snooping binding database, which is also referred to as a DHCP snooping binding table.

For DHCP snooping to work, each switch port must be labeled as trusted or untrusted. Trusted ports are the ports over which the DHCP server is reachable and that will accept DHCP server replies. All other ports should be labeled as untrusted ports and can only source DHCP requests.

Figure 13-1 shows the deployment of DHCP protection mechanisms on the access layer of the network. User ports are designated as untrusted for DHCP snooping, while inter-switch links are designated as trusted, if the DHCP server is reachable through the network core.

Example 13-1 shows the configuration for DHCP snooping on an access layer switch. DHCP snooping must first be enabled globally. DHCP snooping is then explicitly enabled on VLANs 20 through 25. Interfaces Gi0/1 and Gi0/2 are uplinks to another switch where the DHCP server resides. It is configured to be trusted by DHCP snooping so DHCP replies from the server will be allowed. Interfaces Gi0/12 through Gi0/24 are access ports. By default they are untrusted, but DHCP rate limiting is also applied, preventing a flood of DHCP requests to be sourced from the interfaces.

Figure 13-1   DHCP Snooping

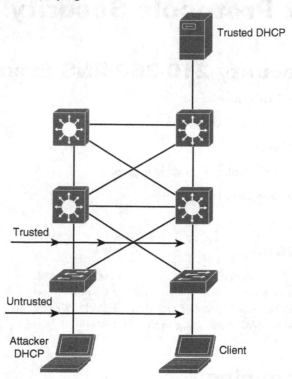

Example 13-1 Configuring DHCP Snooping

```
Switch(config)# ip dhcp snooping
Switch(config)# ip dhcp snooping vlan 20-25
Switch(config)# interface range GigabitEthernet0/1 - 2
Switch(config-if-range)# ip dhcp snooping trust
Switch(config-if-range)# interface range GigabitEthernet0/12 - 24
Switch(config-if-range)# ip dhcp snooping limit rate 15
```

To verify DHCP snooping, use the **show ip dhcp snooping** command and the **show ip dhcp snooping binding** command. Example 13-2 shows the output for both these commands.

Example 13-2 Verifying DHCP Snooping

```
Switch# show ip dhcp snooping
Switch DHCP snooping is enabled
DHCP snooping is configured on following VLANs:
20-25
DHCP snooping is operational on following VLANs:
20-25
DHCP snooping is configured on the following L3 Interfaces:
```

```
Insertion of option 82 is enabled
   circuit-id default format: vlan-mod-port
   remote-id: 0014.c9c6.2a40 (MAC)
Option 82 on untrusted port is not allowed
Verification of hwaddr field is enabled
Verification of giaddr field is enabled
DHCP snooping trust/rate is configured on the following Interfaces:


Interface                 Trusted    Allow option    Rate limit (pps)
----------------------    -------    ------------    ----------------
GigabitEthernet0/1        yes        yes             unlimited
GigabitEthernet0/2        yes        yes             unlimited
GigabitEthernet0/12       no         no              15
GigabitEthernet0/13       no         no              15
<output omitted>
Switch# show ip dhcp snooping binding
MacAddress          IpAddress       Lease(sec) Type            VLAN Interface
-----------------   -------------   ---------- -------------   ---- ----------
00:12:13:47:AF:D2   192.168.20.23   85858      dhcp-snooping   20   GigabitEthernet0/12
00:12:13:47:7D:A1   192.168.20.24   85859      dhcp-snooping   20   GigabitEthernet0/13
Total number of bindings: 2
```

 Video: Configuring DHCP Snooping

Refer to the Digital Study Guide to view this video.

Dynamic ARP Inspection

To prevent ARP spoofing, or "poisoning," a switch can process transit ARP traffic to ensure that only valid ARP requests and responses are relayed. The Dynamic ARP Inspection (DAI) feature of Cisco Catalyst switches prevents ARP spoofing attacks by intercepting and validating all ARP requests and responses. Each intercepted ARP reply is verified for valid MAC-to-IP address bindings before it is forwarded. ARP replies with invalid MAC-to-IP address bindings are dropped. DAI can determine the validity of an ARP reply based on bindings that are stored in a DHCP snooping database. DAI associates each interface with a trusted state or an untrusted state.

In a typical network configuration, configure all access switch ports that are connected to host ports as untrusted and all switch ports that are connected to other switches as trusted. With this configuration, all ARP packets entering a switch from another switch bypass the security check, which is safe because all switches validate the ARP packets as they are sent by hosts that are connected to untrusted access ports.

Example 13-3 shows a sample DAI configuration. It assumes that DHCP snooping has already been enabled. This example builds on Example 13-1. DAI is enabled for VLAN 20 only, while the uplink Gi0/1 is configured as trusted.

Example 13-3 Configuring Dynamic ARP Inspection

```
Switch(config)# ip arp inspection vlan 20
Switch(config)# interface GigabitEthernet0/1
Switch(config-if)# ip arp inspection trust
```

DAI can be verified with the **show ip arp inspection** command, as shown in Example 13-4.

Example 13-4 Verifying Dynamic ARP Inspection

```
Switch# show ip arp inspection


Source Mac Validation      : Disabled
Destination Mac Validation : Disabled
IP Address Validation      : Disabled

 Vlan     Configuration     Operation    ACL Match         Static ACL
 ----     -------------     ---------    ---------         ----------
  20      Enabled           Active
 Vlan     ACL Logging       DHCP Logging      Probe Logging
 ----     -----------       ------------      -------------
  20      Deny              Deny              Off
 Vlan       Forwarded         Dropped      DHCP Drops      ACL Drops
 ----       ---------         -------      ----------      ---------
  20            31               3              3              0
 Vlan     DHCP Permits      ACL Permits  Probe Permits   Source MAC Failures
 ----     ------------      -----------  -------------   -------------------
  20            31               0              0                0
 Vlan     Dest MAC Failures  IP Validation Failures   Invalid Protocol Data
 ----     -----------------  ----------------------   ---------------------
 Vlan     Dest MAC Failures  IP Validation Failures   Invalid Protocol Data
 ----     -----------------  ----------------------   ---------------------
  20            0                    0                        0
```

IP Source Guard

To protect against MAC and IP address spoofing, configure the IP Source Guard (IPSG) security feature. IPSG operates just like DAI, but it looks at every packet, not just the ARP packets. Like DAI, IPSG also requires that DHCP snooping be enabled. Specifically, IPSG is deployed on untrusted Layer 2 access and trunk ports. IPSG restricts the client IP traffic to those source IP addresses that are configured in the binding. Any IP traffic with a source IP address other than that in the IP source binding will be filtered out.

For each untrusted port, there are two possible levels of IP traffic security filtering:

- **Source IP address filter:** IP traffic is filtered based on its source IP address. Only IP traffic with a source IP address that matches the IP source binding entry is permitted.

- **Source IP and MAC address filter:** IP traffic is filtered based on its source IP address in addition to its MAC address; only IP traffic with source IP and MAC addresses that match the IP source binding entry are permitted.

Example 13-5 shows the configuration necessary to enable IPSG. Interface Gi0/12 is configured for source IP address filtering, while Gi0/13 is configured for both source IP and MAC address filtering. This example builds on Example 13-1.

Example 13-5 Configuring IP Source Guard

```
Switch(config)# interface Gigabitethernet0/12
Switch(config-if)# ip verify source
Switch(config-if)# interface Gigabitethernet0/13
Switch(config-if)# ip verify source port-security
```

IPSG can be verified by using the **show ip verify source** command, as shown in Example 13-6.

Example 13-6 Verifying IP Source Guard

```
Switch# show ip verify source
Interface   Filter-type   Filter-mode   IP-address        Mac-address         Vlan
---------   -----------   -----------   ---------------   -----------------   ----
Gi0/12      ip            active        192.168.20.23                         20
Gi0/13      ip-mac        active        192.168.20.24                         20
```

Video: Configuring ID Source Guard

Refer to the Digital Study Guide to view this video.

Port Security

You can use the port security feature to restrict input to an interface by limiting the maximum number of MAC addresses and identifying particular MAC addresses that are allowed to access the port. When you assign secure MAC addresses to a secure port, the port does not forward packets that have source addresses that are outside the group of defined addresses.

Port security allows you to statically specify MAC addresses for a port or permit the switch to dynamically learn a limited number of MAC addresses. By limiting the number of permitted MAC addresses on a port to one, you can use port security to control unauthorized expansion of the network. Limiting the maximum number of MAC addresses on a port also mitigates the CAM table overflow attack.

If a MAC address of a device attached to the port differs from the list of secure addresses, then a port violation occurs, and the port enters the error-disabled state. There are three security violation modes:

- **Protect:** The offending frame is dropped.

- **Restrict:** The offending frame is dropped and an SNMP trap and a syslog message are generated.

- **Shutdown:** The interface is placed in an error-disabled state and an SNMP trap and a syslog message are generated. The port is inactive while in an error-disabled state. Administrative action is required to return the port to a normal state.

Example 13-7 shows a typical port security configuration for a voice port. Three MAC addresses are learned dynamically: two for the access VLAN (one for the PC connected to the phone, and one for the phone before it discovers its voice VLAN) and one for the voice VLAN (once the phone starts sending tagged frames). Violations of this policy result in the port being shut down (error disabled) and the aging timeout for the learned MAC addresses being set to two hours.

Example 13-7 Configuring Port Security

```
Switch(config)# interface gigabitethernet0/10
Switch(config-if)# switchport mode access
Switch(config-if)# switchport access vlan 20
Switch(config-if)# switchport voice vlan 120
Switch(config-if)# switchport port-security
Switch(config-if)# switchport port-security maximum 3
Switch(config-if)# switchport port-security violation shutdown
Switch(config-if)# switchport port-security mac-address sticky
Switch(config-if)# switchport port-security maximum 2 vlan access
Switch(config-if)# switchport port-security maximum 1 vlan voice
Switch(config-if)# switchport port-security aging time 120
```

To verify the port security configuration, use the **show port-security** command, as shown in Example 13-8.

Example 13-8 Verifying Port Security

```
Switch# show port-security
Secure Port   MaxSecureAddr   CurrentAddr   SecurityViolation   Security Action
                (Count)         (Count)         (Count)
-----------------------------------------------------------------------------------
  Gi0/10          3               3               0              Shutdown
-----------------------------------------------------------------------------------
Total Addresses in System (excluding one mac per port)     : 0
Max Addresses limit in System (excluding one mac per port) : 1024
```

```
Switch# show port-security interface gi0/10
Port Security            : Enabled
Port status              : Secure-up
Violation mode           : Shutdown
Maximum MAC Addresses    : 3
Total MAC Addresses      : 3
Configured MAC Addresses : 0
Sticky MAC Addresses     : 3
Aging time               : 120 mins
Aging type               : Absolute
SecureStatic Address Aging : Disabled
Security Violation Count  : 0


Switch# show port-security address
Secure Mac Address Table
-----------------------------------------------------------------------
Vlan    Mac Address      Type            Ports    Remaining Age
                                                     (mins)
----    -----------      ----            -----    -------------
  20    0000.1234.abcd   SecureSticky    Gi0/8       120
  20    0000.1234.5678   SecureSticky    Gi0/8       120
 120    0000.1234.5678   SecureSticky    Gi0/8       120
-----------------------------------------------------------------------
Total Addresses in System (excluding one mac per port)    : 3
Max Addresses limit in System (excluding one mac per port) : 1024
```

 Video: Configuring Port Security

Refer to the Digital Study Guide to view this video.

STP Security Mechanisms

On Day 14, we briefly looked at four STP features that can be used to secure the spanning-tree of a LAN: PortFast, BPDU guard, root guard, and loop guard. This section looks more closely at how each of these features is configured on a Cisco switch.

PortFast

The STP PortFast feature causes an interface that is configured as a Layer 2 access or trunk port to transition from the blocking to the forwarding state immediately, bypassing the listening and learning states. The delay that is caused by the transitions through listening and learning before forwarding can lead to timeouts on DHCP requests and other initialization tasks that take place when a PC boots. You can use PortFast on Layer 2 access ports that connect to a single workstation, phone, or server to allow those devices to connect to the network.

PortFast can be configured globally on all nontrunking ports using the **spanning-tree portfast default** global configuration command. Alternatively, PortFast can be enabled on an interface using the **spanning-tree portfast** interface configuration command.

BPDU Guard

To mitigate STP manipulation, use the root guard and the BPDU guard enhancement commands to enforce the placement of the root bridge in the network and enforce the STP domain borders.

The STP BPDU guard feature is designed to allow network designers to maintain predictability of the active network topology. In a properly configured network, ports that are configured with the PortFast feature should never receive BPDUs. BPDU guard works with the PortFast feature to protect the switched network from the problems that may be caused by the receipt of BPDUs on ports that should not be receiving them. The receipt of unexpected BPDUs may be accidental or may be part of an unauthorized attempt to add a switch to the network.

BPDU guard is enabled on all ports that are configured for PortFast using the **spanning-tree portfast bpduguard default** command in global configuration mode. BPDU guard can also be enabled on interfaces where PortFast is configured, or not configured, using the **spanning-tree bpduguard enable** command in interface configuration mode.

Root Guard

The root guard feature prevents a switch from becoming a root bridge on configured ports. The root guard feature is designed to provide a way to enforce the placement of root bridges in the network. Root guard limits the switch ports from which the root bridge may be negotiated. If a port where Root Guard is enabled receives BPDUs that are superior to BPDUs that the current root bridge is sending, then the port transitions to a root-inconsistent state, which is effectively equal to an STP listening state, and no data traffic is forwarded across that port.

Root guard is best deployed toward ports that connect to switches that should not be the root bridge. Root guard is enabled using the **spanning-tree guard root** command in interface configuration mode.

Loop Guard

Loop guard is a feature designed to provide additional protection against Layer 2 loops. By default, if a non-designated port ceases to receive BPDUs, it will transition to the forwarding state once the max age timer expires. However, what if the switch was not receiving the BPDUs because the switch that was sending the BPDUs had a software failure preventing it from sending BPDUs? That switch would still be able to send and receive data on the interface. This would produce a loop because the non-designated port is now sending and receiving data as well, instead of blocking it. This is all because the BPDUs are no longer arriving on the interface. Loop guard ensures that the non-designated port does not erroneously transition to the forwarding state. Instead, it places it in the loop-inconsistent blocking state and generates a syslog message.

By default, loop guard is disabled on all switch ports. You can enable loop guard as a global default, affecting all switch ports, with the global configuration command **spanning-tree loopguard default**. Instead, you can enable loop guard on a specific switch port by using the interface-configuration command **spanning-tree guard loop**.

Video: Configuring STP Stability Mechanisms

Refer to the Digital Study Guide to view this video.

Activity: Match the Layer 2 Security Feature to Its Description

Refer to the Digital Study Guide to complete this activity.

Packet Tracer Activity: Configure Layer 2 VLAN and STP Security

Refer to the Digital Study Guide to access the PKA file for this activity. You must have Packet Tracer software to run this activity.

Study Resources

For today's exam topics, refer to the following resources for more study.

Resource	Location	Topic
Primary Resources		
CCNA Security Official Cert Guide	9	Securing Layer 2 Technologies
CCNA Security (Networking Academy Curriculum)	6	Securing the Local Area Network
Supplemental Resources		
CCNA Security Complete Video Course	13	Securing Layer 2 Technologies
CCNA Security Portable Command Guide	4	Network Foundation Protection

Check Your Understanding

Refer to the Digital Study Guide to take a ten-question quiz covering the content of this day.

VLAN Security

CCNA Security 210-260 IINS Exam Topics

- 4.6.a Describe the security implications of a PVLAN
- 4.6.b Describe the security implications of a native VLAN

Key Topics

Today we wrap up our review of Layer 2 infrastructure and protocol security. We will first look at two advanced VLAN switch features, namely Private VLANs and PVLAN Edge ports. We will then examine how to apply different types of access control lists (ACL) on a Cisco switch. Finally, we will ensure that the native VLAN is protected from attack.

Private VLANs

The basic definition of a VLAN is that it is a broadcast domain associated with one IP subnet and that inter-VLAN communication is only allowed through a Layer 3 device. It is possible to simplify a multi-VLAN and subnet deployment by using the Private VLAN (PVLAN) feature. PVLANs provide Layer 2 isolation between ports within the same VLAN. For a service provider, this isolation eliminates the need for a separate VLAN and IP subnet per customer.

With PVLANs, a common subnet is subdivided into multiple PVLANs. Communication between hosts is controlled by whether their switchport is configured as isolated, community, or promiscuous. The advantage of using PVLANs is that it simplifies traffic management while conserving IP address space.

A port in a PVLAN can be one of three types:

- **Isolated:** These ports are access ports that are assigned to an isolated VLAN. An isolated port has complete Layer 2 separation from other ports within the same primary PVLAN, except for a promiscuous port. PVLANs block all traffic to isolated ports, except the traffic from promiscuous ports. Traffic that is received from an isolated port is forwarded only to promiscuous ports.

- **Promiscuous:** These ports are access ports that are assigned to a primary VLAN and typically connect to a router or firewall. A promiscuous port can communicate with all ports within the PVLAN, including the community and isolated ports. The default gateway for the segment would likely be hosted on a promiscuous port, given that all devices in the PVLAN need to communicate with that port.

- **Community:** These ports are access ports that are assigned to a community VLAN. Community ports communicate among themselves and with the promiscuous ports. These interfaces are isolated at Layer 2 from all other interfaces in other communities or in isolated ports within their primary PVLAN.

PVLAN ports are associated with a set of supporting VLANs that are used to create the PVLAN structure. A PVLAN uses a VLAN in three ways:

- **As a primary VLAN:** This type of VLAN carries traffic from promiscuous ports to isolated, community, and other promiscuous ports in the same primary VLAN.

- **As an isolated VLAN:** This type of secondary VLAN carries traffic from isolated ports to a promiscuous port.

- **As a community VLAN:** This type of secondary VLAN carries traffic between community ports and to promiscuous ports. You can configure multiple community VLANs in a PVLAN.

Figure 12-1 shows an example of a PVLAN deployment. In this scenario, the primary VLAN is 100, which contains all the ports in the topology. Within VLAN 100, there are two secondary VLANs: 101 and 102. VLAN 101 is an isolated VLAN. PC 1 and PC 2 are isolated and cannot communicate with each other. VLAN 102 is a community VLAN. PC 3 and PC 4 can communicate with each other. PC 3 and PC 4 cannot communicate with PC 1 and PC 2, and vice versa, because they are in different secondary VLANs.

Figure 12-1   PVLAN Topology

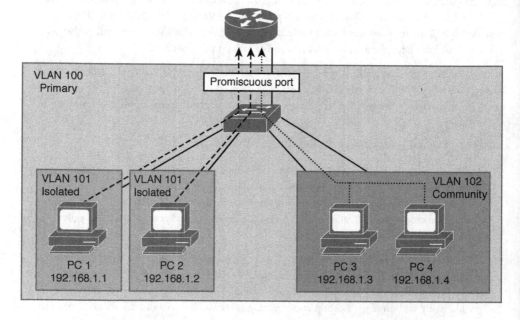

For the PCs to be able to communicate with shared devices or communicate beyond the Layer 2 VLAN, the PVLAN feature supports configuration of promiscuous ports. Promiscuous ports are usually uplink connections to a router for access to the rest of the network. In Figure 12-1, the router uplink is the promiscuous port.

Example 12-1 shows the configuration required to enable the PVLAN feature on the switch in Figure 12-1.

Example 12-1 Configuring PVLANs

```
Switch(config)# vtp mode transparent
Switch(config)# vlan 100
Switch(config-vlan)# private-vlan primary
Switch(config)# vlan 101
Switch(config-vlan)# private-vlan isolated
Switch(config)# vlan 102
Switch(config-vlan)# private-vlan community
Switch(config-vlan)# vlan 100
Switch(config-vlan)# private-vlan association 101,102
Switch(config-vlan)# interface GigabitEthernet 1/0/24
Switch(config-if)# description Trunk-to-Router
Switch(config-if)# switchport trunk encapsulation dot1q
Switch(config-if)# switchport mode trunk
Switch(config-if)# switchport mode private-vlan promiscuous
Switch(config-if)# switchport private-vlan mapping 100 add 101, 102
Switch(config-if)# interface range GigabitEthernet 1/0/1-2
Switch(config-if-range)# description End-User-Ports-In-Isolated-PVLAN
Switch(config-if-range)# switchport mode access
Switch(config-if-range)# switchport mode private-vlan host
Switch(config-if-range)# switchport private-vlan host-association 100 101
Switch(config-if)# interface range GigabitEthernet 1/0/3-4
Switch(config-if-range)# description End-User-Ports-In-Community-PVLA
Switch(config-if-range)# switchport mode access
Switch(config-if-range)# switchport mode private-vlan host
Switch(config-if-range)# switchport private-vlan host-association 100 102
```

Example 12-2 shows the output for the **show vlan private-vlan** and **show interface switchport** commands as they relate to Figure 12-1 and the configuration in Example 12-1.

Example 12-2 Verifying PVLANs

```
Switch# show vlan private-vlan


Primary  Secondary  Type                   Ports
-------  ---------  --------------------   ------------------------
100      101        isolated               Gi1/0/1, Gi1/0/2, Gi1/0/24
100      102        community              Gi1/0/3, Gi1/0/4, Gi1/0/24


Switch# show interfaces Gi1/0/24 switchport | include private-vlan
Administrative Mode: private-vlan promiscuous
```

```
Administrative private-vlan host-association: none
Administrative private-vlan mapping: 100 (VLAN0100) 101 (VLAN101) 102 (VLAN102)
Administrative private-vlan trunk native VLAN: none
Administrative private-vlan trunk Native VLAN tagging: enabled
Administrative private-vlan trunk encapsulation: dot1q
Administrative private-vlan trunk normal VLANs: none
Administrative private-vlan trunk associations: none
Administrative private-vlan trunk mappings: none
Operational private-vlan: 100 (VLAN100) 101 (VLAN0101) 102 (VLAN0102)
```

 Video: Configuring Private VLANs

Refer to the Digital Study Guide to view this video.

PVLAN Edge

In many environments, there is no valid reason for communication between neighbors (forwarding traffic at Layer 2 between ports on the same switch). On client or user VLANs, communication typically goes through central servers in the data center. Blocking communication between neighbors effectively mitigates attacks between neighboring hosts, such as ARP cache poisoning.

Protected ports, also referred to as PVLAN Edge, have the following features:

- The switch does not forward any data traffic (unicast, multicast, or broadcast) from one protected port to any other protected port. Only control traffic is forwarded.

- The forwarding behavior between a protected port and a non-protected port proceeds as usual.

PVLAN Edge is relevant only to the switch on which it is configured. PVLAN Edge provides the same function as PVLAN with regard to promiscuous and isolated ports. What it lacks is community ports. What it offers is a much simpler configuration.

To define a port as a protected port, in interface configuration mode of the port you want to protect, enter the command **switchport protected**. Example 12-3 shows how to configure ports Gi1/0/1 through Gi1/0/24 as protected ports. To return a port to the unprotected state, use the **no switchport protected** interface configuration command.

Example 12-3 Configuring Private VLAN Edge

```
Switch(config)# interface range Gi1/0/1 - 24
Switch(config-if)# switchport protected
```

Example 12-4 shows output from the **show interfaces switchport** command for a port that is secured using PVLAN Edge. The "Protected" status is true if it is a protected port.

Example 12-4 Verifying Private VLAN Edge

```
Switch# show interfaces Gi1/0/1 switchport
Name: Gi1/0/1
Switchport: Enabled
Administrative Mode: dynamic desirable
Operational Mode: static access
Administrative Trunking Encapsulation: dot1q
Operational Trunking Encapsulation: native
Negotiation of Trunking: On
Access Mode VLAN: 1 (default)
Trunking Native Mode VLAN: 1 (default)
Voice VLAN: none
Administrative private-vlan host-association: none
Administrative private-vlan mapping: none
Administrative private-vlan trunk native VLAN: none
Administrative private-vlan trunk encapsulation: dot1q
Administrative private-vlan trunk normal VLANs: none
Administrative private-vlan trunk private VLANs: none
Operational private-vlan: none
Trunking VLANs Enabled: ALL
Pruning VLANs Enabled: 2-1001
Capture Mode Disabled
Capture VLANs Allowed: ALL
Protected: true
Appliance trust: none
```

ACLs on Switches

Access control lists (ACLs) can be applied in three different ways to control traffic flows on Cisco switches:

- **Port ACLs (PACLs):** PACLs provide access control to traffic entering a Layer 2 interface. Cisco multilayer switches do not support PACLs in the outbound direction. You can apply only one IP ACL and one MAC ACL to a Layer 2 interface.

- **Cisco IOS ACLs:** Cisco IOS ACLs provide access control to routed traffic between VLANs and are applied to Layer 3 interfaces in a specific direction (inbound or outbound). Cisco IOS ACLs can also be implemented on switches with switched virtual interfaces (SVIs).

- **VLAN ACLs (VACLs):** Also known as VLAN maps, VACLs provide access control to all traffic on a VLAN. You can apply VLAN maps to all packets that are routed into or out of a VLAN or are bridged within a VLAN in the switch. You do not define VACLs by direction (input or output).

As illustrated in Figure 12-2, for an incoming packet on a physical port, the PACL is applied first. If the packet is permitted by the PACL, the VACL on the ingress VLAN is applied next. If the packet is Layer 3 forwarded and is permitted by the VACL, it is filtered by the Cisco IOS ACLs on the same VLAN. The same process happens in reverse in the egress direction. However, there is currently no hardware support for output PACLs.

Figure 12-2   Interaction Between PACLs, VACLs, and Cisco IOS ACLs

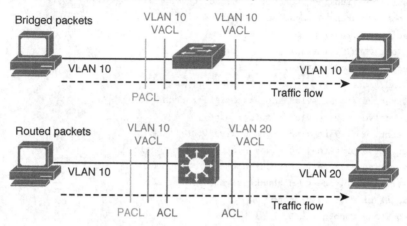

Cisco IOS ACLs (standard, extended, numbered, named) are covered extensively in the CCNA Routing and Switching certification. The focus here will be on PACL and VACL configuration and verification.

PACL Configuration

There are two types of PACLs:

- **IP access list:** This PACL filters IPv4 and IPv6 packets on a Layer 2 port.

- **MAC access list:** This PACL filters packets that are of an unsupported type, based on the fields of the Ethernet frame. A MAC access list is not applied to IP, MPLS, or ARP messages. You can define only named MAC access lists.

NOTE: PACLs cannot filter physical link protocols and logical link protocols, such as CDP, VTP, DTP, PAgP, UDLD, and STP, because the protocols are redirected to the route processor (RP) before the ACL takes effect.

Example 12-5 shows how to configure a MAC PACL and apply it to a Layer 2 interface.

Example 12-5 Configuring a MAC PACL

```
Switch(config)# mac access-list extended MAC-ACL
Switch(config-ext-macl)# permit host 0001.acad.ffff any
Switch(config-ext-macl)# interface gigabitEthernet 1/0/6
Switch(config-if)# mac access-group MAC-ACL in
```

Example 12-6 shows how to configure an IP PACL and apply it to a Layer 2 interface.

Example 12-6 Configuring an IP PACL

```
Switch(config)# ip access-list extended IP-ACL
Switch(config-ext-nacl)# permit ip host 192.168.20.1 any
Switch(config-ext-nacl)# interface gigabitEthernet 1/0/6
Switch(config-if)# ip access-group IP-ACL in
```

Use the **show ip interface** and **show mac access-group interface** commands to verify MAC and IP PACL configurations.

VACL Configuration

VACLs apply to all the traffic on the VLAN. VLAN maps have no direction. To use a VLAN map to filter traffic in a specific direction, you must include an ACL with specific source or destination addresses.

Each VLAN map consists of a series of entries. The order of entries in a VLAN map is important. A packet that comes into the switch is tested against the first entry in the VLAN map. If the packet matches, the action that is specified for that part of the VLAN map is taken. If there is no match, the packet is tested against the next entry in the map. If the packet does not match any of these match clauses, the default is to drop the packet. Three VACL actions are permitted:

- Forward

- Drop

- Redirect

The VACL **match** statement is used to reference an IP ACL or MAC ACL. This command matches the packet (using either the IP or the MAC address) against one or more standard or extended ACLs. Packets are matched only against ACLs of the correct protocol type. IP packets are matched against standard or extended IP ACLs. Non-IP packets are matched only against named MAC extended ACLs.

There are three steps when configuring VACLs. Step one is to define one or more IP or MAC access lists. Step two is to define a VLAN access map that references the ACLs from step one, but also specifies which action to take. Step three is to assign the VLAN access map to a VLAN. Example 12-7 shows a typical VACL configuration. In this scenario, a server resides in the same VLAN as some hosts. We want to prevent the hosts from accessing the server at IP address 192.168.100.100.

Example 12-7 Configuring VACL

```
Switch(config)# access-list 101 permit ip any host 192.168.100.100
Switch(config)# vlan access-map MYMAP 10
Switch(config-access-map)# match ip address 101
Switch(config-access-map)# action drop
```

```
Switch(config-access-map)# vlan access-map MYMAP 20
Switch(config-access-map)# action forward
Switch(config-access-map)# exit
Switch(config)# vlan filter MYMAP vlan-list 200
```

Notice that the ACL uses a **permit** statement to pass the packets to the VLAN access map. The **drop** action is then applied to the packets that were permitted by the ACL. Finally, the VLAN access map is applied to VLAN 200 where the hosts and the server reside. Line 20 of the VLAN access map allows all other communication within and out of the VLAN.

The commands shown in Example 12-8 help verify VACL configurations.

Example 12-8 Verifying VACL

```
Switch# show vlan access-map
Vlan access-map "MYMAP" 10
          match: ip address 101
          action: drop
Vlan access-map "MYMAP" 20
          action: forward

Switch# show vlan filter
VLAN Map Client_VLAN_Map:
            Configured on VLANs: 200
                 Active on VLANs: 200
```

Video: Configuring Port ACLs

Refer to the Digital Study Guide to view this video.

Native VLAN

The IEEE 802.1Q protocol allows operation between equipment from different vendors. All frames, except native VLAN frames, are equipped with a tag when traversing the link.

The native VLAN that is configured on each end of an 802.1Q trunk must be the same. If one end is configured for native VLAN 1 and the other for native VLAN 2, a frame that is sent in VLAN 1 on one side will be received on VLAN 2 on the other. VLAN 1 and VLAN 2 have been segmented and merged. There is no reason this should be required, and connectivity issues will occur in the network. If there is a native VLAN mismatch on either side of an 802.1Q link, Layer 2 loops may occur because VLAN 1 STP BPDUs are sent to the IEEE STP MAC address (0180.c200.0000) untagged.

By default, the native VLAN will be VLAN 1. For the purpose of security, the native VLAN on a trunk should be set to a specific VLAN identifier (VID) that is not used for normal operations elsewhere on the network using the **switchport trunk native vlan** command.

There are several other mechanisms or best practices to minimize authorized access to trunk ports and switch spoofing, including the following:

- Manually configure access ports with the **switchport mode access** command.

- Shut down unused interfaces and place them in a "parking lot" (i.e., an unused VLAN).

- Restrict VLANs on trunk ports with the **switchport trunk allowed vlan** command.

Manually configuring access ports prevents trunks from being dynamic. This configuration is a best practice for ports that are deemed to be only access ports. Shutting down unused ports is a simple practice. This is a best practice regardless of security configuration around switch spoofing, and it aids in preventing connection of wrong ports, incorrect cabling, and so on.

Another configuration to aid in securing trunks is to limit the VLANs on the trunk ports to VLANs needed to pass on the trunk. In a large network, not all VLANs will pass on every trunk port. Reducing the number of VLANs to only interested VLANs helps limit the impact of switch spoofing.

Finally, it is recommended that Dynamic Trunking Protocol (DTP) be disabled when statically configuring switch ports with the **switchport nonegotiate** command.

Example 12-9 shows the commands necessary to secure trunk links, access ports, and the native VLAN. For this scenario, the switch has 24 ports. Ports 1 to 10 are access ports assigned to VLAN 100, ports 11 to 23 are unused and must be disabled and placed in the parking lot VLAN 800, while port 24 is an 802.1Q trunk port. The native VLAN needs to be changed to VLAN 900, and only VLAN 100 should be allowed across the trunk. DTP is disabled on all ports.

Example 12-9 Securing Trunk and Native VLAN

```
Switch(config)# interface range gi1/0/1 - 10
Switch(config-if-range)# switchport mode access
Switch(config-if-range)# switchport access vlan 100
Switch(config-if-range)# switchport nonegotiate
Switch(config-if-range)# interface range gi1/0/11 - 23
Switch(config-if-range)# switchport mode access
Switch(config-if-range)# switchport access vlan 800
Switch(config-if-range)# switchport nonegotiate
Switch(config-if-range)# shutdown
Switch(config-if-range)# interface gi1/0/24
Switch(config-if)# switchport trunk encapsulation dot1q
Switch(config-if)# switchport mode trunk
Switch(config-if)# switchport nonegotiate
Switch(config-if)# switchport trunk native vlan 900
Switch(config-if)# switchport trunk allowed vlan 100
```

Notice in Example 12-9 that the native VLAN has been pruned from the trunk, as only VLAN 100 is permitted. Maintenance protocols, such as CDP and DTP, are normally carried over the native VLAN. Native VLAN pruning will not affect the functionality of these protocols because they will use the native VLAN regardless of configuration.

Activity: Match the Switch Port Security Feature to Its Description

Refer to the Digital Study Guide to complete this activity.

Packet Tracer Activity: Configure IP ACLs

Refer to the Digital Study Guide to access the PKA file for this activity. You must have Packet Tracer software to run this activity.

Study Resources

For today's exam topics, refer to the following resources for more study.

Resource	Location	Topic
Primary Resources		
CCNA Security Official Cert Guide	9	Securing Layer 2 Technologies
CCNA Security (Networking Academy Curriculum)	6	Securing the Local Area Network
Supplemental Resources		
CCNA Security Complete Video Course	13	Securing Layer 2 Technologies
CCNA Security Portable Command Guide	4	Network Foundation Protection

Check Your Understanding

Refer to the Digital Study Guide to take a ten-question quiz covering the content of this day.

Firewall Technologies

CCNA Security 210-260 IINS Exam Topics

- 5.1.a Proxy firewalls

- 5.1.b Application firewall

- 5.1.c Personal firewall

- 5.2.a Firewall operations

- 5.2.b Function of the state table

Key Topics

Today we start our review of firewalls and firewall technologies. We will look at different types of firewalls, as well as different packet-filtering techniques.

Firewall Overview

The word *firewall* commonly describes a system or device that is placed between a trusted network and an untrusted network. Network firewall solutions offer user and application policy enforcement that supplies protection for different types of security threats. These solutions often provide logging capabilities that enable the security administrators to identify, investigate, validate, and mitigate such threats. In a network, a firewall is intended to control what passes from one security zone to another. If a system is compromised in one zone, firewalls help to contain the attack to within that zone. In addition, within a network, firewalls also have the job of preventing unwanted access to secure systems.

Consider the common deployment scenario in Figure 11-1 for a firewall using three zones:

- **Inside:** A private, trusted network

- **Outside:** The public, untrusted Internet

- **DMZ:** A zone containing servers that are accessible by the public Internet

Figure 11-1   Three-Zone Firewall Deployment

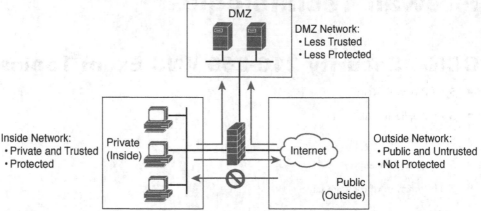

In this scenario, connections from systems on the outside to systems on the inside are forbidden. Connections from the inside to the outside, on the other hand, are generally permitted. However, there may be limitations on the application protocols that are allowed from the inside to the outside. For connectivity from the outside to the DMZ, what is allowed is strictly defined. Access is only allowed to the specific ports on specific servers based on the services that are intended to be provided by the server. Also, it is common to be very restrictive on connections that can be made from servers on the DMZ to systems in other zones.

A firewall can be implemented in various ways, such as packet filtering on routers and switches, dedicated firewall appliances, or complex security systems that include intrusion protection, application awareness, content security, and identity management. All firewalls share the same basic requirements:

- A firewall must be resistant to attacks.

- A firewall must be the only transit point between network zones.

- A firewall enforces the access control policy of the organization.

Firewalls also offer several benefits in a network:

- Prevent the exposure of sensitive hosts, resources, and applications to untrusted users

- Sanitize protocol flow, which prevents the exploitation of protocol flaws

- Block malicious data from servers and clients

- Reduce security management complexity by off-loading most of the network access control to a few firewalls in the network

- Control user access by leveraging AAA

Some organizations have the misconception that a modern firewall provides a complete network security solution. In reality, firewalls should be components in the larger security architecture and solution.

Firewalls have many limitations, such as the following:

- The fact that firewalls concentrate security administration at the critical junctures between network security zones provides a benefit, but it is also a limitation. A misconfiguration of the firewall can have disastrous consequences, as can a hardware failure.

- Because they are implemented at critical points between network security zones, firewalls can introduce performance bottlenecks.

- Firewalls cannot control data paths that circumvent them.

- As with any security mechanism, if the user community does not understand the policies and views them as oppressive, some users may find ways to bypass firewall policy.

- A significant number of intrusions are initiated from within the trusted network. Generally, firewalls can only provide protection between network security zones, not within security zones.

Packet Filtering

The simplest type of firewall is a packet filter. As the name implies, a packet filter looks at individual packets in isolation. Based on the contents of the packet and the configured policy, the packet filter makes a permit or deny decision. Packet filters generally have robust options for differentiating desirable and undesirable packets, such as the following:

- They can filter based on the source and destination IP address at the network layer.

- They can differentiate protocols at the transport layer: TCP, UDP, ICMP, OSPF, and so on.

- When the transport layer is TCP or UDP, source and destination ports can be specified.

- When the transport layer is ICMP, types and codes can be specified.

- When the traffic is TCP, the presence of the ACK bit or the RST bit can be verified. Under normal TCP connection flow, neither of these bits is ever set in the first packet of a new TCP connection.

Packet filtering is commonly implemented on Cisco IOS routers and switches by using ACLs. Although ACLs are simple to implement and have a low impact on network performance, they do have several limitations and weaknesses:

- Their ACLs or rules can be relatively large and difficult to manage.

- They can be deceived into permitting unauthorized access of spoofed packets. Attackers can orchestrate a packet with an IP address that is authorized by the ACL.

- Numerous applications can build multiple connections on random negotiated ports. This makes it difficult to determine which ports are selected and used until after the connection is completed.

ACL packet filters can be used to protect the network infrastructure from specific attacks. Consider the topology in Figure 11-2.

Figure 11-2   Packet Filter ACL

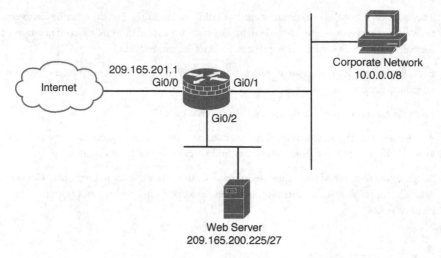

Assume for this scenario the following configuration:

■ The corporate network is using the private IP address space 10.0.0.0/8 and is connected to the edge router's Gi0/1 interface.

■ The web server is hosted on the 209.165.200.224/27 private network, which is connected to the Gi0/2 interface of the edge router.

■ The edge router's Internet-facing interface is Gi0/0 and has a public IP address of 209.165.201.1.

■ The corporate network uses Network Address Translation (NAT) Overload (or Port Address Translation) to access the Internet. NAT and PAT will be explained in detail on Day 10.

■ The edge router uses BGP with the ISP.

■ Internet users are allowed HTTP and HTTPS access to the web server.

■ Corporate network users are allowed Internet access.

Example 11-1 shows the configuration for an ACL applied inbound on the Gi0/0 interface.

Example 11-1   Infrastructure ACL Packet Filter

```
!--- Deny special-use address sources. !--- Refer to RFC 3330
access-list 110 deny ip host 0.0.0.0 any
access-list 110 deny ip 127.0.0.0 0.255.255.255 any
access-list 110 deny ip 192.0.2.0 0.0.0.255 any
access-list 110 deny ip 224.0.0.0 31.255.255.255 any
!--- Filter RFC 1918 space.
access-list 110 deny ip 10.0.0.0 0.255.255.255 any
```

```
access-list 110 deny ip 172.16.0.0 0.15.255.255 any
access-list 110 deny ip 192.168.0.0 0.0.255.255 any
!--- Deny your space as source from entering your AS
access-list 110 deny ip 209.165.200.224 0.0.0.31 any
access-list 110 deny ip host 209.165.201.1 any
!--- Permit BGP.
access-list 110 permit tcp host 209.165.201.2 host 209.165.201.1 eq bgp
access-list 110 permit tcp host 209.165.201.2 eq bgp host 209.165.201.1
|---Permit access to Web server replies
access-list 110 permit tcp any host 209.165.200.225 eq 80
access-list 110 permit tcp any host 209.165.200.225 eq 443
|---Permit corporate network TCP replies
access-list 110 permit tcp any host 209.165.201.1 established
!---Explicit deny
access-list 110 deny ip any any
```

The ACL protects the corporate network from spoofing attacks and illegitimate traffic. It also allows the BGP exchange to occur between the edge router and the ISP. Finally, it allows Internet users to access the web server and permits Internet replies for corporate users. Notice the use of the **established** keyword. When the **established** keyword is specified, the access control entry will match TCP packets between the appropriate IP addresses and TCP ports (in this case, any) as long as either the ACK bit or the RST bit is set in the TCP header of the packet. Also note that the ACL will not permit ICMP ping requests from the Internet or replies back to the corporate network. This access could be added if required.

Proxy and Application Firewalls

A second firewall technology is a proxy server, also known as an application layer gateway. Unlike packet-filtering firewalls, a proxy server does not act as a Layer 3 forwarder. Instead it acts as a Layer 3 termination point. When a proxy server is used as a primary path between two networks, it has an interface in both networks. When a client in one network needs to connect to a remote server in the other network, it connects to the proxy server and the proxy server connects to the other network. This means that there are two separate connections. The remote server does not see a connection from the client. It sees a connection from the proxy server.

The limitation of a proxy server is that it needs to have special coding on a per-application basis. Given the wide variety of network applications, this is very difficult for the firewall vendor to implement. Also, to make the use of the proxy transparent to the end user, the client application may need to have special coding as well.

This limitation, however, can be turned to an advantage when proxy servers are used for particular, high-value applications. In today's networks, it is common to pair a stateful firewall with a proxy server that specializes in web applications. In this case, the stateful firewall explicitly denies HTTP and HTTPS traffic from the internal network to the Internet. It only allows HTTP and HTTPS traffic from the internal network to the proxy server and from the proxy server to the Internet, which forces all HTTP and HTTPS traffic to go through the proxy server. Other applications, however, are controlled by the stateful firewall itself.

Figure 11-3 shows a typical proxy server deployment. A client inside the network is requesting access to a website. The client browser uses a proxy server for all HTTP requests. Perfect examples of proxy gateways performing application layer filtering are the Cisco Web Security Appliance (WSA) and the Cisco Email Security Appliance (ESA). Network security policies force all client connections to go through the proxy server. As shown in Figure 11-3, the browser connects to the proxy server to make requests. Client-side DNS queries and client-side routing to the Internet are not needed when using a proxy server. The client has to reach only the proxy server to make the request.

Figure 11-3   Proxy Server Communication Process

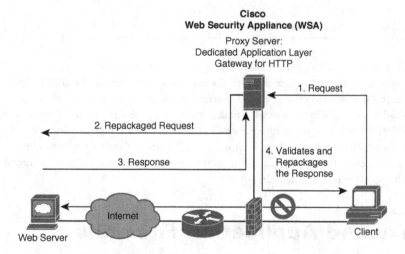

When the proxy server receives the request from a client, it performs user authentication according to the rules applied to it and uses its Internet connection to access the requested website. It forwards only packets that match the firewall rules. On the return route, the proxy server analyzes the packet, including the Layer 5 and Layer 7 header and payload, to ensure that the server allows the content of the reply back in (as an example, checking whether the payload carries hidden malware) before forwarding the packet to the client.

On the other hand, application inspection firewalls ensure the security of applications and services. Some applications require special handling by the firewall application inspection function. Applications that require special application inspection functions are those that embed IP addressing information in the user data packet or that open secondary channels on dynamically assigned ports.

The application inspection function works with NAT to help identify the location of the embedded addressing information. This arrangement allows NAT to translate embedded addresses and to update any checksum or other fields that are affected by the translation.

The application inspection function also monitors sessions to determine the port numbers for secondary channels. Many protocols open secondary TCP or UDP ports. The initial session on a well-known port negotiates dynamically assigned port numbers. The application inspection function monitors these sessions, identifies the dynamic port assignments, and permits data exchange on these ports for the duration of the specific session.

Stateful Firewalls

Whereas a packet filter controls access on a packet-by-packet basis, stateful firewalls control access on a session-by-session basis. This means that when the firewall makes access control decisions, it can take into consideration the rules governing sessions at the transport layer and the application layer along with knowledge of what has previously happened within the session. The data that is associated with what has happened previously within sessions is stored in a state table.

Given an understanding of TCP session rules (three-way handshake, SYN, SYN/ACK, ACK) along with the existence of the state table, stateful firewalls can ensure that those rules are followed. Network attacks often break rules, confusing systems and causing them to behave in unintended fashions. When stateful firewalls recognize that rules are being broken, they will drop offending packets and mitigate the attack. Take for example TCP connections. The connection must begin with a SYN packet. If the policy on the firewall allows the session, the SYN packet is allowed and a new entry in the state table is created. The state table stores information such as the source and destination IP addresses and TCP ports, TCP flags, and sequence numbers. At this point, there is only one valid packet that can follow in this session. It is the server's SYN ACK packet in response to the client's SYN, and it needs to be acknowledging the actual sequence number that was originally presented by the client.

Stateful firewalls can also provide stateful inspection of applications that utilize a control channel to facilitate dynamically negotiated connections. Voice over IP (VoIP) applications are common examples in modern networks. FTP is another example. With FTP, the client connects to the server on TCP port 21, which is the control channel. When the client requests data, a new data channel is opened. This is a dynamically negotiated TCP connection using either port 20 or a dynamically assigned port number.

Like stateless packet filters, ACLs are used to configure access control policy stateful firewalls. But, whereas the ACLs are referenced packet by packet on a stateless packet filter, they are only referenced session by session on a stateful firewall. For example, when a TCP SYN packet is received by a stateful firewall, it checks the ACL configuration to determine if it should allow the connection. If it is a permitted connection, then an entry is created in the state table. The state table now controls the bidirectional flow of all other packets that are associated with that connection. Any non-SYN TCP packet is processed against the state table, not the ACLs. If there is a matching entry in the state table, then the packets are allowed. If there is not a matching entry in the state table, the packets are dropped.

Figure 11-4 shows a successfully established HTTP TCP session that leads to a dynamic ACL rule entry on the outside interface that permits response packets from the web server to the client.

Figure 11-4   Stateful Packet Filtering

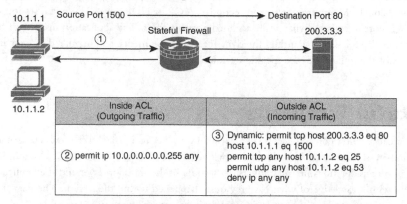

The outside ACL has three permanent entries permitting outside traffic to initiate a connection on 10.1.1.2. Our firewall also has an ACL on its inside interface, permitting traffic from inside users to anywhere outside.

1. An inside user initiates a connection.
2. The user's connection is tested against the inbound ACL on the inside interface.
3. If the traffic is permitted to progress from inside to outside, the firewall inserts a dynamic entry in the inbound ACL of the outside interface to allow the reply traffic to come in to reach the inside user.

Next-Generation Firewalls

Firewalls have now evolved beyond simple packet filtering and stateful inspection. Most companies are deploying next-generation firewalls to block modern threats such as advanced malware and application layer attacks.

Features that can be included in a next-generation firewall include

- Standard firewall capabilities like stateful inspection

- Integrated intrusion prevention

- Application awareness and control to see and block risky apps and URLs

- Context awareness that tracks who is connecting, to what, from where, using which device, and at what time

- Advanced malware protection that can provide detection, blocking, tracking, analysis, and remediation

- Secure Internet access with VPN and NAT

- Upgrade paths to include future information feeds

- Techniques to address evolving security threats

In September 2014, Cisco announced the integration of Sourcefire's FirePOWER Next-Generation IPS (NGIPS) services into the Cisco Adaptive Security Appliance (ASA). Designed with advanced malware protection, the Cisco ASA with FirePOWER services is also called the Cisco ASA Next-Generation Firewall because it is an adaptive, threat-focused firewall. It is designed to provide defense across the entire attack continuum, which includes before, during, and after attacks.

Video: Cisco ASA Next-Generation Firewalls

Refer to the Digital Study Guide to view this video.

Personal Firewall

A personal firewall is typically a software program that is installed on an endpoint device to protect the device itself. Most modern operating systems have integrated personal firewalls. We will look more closely at this type of firewall on Day 2 when we review endpoint security.

Activity: Match the FirewallType to Its Description

Refer to the Digital Study Guide to complete this activity.

Study Resources

For today's exam topics, refer to the following resources for more study.

Resource	Location	Topic
Primary Resources		
CCNA Security Official Cert Guide	14	Understanding Firewall Technologies
CCNA Security (Networking Academy Curriculum)	4	Implementing Firewall Technologies
Supplemental Resource		
Cisco ASA (3rd ed.)	1	Introduction to Security Technologies

Check Your Understanding

Refer to the Digital Study Guide to take a ten-question quiz covering the content of this day.

Cisco ASA NAT Implementation

CCNA Security 210-260 IINS Exam Topics

- 5.3.a Static

- 5.3.b Dynamic

- 5.3.c PAT

- 5.3.d Policy NAT

- 5.3.e Verify NAT operations

Key Topics

Today we are reviewing Network Address Translation (NAT) and how to deploy it on a Cisco ASA.

NAT Fundamentals

NAT operates on Layer 3 forwarding devices to provide address simplification and conservation. The most common use of NAT is to allow networks using private IPv4 network addresses to connect to the public Internet. NAT translates the private addresses that are used in the internal network into public addresses that can be routed across the Internet. As part of this functionality, you can configure NAT to use only one address for the entire network to connect to the outside world. Using only one address effectively hides the internal network, thus providing additional security.

Multiple device types can be configured to perform NAT services. Although firewalls are most common, routers and Layer 3 switches are also capable of deploying this service.

Cisco defines the following list of NAT terms:

- **Inside local address:** The IPv4 address that is assigned to a host on the inside network. The inside local address is likely to be one that falls within the RFC 1918 reserved private IPv4 address spaces.

- **Inside global address:** A globally routable IPv4 address that represents one or more inside local IPv4 addresses to the outside world.

- **Outside local address:** The IPv4 address of an outside host as it appears to the inside network. Not necessarily a public address, the outside local address is allocated from a routable address space.

- **Outside global address:** The IPv4 address that is assigned to a host on the outside network by the host owner. The outside global address is allocated from a globally routable address or network space.

NAT eliminates the need to readdress all hosts that require external access, saving time and money. NAT also conserves addresses through application port-level multiplexing. In other words, internal hosts can share a single registered IPv4 address for all external communications. In this type of configuration, relatively few external addresses are required to support many internal hosts, thus conserving IPv4 addresses.

Figure 10-1 illustrates an ASA that is translating the source address as the packet is forwarded from inside to outside, and reversing the translation on the reply that returns. The steps that are taken are as follows:

1. Host 192.168.1.1 sends a packet to the Web Server.

2. The ASA performs address translation according to the NAT table and the NAT configuration.

3. The ASA replaces the inside local address 192.168.1.1 with the inside global address 209.165.200.225 and forwards the packet.

4. The Web Server receives the packet with 209.165.200.225 as the source address. When it replies, it specifies a destination address of 209.165.200.225.

5. When the ASA receives the packet, it checks the NAT table and finds the entry that is associated with the inside global address of 209.165.200.225.

6. The ASA replaces the inside global address 209.165.200.225 with the inside local address 192.168.1.1 and forwards the packet.

Figure 10-1   NAT Process

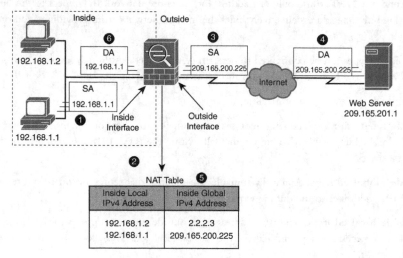

NAT requirements will vary from situation to situation. The following deployment modes are available to address varying requirements:

- **Static NAT:** Maps a private IPv4 address to a public IPv4 address. One-to-one static NAT is particularly useful when a device must be accessible from outside the network.

- **Dynamic NAT:** Maps a private IPv4 address to a public IPv4 address from a pool of public IPv4 addresses.

- **Dynamic PAT (NAT Overload):** Maps multiple private IPv4 addresses to a single public IPv4 address by using the source port to distinguish between translations. That single IPv4 address may be the IPv4 address of the NAT device itself.

- **Static PAT:** Imagine a network that has just one single public IPv4 address, and this IPv4 address must be used by the firewall that connects the network to the Internet. It must also be used as the PAT address for all outbound connections. If this network must also support a DMZ server, then static PAT can be used. For example, TCP port 80 may be reserved for PAT translation to the HTTP service on the DMZ server. Static PAT is sometimes called port forwarding.

- **Policy NAT:** Uses extended criteria, such as source addresses, destination addresses, and transport layer ports, to specify the translation. For example, traffic that is destined to a particular partner network may be translated to a specific address using PAT while traffic destined elsewhere is translated using a dynamic NAT pool.

NAT on Cisco ASA

Cisco ASA can translate an internal private address to a global public address when packets are destined for the public network. With this method, also known as *inside NAT*, the ASA converts the global address of the return traffic to the original internal address. Inside NAT is used when traffic originates from a higher-security–level interface, such as the inside interface, and is destined for a lower-security–level interface, such as the outside interface.

Optionally, the hosts on the lower-security–level interface can be translated when traffic is destined for a host on the higher-security–level interface. This method, known as *outside NAT*, is useful when you want a host on the outside network to appear as one of the internal IP addresses.

In Figure 10-2, a host on the outside network, 209.165.201.1, sends traffic to a host on the inside network, 192.168.10.10, by using its global IP address as the destination address (209.165.200.226). Cisco ASA converts the source IP address to 192.168.10.100 while changing the destination IP address to 192.168.10.10. Because both the source and destination IP addresses are changing, this is also known as *bidirectional NAT*.

Cisco ASA software uses an object-oriented configuration when deploying NAT. By creating an object for every host, translated address, and service that is used in translations, it is easier to understand how the NAT configuration is used. With Cisco ASA, you can configure translations as network objects that are added to the configuration.

Figure 10-2   Dynamic NAT

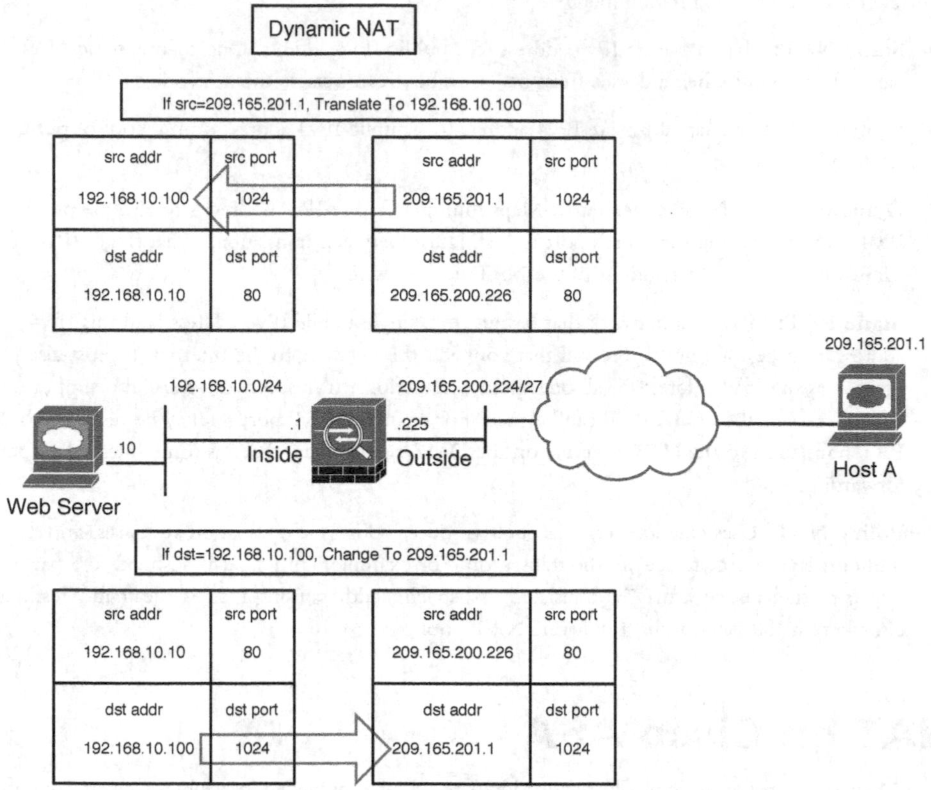

The concept of a "network object" is defined as a single IP address or network. The host or subnet that is defined in the network object is used to identify the real (nontranslated) address in a NAT configuration. ACLs that permit traffic from a lower-security-level interface to a higher-security-level interface reference the real (nontranslated) address instead of the mapped (translated) address of the inside hosts.

Cisco ASA uses the concept of a NAT table to build NAT configuration entries. The NAT sections are read by the ASA from top to bottom. The first translation match that is found is used. The NAT table has three sections:

- **Manual NAT (first section):** The manual NAT section enables the administrator to define translations that the appliance compares before the other two sections. These translations are usually very precise.

- **Auto NAT (second section):** The Auto NAT section, also referred to as object NAT, contains translations that are defined in the object itself. This section allows each object definition to include a single translation for every object that is configured. These translations are usually static translations for servers that have clients connecting to them from the Internet or are dynamic translations for clients connecting to the Internet.

- **Manual NAT after Auto NAT (third section):** The manual NAT section that comes after the Auto NAT section contains more general translations that are not handled by the prior two sections.

As we go through the different implementations of NAT, we will verify and analyze the NAT table with the appropriate **show** commands.

We will use the reference topology in Figure 10-3 to deploy four different versions of NAT: static NAT, dynamic NAT, dynamic PAT, and policy NAT. The topology includes an inside interface using 10.1.1.0/24, a DMZ using 172.16.1.0/24, and an outside interface using 209.165.201.0/27.

For simplicity, the simulated Internet devices are also hosted on the 209.165.201.0/27 network.

Figure 10-3   NAT Reference Topology

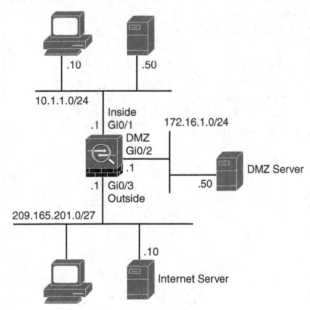

Static NAT

Static NAT defines a fixed translation of an inside host or subnet address to a global routable address or subnet. The security appliance uses the one-to-one methodology by assigning one global IP address to one inside IP address. Additionally, the inside hosts are assigned the same IP address whenever the security appliance translates the packets going through it. This is a recommended solution in scenarios in which an organization provides services such as email, web, DNS, and FTP for outside users. Using static NAT, the servers use the same global IP address for all the inbound and outbound connections.

For our scenario, we want to create a static NAT mapping for the DMZ server located at 172.16.1.50. The translated or mapped address should be 209.165.201.2. We will also use the Auto NAT feature to help create the rule.

Using ASDM, navigate to **Configuration > Firewall > Objects > Network Objects/Groups**. Start configuration by choosing **Add > Network Object**. As shown in Figure 10-4, define parameters of the object you want to create; in this case the object is the DMZ server. Enter the type and IP address of the object you are defining. Here the DMZ server is defined as a Host object with an IP address of 172.16.1.50. Then check the **Add Automatic Address Translation Rules** check box to use Auto NAT, and enter the translated IP address information.

Figure 10-4   ASDM Static NAT Configuration (Step 1)

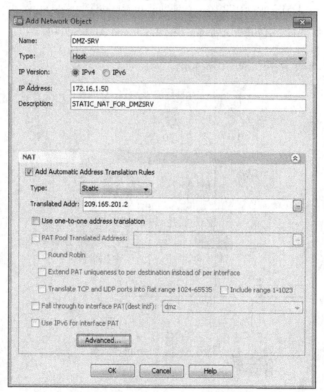

As a result of this configuration, the DMZ server residing at IP address 172.16.1.50 will be statically translated to IP address 209.165.201.2.

Next, we must define a traffic direction for the NAT translation to occur. Click the **Advanced** button to define the source and destination interfaces for the desired translation. Figure 10-5 shows the DMZ server on the DMZ interface will have its IP address statically translated to and from traffic on the outside interface. Click **OK** to close the Advanced NAT Settings dialog box.

Figure 10-5   ASDM Static NAT Configuration (Step 2)

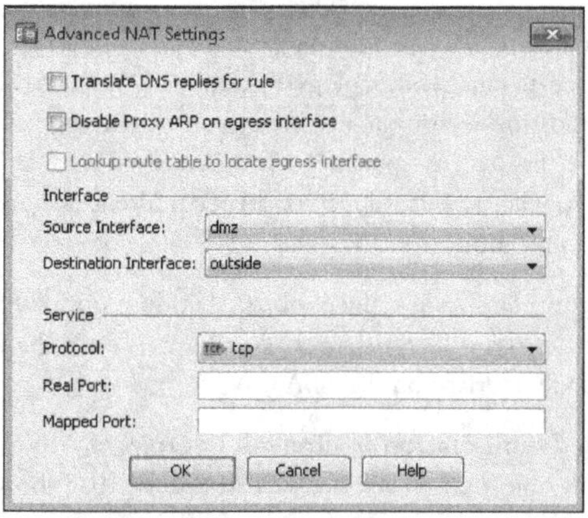

Example 10-1 shows the commands created by ASDM and pushed to the ASA.

Example 10-1 Static NAT CLI

```
object network DMZ-SRV
  host 172.16.1.50
  description STATIC_NAT_FOR_DMZSRV
  nat (dmz,outside) static 209.165.201.2
```

To verify the static NAT configuration from ASDM, choose **Tools > Command Line Interface**. Either type **show xlate** or select it from the drop-down list in the Single Line command field. Click **Send**. Figure 10-6 confirms that the ASA has one static NAT rule in use for the DMZ server.

Figure 10-6   ASDM Static NAT Verification

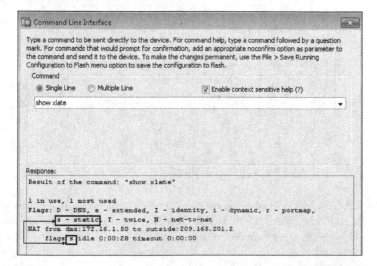

Dynamic NAT

Dynamic NAT assigns a random IP address from a preconfigured pool of global IP addresses. The security appliance uses a one-to-one methodology by allocating one global IP address to an inside IP address. Hence, if 100 hosts reside on the inside network, then you have at least 100 addresses in the pool of addresses. After the security appliance has built a dynamic NAT entry for an inside host, any outside machine can connect to the assigned translated address, assuming that the security appliance allows the inbound connection.

Usually you would configure translation using a subnet that does not physically exist. For simplicity of routing in our scenario, we will create a pool of addresses from the 209.165.201.0/27 subnet that is assigned to the outside interface on the ASA.

Using ASDM, navigate to **Configuration > Firewall > Objects > Network Objects/Groups**. Select the **inside-network** object group and click **Edit**. Figure 10-7 shows that the network object has been named inside-network, that Auto NAT will be used, and that the type is set to Dynamic translation.

Figure 10-7   ASDM Dynamic NAT Configuration (Step 1)

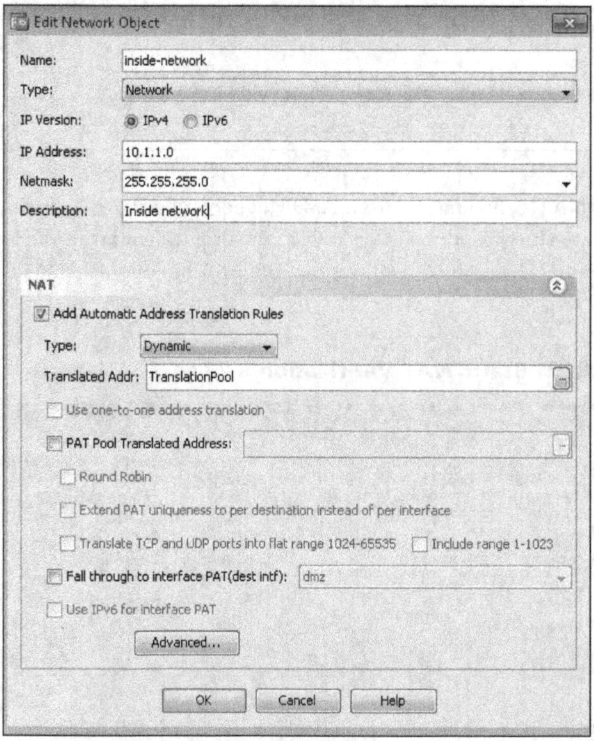

The Translated Addr field is defined as a network object. Click the ellipsis (**...**) button in the Translated Addr field. Choose **Add > Network Object** in the Browse Translated Addr window to open the Add Network Object window. Figure 10-8 shows the creation of the dynamic NAT address pool.

Figure 10-8   ASDM Dynamic NAT Configuration (Step 2)

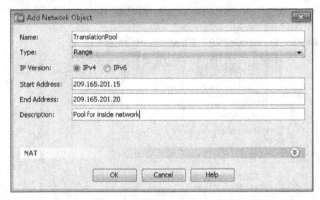

The address pool has been named TranslationPool, and it covers a range of addresses from 209.165.201.15 to 209.165.201.20.

Click **OK** to return to the Browse Translated Addr window. Notice that the newly created address pool is highlighted, as shown in Figure 10-9. Click the **Translated Addr** button to select it, and click **OK** to return to the Edit Network Object window.

Figure 10-9   ASDM Dynamic NAT Configuration (Step 3)

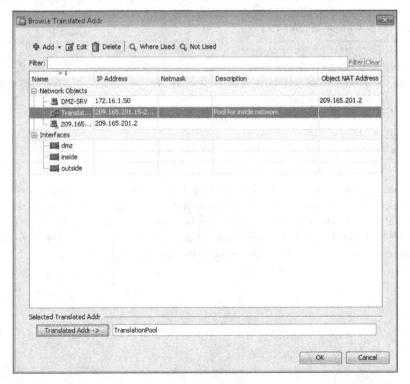

Click the **Advanced** button to open the Advanced NAT Settings dialog box. Set the Source Interface to **inside** and the Destination Interface to **outside**, as shown in Figure 10-10.

Figure 10-10   ASDM Dynamic NAT Configuration (Step 4)

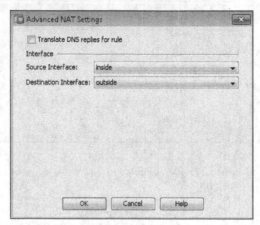

Click **OK** to return once again to the Edit Network Object window. Click **Apply** in the next window. The Preview CLI Commands window opens, displaying the commands that will be sent to the ASA, as shown in Example 10-2. Click **Send** to deploy the configuration to the ASA.

Example 10-2 Dynamic NAT CLI

```
object network TranslationPool
 range 209.165.201.15 209.165.201.20
 description Pool for inside network
object network inside-network
 subnet 10.1.1.0 255.255.255.0
 description Inside network
 nat (inside,outside) dynamic TranslationPool
```

To verify the dynamic NAT configuration, first trigger translation by initiating a connection from the inside network to the outside network. Then from ASDM, select **Tools > Command Line Interface**. Either type **show xlate** or select it from the drop-down list in the Single Line command field. Click **Send**. Figure 10-11 confirms that the ASA has one static NAT rule in use for the DMZ server and one dynamic NAT rule for the inside device at 10.1.1.10.

Figure 10-11   ASDM Dynamic NAT Verification

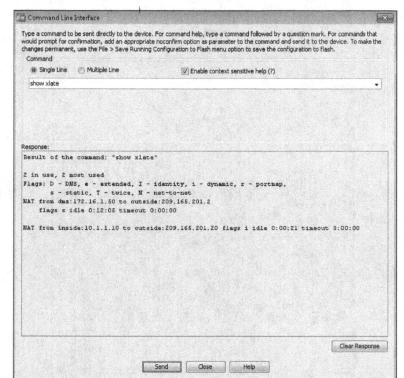

Dynamic PAT

With dynamic PAT, the security appliance builds the address translation table by looking at the Layer 3 and Layer 4 header information. It is the most commonly deployed scenario because multiple inside machines can get outside connectivity through one global IP address. In dynamic PAT, the security appliance uses the source IP addresses, the source ports, and the IP protocol information (TCP or UDP) to translate an inside host.

The goal in this third scenario is to modify the previous dynamic NAT configuration so as to change it to use dynamic PAT on the outside interface of the ASA for translation.

From ASDM, navigate to **Configuration > Firewall > Objects > Network Objects/Groups**. Double-click the **inside-network** object group to open the Edit Network Object window. Change the NAT type to **Dynamic PAT (Hide)**, and also change the Translated Addr field to **outside**. Notice that as you start to type the word "outside" in the Translated Addr field, ASDM suggests the completion for you, as shown in Figure 10-12.

Figure 10-12 ASDM Dynamic PAT Configuration

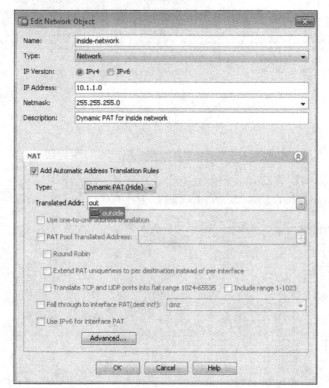

Click **OK**, and then click **Apply** to send the new configuration to the ASA. ASDM displays a message asking if it should clear the translation table. Click **Yes** to open the Preview CLI Commands window, which shows the commands produced by ASDM, as shown in Example 10-3. Click **Send** to enable dynamic PAT on the ASA.

Example 10-3 Dynamic PAT CLI

```
object network inside-network
 nat (inside,outside) dynamic interface
clear xlate interface inside local 10.1.1.0 netmask 255.255.255.0
```

To verify the dynamic PAT configuration, first trigger translation by initiating a connection from the inside network to the outside network. Then from ASDM, select **Tools > Command Line Interface**. Either type **show xlate** or select it from the drop-down list in the Single Line command field. Click **Send**. Figure 10-13 confirms that the ASA has one static NAT rule in use for the DMZ server and dynamic PAT rules for the inside device at 10.1.1.10. Notice the ASA maintaining the original TCP source port during translation.

Figure 10-13   ASDM Dynamic PAT Verification

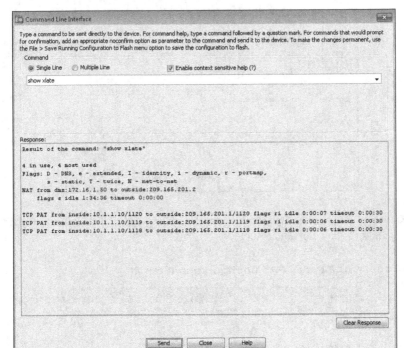

Policy NAT

Policy NAT translates the IP address of the packets passing through the security appliance only if those packets match a defined criterion or policy. You define the policy by identifying interesting traffic through the use of ACLs or by using manual NAT and identifying specific traffic. If traffic matches the defined entries in the ACL, then the original source or destination address can be translated to a different address.

The goal in this fourth scenario is to configure a policy that translates the IP address of the inside server (10.1.1.50) to 209.165.201.30 when it communicates with the Internet server. This policy should not affect translation from the inside server to any other systems. For other connections to the outside, the inside server will still use the dynamic PAT configuration.

We need to start by configuring host objects associated with the real and translated addresses. In ASDM, navigate to **Configuration > Firewall > Objects > Network Objects/Groups**. Choose **Add > Network Object** to define a first object for the inside server using its private internal address, as shown in Figure 10-14.

Figure 10-14 ASDM Policy PAT Configuration (Step 1)

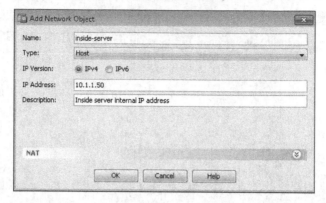

Click **OK** and repeat the process by creating another network object, this time for the Internet server's IP address, as shown in Figure 10-15.

Figure 10-15 ASDM Policy PAT Configuration (Step 2)

Click **OK** and repeat the process a third time, this time for the public IP address the inside server will use when communicating with the Internet server, as shown in Figure 10-16.

Click **OK** and confirm that there are now three new network objects configured on the ASA. Click **Apply** and notice the Preview CLI Commands window opens displaying the commands that will be sent to the ASA, as shown in Example 10-4. Click **Send** if they appear correct.

Figure 10-16   ASDM Policy PAT Configuration (Step 3)

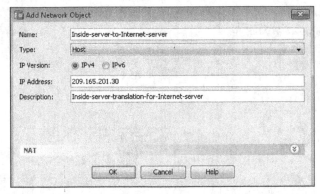

Example 10-4 Policy NAT CLI (Part 1)

```
object network Inside-server-to-Internet-server
 host 209.165.201.30
 description Inside-server-translation-for-Internet-server
object network Internet-server
 host 209.165.201.10
 description Internet server public IP address
object network inside-server
 host 10.1.1.50
 description Inside server internal IP address
```

To define the manual translation of the inside server for connections to the Internet server, use ASDM and navigate to **Configuration > Firewall > NAT Rules**. The NAT Rules table appears. There are currently two Network Object NAT rules defined, one for our static NAT and one for our dynamic PAT.

When configuring manual NAT entries, they can be placed either before or after the Object NAT rules. We want this new policy NAT configuration to have higher precedence than the dynamic PAT rule. Click **Add > Add NAT Rule Before "Network Object" NAT Rules**. The Add NAT Rule window opens.

Select the inside server for the source address, select the Internet server for the destination, and, under the Action: Translated Packet section, select Inside-server-to-Internet-server for the Source Address. Notice in Figure 10-17 that as soon as you start typing in the address fields, ASDM suggests completions for you.

Figure 10-17   ASDM Policy PAT Configuration (Step 4)

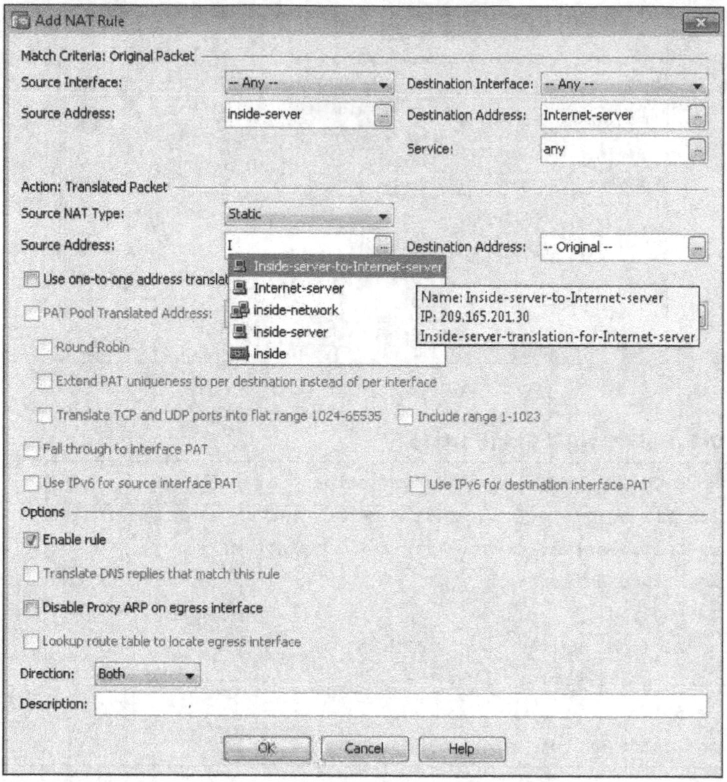

Click **OK** to return to the NAT Rules window. The new rule should appear above the Network Object NAT rules. Clicking **Apply** makes the Preview CLI Commands window open and shows the command that will be sent to the ASA, as shown in Example 10-5.

Example 10-5 Policy NAT CLI (Part 2)

```
nat 1 source static inside-server Inside-server-to-Internet-server destination
static Internet-server Internet-server
```

Click **Send** to confirm.

To verify the policy NAT configuration, first trigger translation by initiating a connection from the inside server to the Internet server. Then from ASDM, select **Tools > Command Line Interface**. Either type **show xlate** or select it from the drop-down list in the Single Line command field. Click **Send**. Figure 10-18 confirms that the ASA has one static NAT rule in use for the DMZ server two policy NAT rules for the inside server at 10.1.1.50 and the Internet server at 209.165.201.10. Notice active PAT translations as well, confirming that other outbound connections initiated by the internal server are still functioning.

Figure 10-18   ASDM Policy PAT Verification

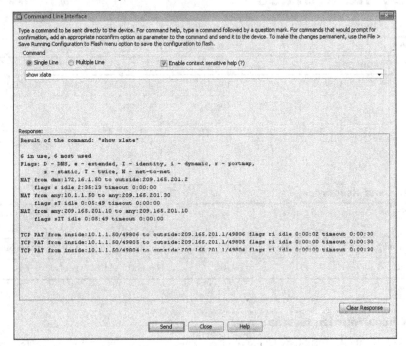

Video: Configuring NAT on Cisco ASA with ASDM

Refer to the Digital Study Guide to view this video.

Activity: Match the NAT Terminology to Its Description

Refer to the Digital Study Guide to complete this activity.

Study Resources

For today's exam topics, refer to the following resources for more study.

Resource	Location	Topic
Primary Resources		
CCNA Security Official Cert Guide	14	Understanding Firewall Fundamentals
	16	Configuring Basic Firewall Policies on Cisco ASA
CCNA Security (Networking Academy Curriculum)	9	Implementing the Cisco Adaptive Security Appliance
	10	Advanced Cisco Adaptive Security Appliance
Supplemental Resources		
CCNA Security Complete Video Course	11	Configuring Basic Firewall Policies on Cisco ASA
CCNA Security Portable Command Guide	21	Configuring Cisco ASA Advanced Settings
Cisco ASA (3rd ed.)	10	Network Address Translation

Check Your Understanding

Refer to the Digital Study Guide to take a ten-question quiz covering the content of this day.

Cisco IOS Zone-Based Policy Firewall

CCNA Security 210-260 IINS Exam Topics

- 5.4 Implement Zone-Based Firewall

Key Topics

Today we are reviewing the Cisco IOS Zone-Based Policy Firewall (ZPF) on Cisco routers. The ZPF changes the original implementation of Cisco IOS Classic Firewall stateful inspection from the older, interface-based model to a more flexible, more easily understood zone-based configuration model. Today focuses on the features of Cisco IOS ZPF and how to configure and verify them from the CLI.

ZPF Concepts

ZPF offers an easily understood zone-based configuration model. Interfaces are assigned to zones, and an inspection policy is applied to traffic moving between the zones. You can group physical and virtual interfaces into zones. Interzone policies offer considerable flexibility and granularity, which enables you to apply different inspection policies to multiple host groups that are connected to the same router interface, as shown in Figure 9-1.

Figure 9-1   Cisco IOS ZPF Traffic Flows

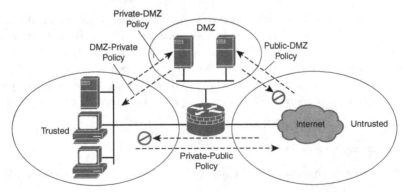

Figure 9-1 shows a typical three-zone network with the following inspection policies:

- **Public-DMZ:** DMZ policy that sets the rules for traffic originating from the untrusted zone with the DMZ as destination

- **DMZ-Private:** Private policy that sets the rules for the traffic originating from the DMZ with the trusted zone as destination

- **Private-DMZ:** DMZ policy that sets the rules for the traffic originating from the trusted zone with the DMZ as destination

- **Private-Public:** Public policy that sets the rules for the traffic originating from the trusted zone with the untrusted zone as destination

Rules are bidirectional. As an example, traffic originating from the trusted zone going to the DMZ would be allowed to return due to the Private-DMZ policy, which would permit the connection and allow the return traffic to come back in the trusted zone. The DMZ-Private policy is not involved for return traffic that originated from the trusted network and for which the reply is now going from the DMZ to the trusted network. The DMZ-Private policy is only needed for traffic originating from the DMZ and destined for the trusted network.

Cisco IOS ZPFs are configured with the Cisco Common Classification Policy Language (C3PL), which uses a hierarchical structure to define inspection for network protocols and the groups of hosts to which the inspection will be applied. Cisco IOS ZPF supports the following features:

- Stateful inspection

- Application inspection

- URL filtering

- Per-policy connection parameters

- Transparent firewall

- Virtual routing and forwarding (VRF)-aware firewall

ZPF Zones and Zone Pairs

Zones establish the security borders of your network. A zone defines a boundary where traffic is subjected to policy restrictions as it crosses to another region of your network. The default policy of a ZPF between zones is to "deny all." If no policy is explicitly configured, all traffic moving between zones is blocked. The C3PL structure is similar to the Modular QoS CLI (MQC) structure in which class maps are used to categorize traffic and policy maps are used to specify policy to be applied to each traffic category. C3PL will be discussed in more detail in the next section.

Key benefits of firewall ZPF are as follows:

- It is not dependent on ACLs.

- The router security posture is restrictive (which means block unless explicitly allowed).

- C3PL makes policies easy to read and troubleshoot.

- One policy affects any given traffic instead of needing multiple ACL and inspection actions.

A zone is a collection of networks that is reachable over a specific set of router interfaces and is designated to belong to the same zone. ZPF access control policies then control access between two or more zones that are configured on the router. C3PL, a flexible configuration language, allows you to specify simple or complex access policies in a manageable manner.

Once zones are created, default rules apply. These default rules will be presented in more detail later. However, default rules generally allow unrestricted access between interfaces that belong to the same zone, while denying all interzone traffic. Also note that an interface can belong only to one zone.

A zone pair allows you to specify a unidirectional firewall policy between two security zones, thus changing the default policy. The direction of the traffic is indicated by specifying a source zone and a destination zone. You must first define the source and destination zones before they can be referenced in a new zone pair.

The self zone is a system-defined zone. It does not have any interfaces as members. A zone pair that includes the self zone, along with the associated policy, applies to traffic directed to the router or traffic that is generated by the router. It does not apply to traffic through the router.

Introduction to C3PL

There are three major components to C3PL, as shown in Figure 9-2: class map, policy map, and service policy.

Figure 9-2   C3PL Components

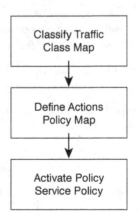

- Class maps: Identify traffic at OSI Layers 3 through 7. Use multiple matching criteria.

Classify Traffic
Class Map

- Policy maps: Define policy for traffic at Layers 3 through 7.

Define Actions
Policy Map

- Service policies: Activate policy maps for traffic flows on specific direction of zone pairs.

Activate Policy
Service Policy

To create firewall policies using C3PL, complete the following tasks:

- Define the match criterion in a class map.

- Associate policy actions to impose on the matched traffic with a policy map.

- Specify where to apply a policy map by referencing the policy map and a zone pair within a service policy.

Class Maps

A class map provides a way to specify the criteria to differentiate traffic into categories. Normally you define a class so that you can apply policy actions to the categorized traffic. Policy actions include inspect, drop, and pass.

C3PL policies are modular, object-oriented, and hierarchical in nature:

- **Modular and object-oriented:** This trait gives the firewall administrator the flexibility to create building-block objects such as class maps and policy maps, and reuse them within a given policy and across policies.

- **Hierarchical:** This feature results in powerful policies that can be expanded to include customized inspection, application layer rules, and advanced inspection features.

A policy map is applied to traffic flows that traverse a zone pair by using service policies. The policy map processes traffic flows by matching sessions against one or more class map objects, and performing policy actions that are defined for the matched class.

In a sense, policy maps are "if-then-else" statements, something similar to saying: "**If** a traffic flow matches the first class map, **then** the associated action is performed, and no other class map in the same policy is evaluated. **Else**, if the traffic flow matches the next class map in the configuration, **then** the associated action is performed." If traffic is not matched by any class map in a policy, a default action is performed.

The following are characteristics of class map objects that you should consider:

- Class maps that analyze Layer 3 and Layer 4 traffic can categorize the traffic that is based on the following criteria:

  - **Access group:** A standard, extended, or named ACL can filter traffic that is based on source and destination IP addresses and source and destination ports.

  - **Protocol:** The class map can identify Layer 4 protocols such as TCP, UDP, and ICMP, and application services such as HTTP, SMTP, and DNS.

  - **Class map:** A subordinate class map that provides additional match criteria can be nested inside another class map.

- Each class map can have multiple match statements. The match type defines how multiple match statements are processed to match the class:

  - If **match-any** is specified, traffic must meet only one of the match criteria in the class map.

  - If **match-all** is specified, traffic must match all the class map criteria to belong to that particular class.

Policy Maps

When configuring a policy map, keep in mind that class maps are evaluated in the order in which they are configured and added to the policy map. In addition to user-defined classes, a system-defined class map that is named class-default represents all packets that do not match any of the user-defined classes in a policy, and for which the default action is drop.

Cisco IOS ZPF supports the following four policy actions:

- **Inspect:** This action configures stateful packet inspection. The traffic is allowed as long as it obeys the rules of the associated protocols.

- **Drop:** This action is analogous to deny in an ACL.

- **Pass:** This action is analogous to permit in a stateless ACL-based firewall. The pass action does not track the state of connections or sessions within the traffic. Pass allows the traffic in only one direction. A corresponding policy must be applied to allow return traffic to pass in the opposite direction.

- **Log:** It is possible to log the information of the session, but this is only available for drop actions.

Service Policy

Service policy assignments are unidirectional, as defined by the zone pair to which the policy map is assigned. Zone pairs define the direction by specifying the source zone and the destination zone. A policy map that is applied to a given zone pair will match traffic and perform an action for that traffic in the direction that is defined by the zone pair. In other words, the policy map applies to traffic originating at the source zone and flowing toward the destination zone.

Exactly one service policy may be applied to a given zone pair at any given time. If you apply a different service policy to a zone pair that already has a service policy, you will overwrite the previous service policy.

Default Policies and Traffic Flows

The membership of the router network interfaces in zones is subject to several rules governing interface behavior as is the traffic moving between zone member interfaces:

- A zone must be configured before you can assign interfaces to the zone.

- You can assign an interface to only one security zone.

- Traffic is implicitly allowed to flow by default among interfaces that are members of the same zone.

- To permit traffic to and from a zone member interface, a policy allowing or inspecting traffic must be configured between that zone and any other zone.

- Traffic cannot flow between a zone member interface and any interface that is not a zone member. You can apply pass, inspect, and drop actions only between two zones.

- Interfaces that have not been assigned to a zone function as classical router ports and might still use legacy stateful inspection configuration.

- If you do not want an interface on the router to be part of the zone-based firewall policy, it might be necessary to put that interface in a zone and configure a "pass all" policy between that zone and any other zone to which traffic flow is desired.

■ From the preceding rules, it follows that if traffic is to flow among all the interfaces in a router, all the interfaces must be part of the zoning model (each interface must be a member of a zone).

The rules for a zone-based policy firewall are different when the router is involved in the traffic flow, whether as the source of traffic or the destination. A zone-based policy firewall is used to control router administration where the router is the destination.

When an interface is configured to be a zone member, the hosts that are connected to the interface are included in the zone, but traffic flowing to and from the interfaces of the router is not controlled by the zone policies. Instead, all the IP interfaces on the router are automatically made part of the self zone when a zone-based policy firewall is configured. In order to limit IP traffic moving to the IP addresses of the router from the various zones on a router, policies must be applied to block, allow, or inspect traffic between the zone and the self zone of the router, and vice versa. If there are no policies between a zone and the self zone, all traffic is permitted to the interfaces of the router without being inspected.

A zone pair that includes the self zone, along with the associated policy, applies to traffic that is directed to the router or traffic that the router generates. It does not apply to traffic traversing the router.

ZPF Configuration and Verification

The following procedure can be used to configure a zone-based policy firewall:

1. Define zones.

2. Define zone pairs.

3. Define class maps that describe traffic that must have a policy applied to it as it crosses a zone pair.

4. Define policy maps to apply action to the traffic of your class map.

5. Apply policy maps to zone pairs.

6. Assign interfaces to zones.

Before going through a complete configuration example, let's review some of the options available when configuring class maps and policy maps.

Configuring Class Maps

Class maps define the traffic that the firewall selects for policy application. Layer 4 class maps sort the traffic that is based on the following criteria, which are specified using the **match** command in a class map:

■ **Access group:** A standard, extended, or named ACL can filter traffic that is based on source and destination IP address and source and destination port.

- **Protocol:** Layer 4 protocols (TCP, UDP, and ICMP) and application services such as HTTP, SMTP, DNS, etc.

- **Class-map:** A subordinate class map that provides additional match criteria can be nested inside another class map.

Example 9-1 shows three different class maps: PRIVATE-NET, where a named ACL is being used to match traffic; WEB-TRAFFIC, where Layer 7 applications are being matched; and INTERNET-TRAFFIC, where a class map contains subordinate class maps.

Example 9-1   Class Map Configuration Example

```
class-map type inspect match-all PRIVATE-NET
 match access-group name MYNET
class-map type inspect match-any WEB-TRAFFIC
 match protocol http
 match protocol https
 match protocol dns
class-map type inspect match-all INTERNET-TRAFFIC
 match class-map PRIVATE-NET
 match class-map WEB-TRAFFIC
```

Configuring Policy Maps

The policy map applies firewall policy actions to one or more class maps to define the service policy that will be applied to a security zone pair. When an inspect-type policy map is created, a default class named class class-default is applied at the end of the class. The class class-default's default policy action is drop, but can be changed to pass. The log option can be added with the drop action. Inspect cannot be applied on class class-default.

Example 9-2 shows the configuration of a policy map that uses a class map from Example 9-1. Notice that the **inspect** action is being used. The **inspect** action offers state-based traffic control. For example, if traffic from a private zone to an Internet zone is inspected, the router maintains connection or session information for TCP and UDP traffic. Therefore, the router permits return traffic that is sent from Internet-zone hosts in reply to private-zone connection requests.

Example 9-2   Policy Map Configuration Example

```
policy-map type inspect INTERNET-ACCESS
 class type inspect INTERNET-TRAFFIC
  inspect
```

Configuration and Verification

Figure 9-3 shows the topology for the following ZPF configuration example.

Figure 9-3   ZPF Configuration Example

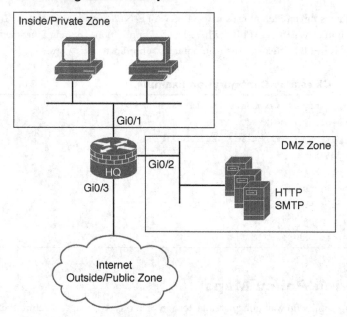

We will configure and verify a Cisco IOS ZPF to provide access control between the three zones indicated in Figure 9-3. HTTP, SMTP, and ICMP will be allowed to the DMZ from both the inside and outside zones. General TCP and UDP applications and ICMP will be allowed from the inside to the outside. Nothing will be allowed to initiate from the outside destined to the inside. No policy will be defined using the DMZ as the source zone, so sessions will not be allowed to originate from the DMZ.

Example 9-3 shows the commands necessary to configure the ZPF on router HQ according to our scenario.

Example 9-3   ZPF Configuration Example

```
HQ(config)# zone security inside
HQ(config-sec-zone)# exit
HQ(config)# zone security dmz
HQ(config-sec-zone)# exit
HQ(config)# zone security outside
HQ(config-sec-zone)# exit
HQ(config)# interface gi0/1
HQ(config-if)# zone-member security inside
HQ(config-if)# interface gi0/2
HQ(config-if)# zone-member security dmz
```

```
HQ(config-if)# interface gi0/3
HQ(config-if)# zone-member security outside
HQ(config-if)# exit
HQ(config)# class-map type inspect match-any To-DMZ
HQ(config-cmap)# match protocol http
HQ(config-cmap)# match protocol smtp
HQ(config-cmap)# match protocol icmp
HQ(config-cmap)# exit
HQ(config)# class-map type inspect match-any In-To-Out
HQ(config-cmap)# match protocol tcp
HQ(config-cmap)# match protocol udp
HQ(config-cmap)# match protocol icmp
HQ(config-cmap)# exit
HQ(config)# policy-map type inspect To-DMZ-Traffic
HQ(config-pmap)# class type inspect To-DMZ
HQ(config-pmap-c)# inspect
HQ(config-pmap-c)# exit
HQ(config)# policy-map type inspect In-To-Out-Traffic
HQ(config-pmap)# class type inspect In-To-Out
HQ(config-pmap-c)# inspect
HQ(config-pmap-c)# exit
HQ(config)# zone-pair security Out-To-DMZ source outside destination dmz
HQ(config-sec-zone-pair)# service-policy type inspect To-DMZ-Traffic
HQ(config-sec-zone-pair)# exit
HQ(config)# zone-pair security In-To-DMZ source inside destination dmz
HQ(config-sec-zone-pair)# service-policy type inspect To-DMZ-Traffic
HQ(config-sec-zone-pair)# exit
HQ(config)# zone-pair security In-To-Out source inside destination outside
HQ(config-sec-zone-pair)# service-policy type inspect In-To-Out-Traffic
HQ(config-sec-zone-pair)# exit
HQ(config)# exit
HQ# show zone security
zone self
Description: System Defined Zone

zone inside
 Member Interfaces:
  GigabitEthernet0/1

zone dmz
 Member Interfaces:
  GigabitEthernet0/2

zone outside
 Member Interfaces:
```

```
 GigabitEthernet0/3
HQ# show zone-pair security
Zone-pair name Out-To-DMZ
    Source-Zone outside  Destination-Zone DMZ
    service-policy To-DMZ-Traffic
Zone-pair name In-To-DMZ
    Source-Zone inside  Destination-Zone DMZ
    service-policy To-DMZ-Traffic
Zone-pair name In-To-Out
    Source-Zone inside  Destination-Zone outside
    service-policy In-To-Out-Traffic
```

To view the state table while live sessions are being monitored by the ZPF, use the **show policy-map type inspect zone-pair** command.

Video: IOS Zone-Based Policy Firewall

Refer to the Digital Study Guide to view this video.

Activity: Match the ZPF Terminology to Its Description

Refer to the Digital Study Guide to complete this activity.

Packet Tracer Activity: Configure IOS Zone-based Policy Firewall (ZPF)

Refer to the Digital Study Guide to access the PKA file for this activity. You must have Packet Tracer software to run this activity.

Study Resources

For today's exam topics, refer to the following resources for more study.

Resource	Location	Topic
Primary Resources		
CCNA Security Official Cert Guide	15	Implementing Cisco IOS Zone-Based Firewalls
CCNA Security (Networking Academy Curriculum)	4	Implementing Firewall Technologies
Supplemental Resources		
CCNA Security Complete Video Course	10	Implementing Cisco IOS Zone-Based Firewalls
CCNA Security Portable Command Guide	12	Configuring Zone-Based Firewalls

Check Your Understanding

Refer to the Digital Study Guide to take a ten-question quiz covering the content of this day.

Cisco ASA Firewall Concepts

CCNA Security 210-260 IINS Exam Topics

- 5.5.e Describe modes of deployment (routed firewall, transparent firewall)
- 5.5.f Describe methods of implementing high availability
- 5.5.g Describe security contexts
- 5.5.h Describe firewall services

Key Topics

Today we are introducing the Cisco Adaptive Security Appliance (ASA). We will cover its features and modes of deployment within a network.

Cisco ASA Family

The Cisco ASAs are purpose-built solutions that integrate firewall, VPN, IPS, and content security services in a unified platform. The Cisco ASA is fundamentally a stateful packet filter with application inspection and control, with a rich set of additional integrated software and hardware features such as advanced malware protection, URL filtering, intrusion protection, and clientless VPN access.

The Cisco ASA provides intelligent threat defense that stops attacks before they penetrate the network perimeter, controls network and application activity, and delivers secure remote-access and site-to-site connectivity. This multifunction network security appliance family provides security breadth, precision, and depth for protecting business networks of all sizes, while reducing the overall deployment and operations costs that are associated with implementing comprehensive multilayer security.

Cisco offers several models of the ASA to meet customer needs, ranging from remote/teleworker models to high-end data center models. Figure 8-1 shows the complete ASA 5500-X family.

The CCNA Security certification exam focuses on configuring and managing the ASA 5506-X. Figure 8-2 illustrates the front panel of the ASA 5506-X. Figure 8-3 illustrates the back panel of the Cisco ASA 5506-X.

Figure 8-1   Cisco ASA 5500-X Family

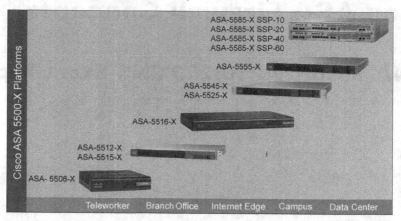

Figure 8-2   Cisco ASA 5506-X Front Panel

Figure 8-3   Cisco ASA 5506-X Back Panel

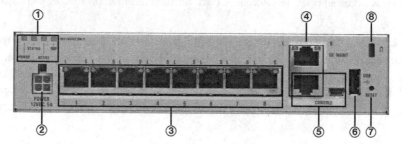

The rear panel has the following components:

1. **Status LEDs.** The Power LED lights up solid green when power is applied to the ASA. The Status LED lights up solid green when the ASA is functioning normally. An amber Status LED indicates a critical alarm such as a major hardware failure, over-temperature condition, or a power voltage issue. The Active LED lights up solid green when a high availability (HA) failover pair is functioning normally, and lights up amber if the unit is the standby device in an HA pair. The wLAN LED only lights up if the ASA contains a wireless access point. This feature is available in the ASA 5506W-X.

2. **Power cord socket.** The ASA is powered on as soon as you plug in the AC power supply.

3. **Network data ports.** Eight Gigabit Ethernet RJ-45 network interfaces numbered Gigabit Ethernet 1/1 through Gigabit Ethernet 1/8. The network ports support auto MDI/X as well as auto-negotiation for interface speed, duplex, and other negotiated parameters, and they are MDI/MDIX compliant. The Link status (L) LED lights up to indicate when the port is in use, flashing when there is activity. The Connection-speed status (S) LED lights up differently depending on the speed (one blink every three seconds = 10 Mbps; two rapid blinks = 100 Mbps; three rapid blinks = 1000 Mbps).

4. **Management port.** A Gigabit Ethernet interface (interface Management1/1) restricted to network management access only. Connect with an RJ-45 cable. This interface is up by default but has no IP address configured. It is reserved for use by the ASA's FirePOWER module.

5. **Console ports.** Two serial ports, a standard RJ-45 and a mini-USB Type B, are provided for management access via an external system.

6. **USB port.** A standard USB Type A port is provided that allows the attachment of an external device, such as mass storage.

7. **Reset button.** A small recessed button that, if pressed for longer than three seconds, resets the ASA to its default "as-shipped" state following the next reboot. Configuration variables are reset to factory default. However, the flash is not erased and no files are removed.

8. **Lock slot.** The slot accepts a standard Kensington T-bar locking mechanism for securing the ASA.

Cisco also supports the virtualization of computing infrastructure by taking advantage of the increased power availability of modern x86 servers. The Cisco Adaptive Security Virtual Appliance (ASAv) brings the power of ASAs to the virtual domain. The Cisco ASAv operates as a VM using the server's interfaces to process traffic. Like the physical Cisco ASA devices, the ASAv also supports site-to-site VPN, remote-access VPN, and clientless VPN functionalities.

ASA Features and Services

The heart of the ASA is an application-aware stateful packet inspection algorithm, which controls flows between networks that are controlled by the ASA. The connection-oriented stateful packet inspection algorithm design creates session flows based on source and destination addresses and ports. The algorithm randomizes TCP sequence numbers, port numbers, and additional TCP flags before completion of the connection. This function is always in operation, monitoring return packets to ensure that they are valid, and it transparently allows any additional dynamic transport layer sessions of the same application session. This fundamental function of the ASA allows you to minimize host and application exposure and allow only the minimal traffic on OSI network and transport layers that is required to support your applications.

The ASA also provides rich Application Visibility and Control (AVC) services, enabling you to verify the conformance of application layer protocols and prevent many tunneling attempts and application layer attacks that violate protocol specifications.

The ASA includes support for many different flavors of NAT, including inside and outside NAT, policy (destination-sensitive) NAT, one-to-one and one-to-many NAT, and port forwarding (dynamic and static PAT).

The ASA supports rich IP routing functionality for both static and dynamic routing. It integrates with IPv6 networks natively, to provide access control between IPv6 security domains.

The ASA integrates a DHCP server and client. It natively integrates with multicast networks.

In addition to these basic features, the ASA offers four advanced services:

- **ASA virtualization:** A single ASA can be partitioned into multiple virtual devices. Each virtual device is called a security context. Each context is an independent device, with its own security policy, interfaces, and administrators. Multiple contexts are similar to having multiple standalone devices. We will discuss ASA security contexts in the next few sections.

- **High availability with failover:** Two identical ASAs can be paired into an active/standby failover configuration to provide device redundancy. Both platforms must be identical in software, licensing, memory, and interfaces. We will discuss ASA high availability in an upcoming section.

- **Identity firewall:** The ASA provides optional, granular access control based on an association of IP addresses to Windows Active Directory login information. For example, when a client attempts to access an inside protected resource, it must first be authenticated using the Microsoft Active Directory Identity–based firewall services.

- **FirePOWER:** Cisco ASA now offers, in one device, next-generation intrusion prevention (NGIPS), advanced malware protection (AMP), and URL filtering. We will look at these new features during the last few days of our review.

ASA Deployments

The ASA offers different modes of deployment. The modes are known as routed mode and transparent mode. The mode of deployment that is used will depend upon your network requirements and needs. The modes of deployment have the following characteristics:

- **Routed mode:** The ASA supports RIP (versions 1 and 2), OSPF, EIGRP, and BGP dynamic routing protocols to integrate into existing routing infrastructures. Where dynamic routing is not available, the ASA can use static route tracking to determine neighbor or path health instead. This is the most commonly used mode of deployment.

- **Transparent (bridged) mode:** The ASA includes the ability to operate in a secure bridging mode as a Layer 2 device to provide rich OSI Layers 2 through 7 security services for the protected network. This ability enables businesses to deploy security appliances into existing network environments without requiring readdressing of the network. Although the security appliance can be invisible to devices on both sides of a protected network, you can manage it via a management IP address (which can be hosted on a separate management interface, if required).

ASA High Availability

The ASA has three redundancy options to provide for maximum uptime and system availability:

- **Active/Standby failover model:** One security appliance actively processes user traffic, whereas the other unit acts as a hot standby, prepared to take over if the active unit fails. Figure 8-4 shows an example of an active/standby failover topology.

Figure 8-4   Cisco ASA Active/Standby Failover Example

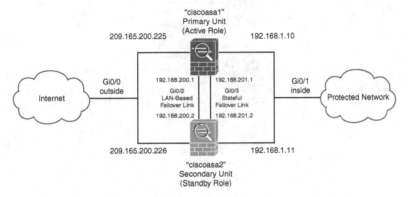

- **Active/Active failover model:** Both security appliances can actively process user traffic and can tolerate the failure of one device in the failover cluster. Figure 8-5 shows an example of an active/active failover topology. This example is somewhat more complex and introduces the concept of security contexts. Three security contexts are used. Failover group 1 should contain the admin and ContextB contexts, with the primary ASA normally having the active role. Failover group 2 should contain only ContextA, normally active on the secondary ASA. We will discuss security contexts in the following section.

- **Clustering:** This feature lets you group multiple ASAs as a single logical device. A cluster provides all the convenience of a single device (management, integration into a network) while achieving the increased throughput and redundancy of multiple devices. Figure 8-6 illustrates a two-unit cluster in Spanned EtherChannel mode. Inside and outside interfaces use two separate cluster-spanned EtherChannels in this example. These interfaces connect to two different switches, which are connected using a virtual port channel (vPC). TenGigabitEthernet0/6 and 0/7 interfaces on both cluster members bundle into the inside EtherChannel; both members respond to the virtual IP address of 192.168.1.1 on this link. TenGigabitEthernet0/8 and 0/9 interfaces similarly bundle into the outside EtherChannel with the virtual IP address of 172.16.125.1.

Figure 8-5   Cisco ASA Active/Active Failover Example

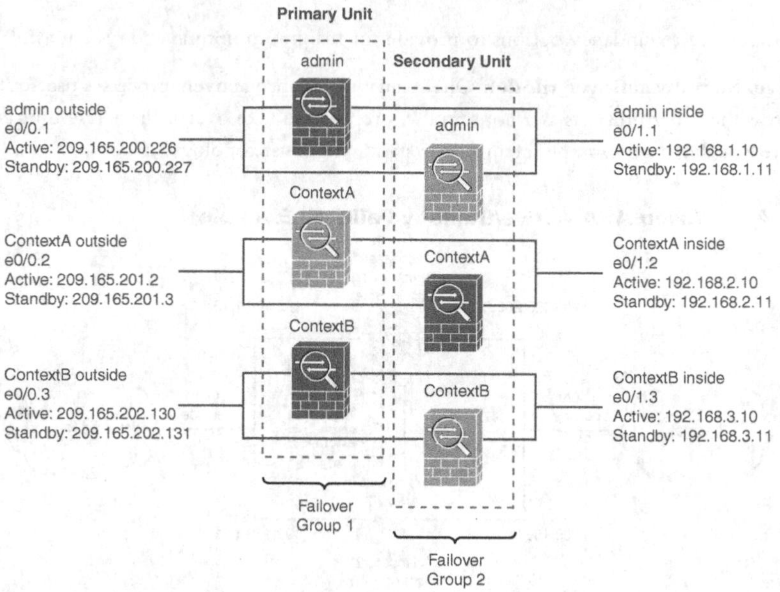

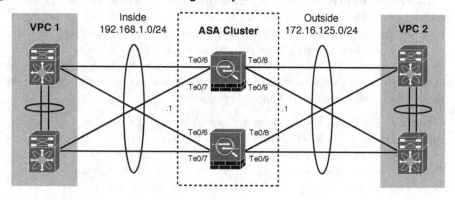

Figure 8-6   Cisco ASA Clustering Example

To facilitate failover, the ASAs participating in a failover pair (active/active or active/standby) pass between themselves information about the state of each device. Following are two types of failover links:

- LAN-based failover links
- Stateful failover links

With LAN-based failover links, the failover messages are transferred over Ethernet connections. LAN-based failover links provide message encryption and authentication using a manual pre-shared key (PSK) for added security. LAN-based failover links require an additional Ethernet interface on each ASA to be used exclusively for passing failover communications between two security appliance units.

The stateful failover interface passes per-connection stateful information to the standby ASA unit. Stateful failover requires an additional Ethernet interface on each security appliance with a minimum speed of 100 Mbps to be used exclusively for passing state information between the two ASAs. The LAN-based failover interface can also be used as the stateful failover interface.

ASA Contexts

You can partition a single ASA into multiple virtual firewalls that are known as security contexts. Each context is an independent firewall with its own security policy, interfaces, and administrators. Having multiple contexts is like having multiple standalone firewalls. You must first configure the security appliance that will host multiple security contexts into "multiple mode" to support virtualization. Most of the single-mode Cisco ASA security appliance features are also supported in multiple-context mode, including static routing, select dynamic routing protocols, access control features, security modules, and management features. Figure 8-7 shows a scenario where an ASA has been virtualized. Each dotted box represents a security context that is inspecting and protecting the packets flowing through it. The encompassing solid box represents the physical Cisco ASA that contains these multiple security contexts.

Figure 8-7   Cisco ASA Virtualization

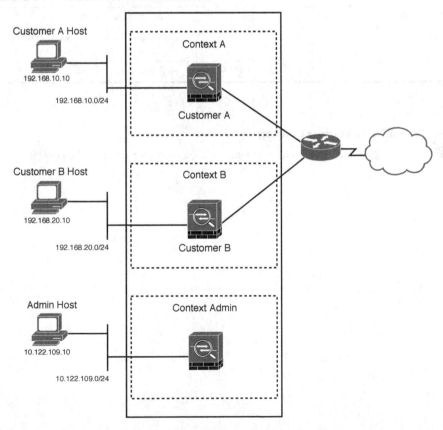

Video: Introducing the Cisco ASA

Refer to the Digital Study Guide to view this video.

Activity: Match the ASA Feature or Service to Its Descriptions

Refer to the Digital Study Guide to complete this activity.

Study Resources

For today's exam topics, refer to the following resources for more study.

Resource	Location	Topic
Primary Resources		
CCNA Security Official Cert Guide	16	Configuring Basic Firewall Policies on Cisco ASA
CCNA Security (Networking Academy Curriculum)	9	Implementing the Cisco Adaptive Security Appliance
Supplemental Resources		
CCNA Security Complete Video Course	9	Understanding Firewall Fundamentals
CCNA Security Portable Command Guide	18	Introduction to the ASA
Cisco ASA (3rd ed.)	2	Cisco ASA Product and Solution Overview
	16	High Availability

Check Your Understanding

Refer to the Digital Study Guide to take a ten-question quiz covering the content of this day.

ASA Firewall Configuration

CCNA Security 210-260 IINS Exam Topics

- 5.5.a Configure ASA access management

- 5.5.b Configure security access policies

- 5.5.c Configure Cisco ASA interface security levels

- 5.5.d Configure default Cisco Modular Policy Framework (MPF)

Key Topics

Today we will look at the ASA's default configuration and establishing initial connectivity using both the CLI and ASDM. We will then configure interfaces, objects, object groups, and service policy rules using Cisco's Modular Policy Framework (MPF).

ASA Default Configuration

Figure 7-1 shows the recommended initial network deployment for the ASA 5506-X with the ASA FirePOWER module. This recommendation is based on the default factory configuration, which is shown in Example 7-1.

Figure 7-1   Cisco ASA 5506-X Deployment Topology

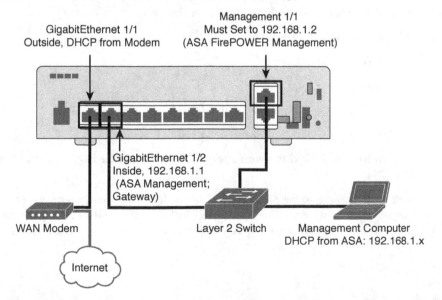

Example 7-1   ASA 5506-X Factory Default Configuration

```
interface Management1/1
 management-only
 no nameif
 no security-level
 no ip address
 no shutdown
interface GigabitEthernet1/1
 nameif outside
 security-level 0
 ip address dhcp setroute
 no shutdown
interface GigabitEthernet1/2
 nameif inside
 security-level 100
 ip address 192.168.1.1 255.255.255.0
 no shutdown
object network obj_any
 subnet 0.0.0.0 0.0.0.0
 nat (any,outside) dynamic interface
http server enable
http 192.168.1.0 255.255.255.0 inside
dhcpd auto_config outside
dhcpd address 192.168.1.5-192.168.1.254 inside
dhcpd enable inside
logging asdm informational
```

This factory default configuration confirms the following behavior:

- Inside interface is GigabitEthernet1/2.

- Outside interface is GigabitEthernet1/1.

- Inside to outside traffic flow is allowed.

- The outside IP address will be obtained via DHCP from the modem or ISP.

- The inside IP address is 192.168.1.1/24.

- DHCP is enabled for inside clients using a pool of IP addresses in the range 192.168.1.5 to 192.168.1.254.

- Management1/1 belongs to the ASA FirePOWER module. The interface is up, but otherwise unconfigured on the ASA. The ASA FirePOWER module can then use this interface to access the ASA inside network and use the inside interface as the gateway to the Internet.

> **NOTE:** Do not configure an IP address for this interface in the ASA configuration. Only configure an IP address in the FirePOWER setup and use 192.168.1.2/24 in that case. You should consider this interface as completely separate from the ASA in terms of routing. You can connect inside and management on the same network because the management interface acts like a separate device that belongs only to the ASA FirePOWER module.

- ASDM access is enabled for inside hosts, using a blank username and a blank password by default.

- Privilege EXEC mode access is enabled using a blank password by default.

- Dynamic PAT is enabled for all inside and management hosts.

ASA Management Access

Some of the first steps in deploying the ASA are to establish CLI and Cisco Adaptive Security Device Manager (ASDM) access. Cisco ASDM is a GUI configuration tool that is designed to facilitate the setup, configuration, monitoring, and troubleshooting of the ASA. The ASA uses a CLI command set that is based on Cisco IOS Software. The appliance provides five configuration modes, similar to Cisco IOS devices:

- **ROM monitor:** A special mode that allows you to update the ASA image over the network or perform password recovery.

- **User EXEC mode:** Available when first accessing the ASA. Provides a restricted view of the security appliance settings.

- **Privileged EXEC mode:** Enables changing of current settings.

- **Global configuration mode:** Enables changing of system configurations.

- **Specific configuration modes:** Enables changing of configurations that are specific to part of the security appliance. For example, interface settings.

For initial configuration of the ASA, access the CLI directly from the console port. For remote management, it is possible to enable Telnet, SSH, and ASDM access via HTTPS.

To identify an inside client at IP address 192.168.1.10 that is allowed to connect to the ASA using Telnet, SSH, and ASDM via HTTPS, perform from global configuration mode the configuration steps shown in Example 7-2. Although HTTPS is enabled as part of the factory default, it is included here for completeness.

Example 7-2   ASA Remote Management Access

```
ciscoasa(config)# password cisco12345
ciscoasa(config)# telnet 192.168.1.10 255.255.255.255 inside
ciscoasa(config)# crypto key generate rsa modulus 1024
ciscoasa(config)# ssh 192.168.1.10 255.255.255.255 inside
ciscoasa(config)# username admin password adminpass encrypted privilege 15
```

```
ciscoasa(config)# aaa authentication ssh console LOCAL
ciscoasa(config)# http server enable
ciscoasa(config)# http 192.168.1.10 255.255.255.255 inside
ciscoasa(config)# aaa authentication http console LOCAL
```

In this example, the cisco12345 password will be used for Telnet connections, whereas the AAA local database will be used for SSH and ASDM connections via HTTPS. A 1024–bit RSA key is generated for encrypting SSH and HTTPS traffic. The admin user has been assigned a privilege level of 15, and the password (adminpass) will be encrypted in the running-config.

Video: Configuring ASA Management Access

Refer to the Digital Study Guide to view this video.

ASA Interfaces

To make an ASA operational, you must configure, at minimum, basic interface configuration parameters. These include IP address, interface name, and security levels. Also, the interface must be enabled from its initial shutdown state, unless you are using interfaces already enabled thanks to the factory default configuration.

In the Cisco ASA, default access control is based on interface security levels. Each interface must have a security level from 0 (lowest) to 100 (highest). For example, you should assign your most secure network, such as the inside host network, to level 100, while the outside network connected to the Internet can be level 0. Other networks, such as DMZs, can be assigned a level in between. You can assign multiple interfaces to the same security level.

Security levels define the level of trustworthiness of interfaces. The higher the level, the more trusted the interface. The specific values are not really important, but the relationship between the values is. Traffic flows are defined as inbound or outbound like this:

- Inbound traffic travels from a less trusted interface to a more trusted interface. That is, from a lower security level to a higher security level. For example, outside to inside.

- Outbound traffic travels from a more trusted interface to a less trusted interface. That is, from a higher security level to a lower security level. For example, inside to outside.

The security level controls network access. By default, there is an implicit permit for connections from a higher-security-level interface to a lower-security-level interface (outbound). Hosts on the higher-security-level interface can initiate connections to any host on a lower-security-level interface. Also by default, there is an implicit deny for connections from a lower-security-level interface to a higher-security-level interface (inbound). Hosts on a lower-security-level interface are not allowed to initiate connections to a host on a higher-security-level interface. This default behavior can be overridden by applying an access list to an interface.

Figure 7-2 illustrates an example of security levels in action. The traffic flows from Inside to DMZ and from Inside to Outside are permitted by default, because they go from more trusted to less trusted interfaces. In a real network, this means that internal users on the inside interface can access resources on the DMZ. They can also initiate connections to the Internet.

Figure 7-2   Cisco ASA Traffic Flow

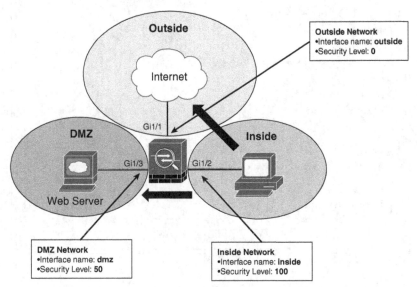

By the same token, traffic that is sourced on the outside network, originating from the Internet and going into either the DMZ or the inside network, is denied by default. In addition, traffic sourced from the DMZ and going to the inside network is denied by default. Stateful inspection allows return traffic from the lower-security-level interfaces for any connections that originated from the higher-security-level interface.

Example 7-3 shows the CLI configuration of interface GigabitEthernet1/3, which will be used for DMZ services on the ASA in Figure 7-2. The interface is configured with an IP address of 172.16.1.1/24 and a security level of 50, and is given the name dmz.

Example 7-3   ASA DMZ Interface Configuration

```
ciscoasa(config)# interface gigabitethernet1/3
ciscoasa(config)# no shutdown
ciscoasa(config)# nameif dmz
ciscoasa(config)# security-level 50
ciscoasa(config)# ip address  172.16.1.1 255.255.255.0
```

Figure 7-3 shows the same configuration being done instead with ASDM (v7.4).

Figure 7-3   ASA ASDM DMZ Interface Configuration

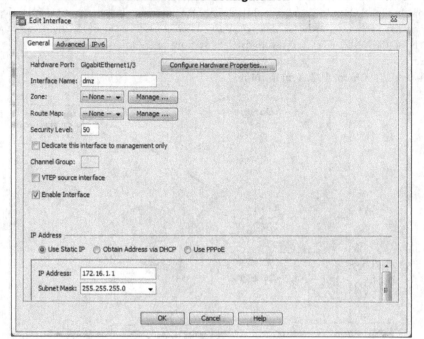

ASA Access Rules

The ASA provides the administrator with a rich set of access control methods that can tightly control access between networks. This section discusses the most fundamental of these controls: interface access rules that enforce a basic Layer 3 and Layer 4 policy.

Interface access rules are a per-interface ordered list of permit and deny rules, evaluated sequentially from the top down.

When deploying ASA appliances, your access policy is made up of one or more access rules per interface and, optionally, a set of global access rules that affects all interfaces. An access rule permits or denies sessions. The determination of whether to permit or deny a session can be based on the protocol, a source and destination IP address or network, and optionally the source and destination ports.

The order of rules is important. When the ASA decides whether to permit or deny a session, the appliance tests the initial packet against each rule in the order in which the rules are listed. After a match is found, no more rules are checked.

There is an implicit deny-all rule at the end of the global access rule list. The global access rule list is appended to the end of interface access rule lists.

For all statefully managed protocols and applications, the ASA interface access rules only need to permit the initial packet per session. The state table is used to provide access control for subsequent packets that are associated with the session.

Applying interface access control lists (ACLs) on security appliance interfaces is optional. If you do not apply interface access rules to a specific interface, the appliance applies a default access policy:

- All outbound (i.e., to lower-security-level interfaces) connections for hosts on that interface are permitted.

- All inbound (i.e., to higher-security-level interfaces) connections for hosts on that interface are denied.

ACLs that permit traffic from a lower-security-level interface to a higher-security-level interface reference the "real" (nontranslated) IP address instead of the "mapped" (translated) IP address of the inside hosts.

You can apply interface access rules on the input or output direction of the ASA interface. You can optionally apply a global access rule.

Interface access rules that you apply inbound on the interface control the connections that the security appliance accepts from hosts on that interface. Interface access rules that are applied outbound on the interface control the connections that are forwarded to hosts on that interface. The global access rule, if configured, applies to all traffic that does not match any interface access rules.

To configure or view access rules within ASDM, choose **Configuration > Firewall > Access Rules**. Figure 7-4 shows the default view of the Access Rules table on an ASA that does not have any explicit interface access rules or any explicit global access rules configured. With no explicit rules configured, the security appliance permits all connections that arrive to an interface, if these connections are routed to interfaces with lower security levels.

Figure 7-4   ASA ASDM Access Rules Table

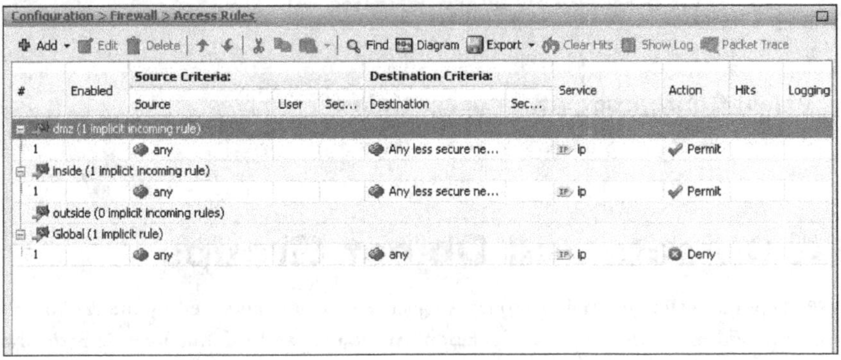

To add and apply a specific access rule to an interface, click the **Add** button to open the Add Access Rule window, shown in Figure 7-5. In this case, the inside network 192.168.1.0/24 is being permitted HTTP access to an external server at 209.165.201.10.

Figure 7-5   ASA ASDM Add Access Rule Window

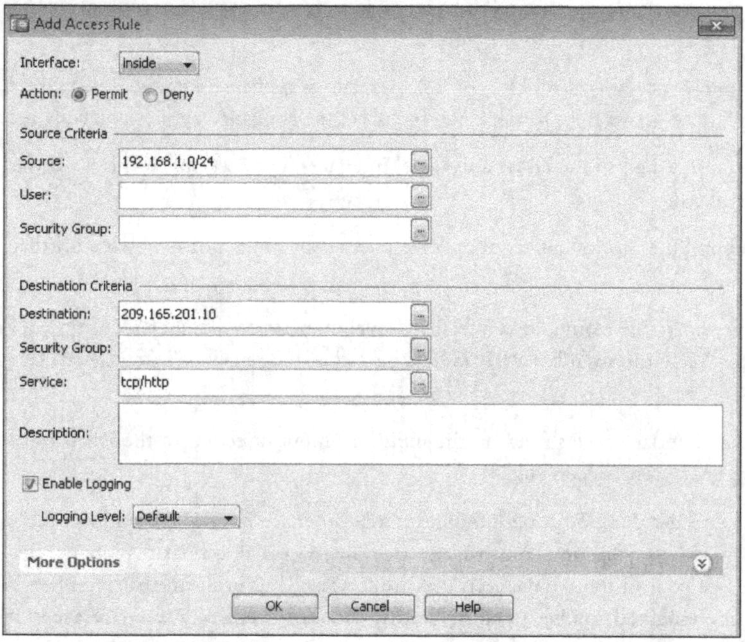

Add Access Rule

Interface: inside ▾
Action: ◉ Permit ○ Deny

Source Criteria

Source: 192.168.1.0/24
User:
Security Group:

Destination Criteria

Destination: 209.165.201.10
Security Group:
Service: tcp/http

Description:

☑ Enable Logging
    Logging Level: Default ▾

More Options   ⊗

OK   Cancel   Help

Example 7-4 shows the equivalent CLI commands generated by the ASDM. Notice that the ASA access rule syntax is similar to an ACL on a Cisco IOS router.

Example 7-4   ASA CLI Access Rule Commands

```
access-list inside_access_in line 1 extended permit tcp 192.168.1.0 255.255.255.0
  host 209.165.201.10 eq http
access-group inside_access_in in interface inside
```

Video: Configuring ASA Access Rules

Refer to the Digital Study Guide to view this video.

ASA Objects and Object Groups

The ASA supports objects and object groups. Objects are created and used by the ASA in place of an inline IP address in any given configuration. An object can be defined with a particular IP address, an entire subnet, a range of addresses, a protocol, or a specific port or range of ports. The object can then be reused in several configurations.

The advantage of this feature is that when an object is modified, the change is automatically applied to all rules that use the specified object. Therefore, using objects makes it easy to maintain configurations.

Objects can be attached or detached from one or more object groups when needed, ensuring that the objects are not duplicated, but can be reused wherever needed. These objects can be used in NAT (as we saw in detail on Day 10), access lists, and object groups.

There are two types of objects that can be configured:

- **Network object:** Contains a single IP address and subnet mask. Network objects can be of three types: host, subnet, or range.

- **Service object:** Contains a protocol and optional source and/or destination port.

The ASA supports various types of object groups:

- **Network:** A network-based object group specifies a list of IP host, subnet, or network addresses.

- **Service:** A service-based object group is used to group TCP, UDP, or TCP and UDP ports into an object. The ASA enables the creation of a service object group that can contain a mix of TCP services, UDP services, ICMP-type services, and any protocol, such as ESP, GRE, and TCP.

- **Security:** A security object group can be used in features that support Cisco TrustSec by including the group in an extended ACL, which in turn can be used in an access rule.

- **User:** Both locally created and imported Active Directory user groups can be defined for use in features that support the Identity Firewall.

- **ICMP-type:** The ICMP protocol uses unique types to send control messages (RFC 792). The ICMP-type object group can group the necessary types required to meet an organization's security needs, such as to create an object group called ECHO to group echo and echo-reply.

Network object and network object group configuration can be accessed by following the ASDM menu path **Configuration > Firewall > Objects > Network Objects/Groups** and clicking **Add**, as shown in Figure 7-6.

Figure 7-6   ASA ASDM Network Object/Object Groups Window Add Menu

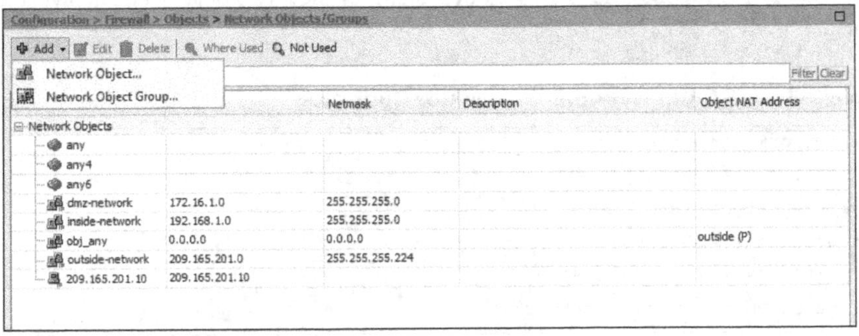

Figure 7-7 shows the creation of an object for Admin_host1 at IP address 192.168.1.10, and Figure 7-8 shows the creation of an object for the inside network using 192.168.1.0/24.

Figure 7-7   ASA ASDM Admin Host Network Object Creation

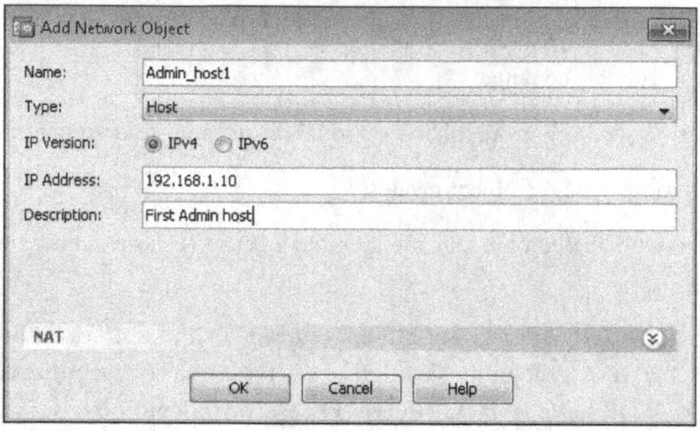

Figure 7-8   ASA ASDM Inside Network Object Creation

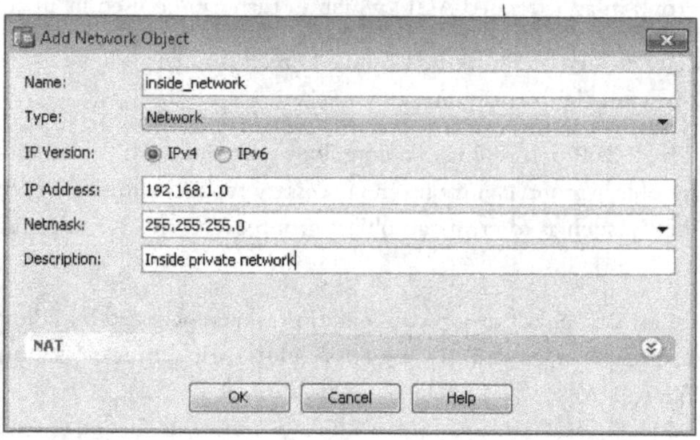

Example 7-5 shows the commands generated by ASDM for these two objects after applying the configuration to the ASA.

Example 7-5   ASA CLI Network Object Configuration

```
object network Admin_host1
 host 192.168.1.10
 description First Admin host
object network inside_network
 subnet 192.168.1.0 255.255.255.0
 description Inside private network
```

To create an object group, let's now assume that there are two Admin hosts, Admin_host1 at address 192.168.1.10 and Admin_host2 at address 192.168.1.11. Figure 7-9 shows the Add Network Object Group window where you can enter the object group name, description, and assign group members. In this case, an object group called Admin_hosts is configured. Selecting an existing object on the left and clicking **Add** allows you to assign the group members.

Figure 7-9   ASA ASDM Add Network Object Group Window

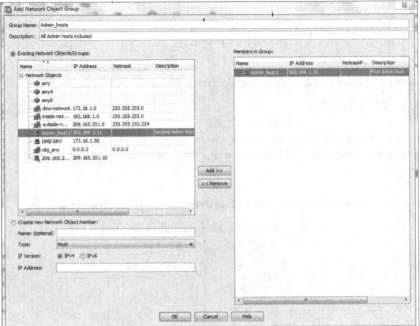

Example 7-6 shows the commands generated by ASDM for this object group after applying the configuration to the ASA.

Example 7-6   ASA CLI Network Object Group Configuration

```
object-group network Admin_hosts
 description All Admin hosts included
 network-object object Admin_host1
 network-object object Admin_host2
```

Figure 7-10 confirms that a new object group called Admin_hosts has been defined and includes Admin_host1 and Admin_host2.

Figure 7-10   New Object Group in ASA ASDM Network Objects/Groups Window

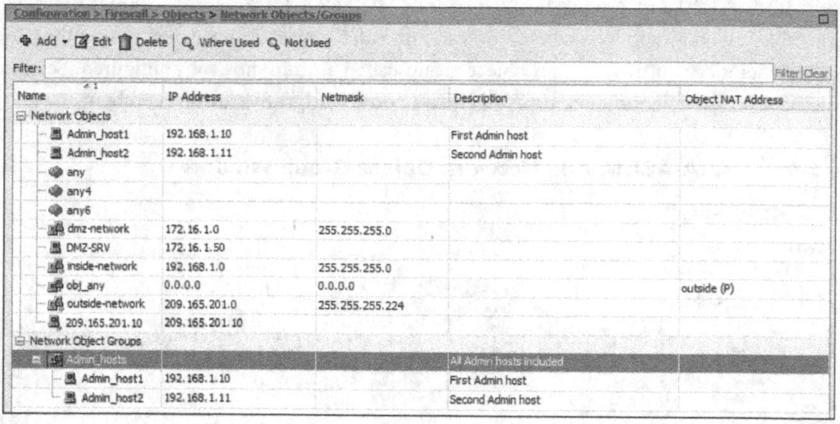

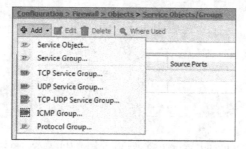

Service object and service group configuration can be accessed by following the ASDM menu path **Configuration > Firewall > Objects > Service Objects/Groups** and clicking **Add**, as shown in Figure 7-11.

Figure 7-11   ASA ASDM Service Objects/Groups Window Add Menu

Notice in Figure 7-11 that there are seven types of service groups that can be created. The most generic and flexible of these is the IP service group. You can group any service into an IP service group. Figure 7-12 shows the creation of an IP service group called Web_access that has TCP/HTTP, TCP/HTTPS, and UDP/DNS services added as group members.

Figure 7-12 ASA ASDM Add Service Group Window

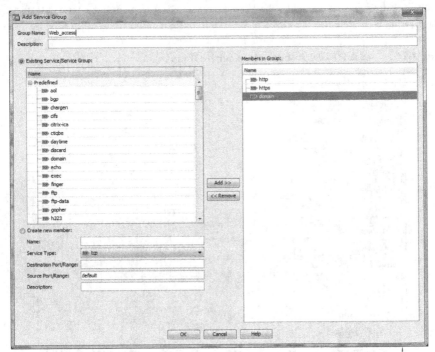

Example 7-7 shows the commands generated by ASDM for this service group after applying the configuration to the ASA.

Example 7-7 ASA CLI Service Group Configuration

```
object-group service Web_access
 service-object tcp destination eq http
 service-object tcp destination eq https
 service-object udp destination eq domain
```

Figure 7-13 confirms that the new service group has been created and will inspect traffic matching the HTTP, HTTPS, and DNS protocols.

Figure 7-13 ASA ASDM Service Group Verification

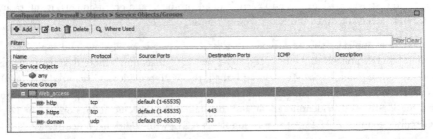

All these newly created objects, object groups, and service groups can now be used when defining firewall access rules. For example, the Web_access service group could be applied to the inside interface for traffic destined to the DMZ server. This configuration can be seen in Figure 7-14.

Figure 7-14   ASA ASDM Access Rule with Objects

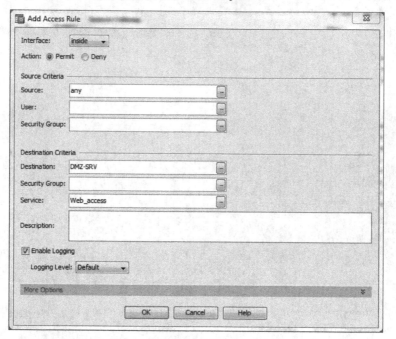

Video: Configuring ASA Network and Service Objects and Object Groups

Refer to the Digital Study Guide to view this video.

ASA Modular Policy Framework

Earlier today we covered interface ACLs and how you can use them to control access through an ASA. With ACLs alone, packets are permitted or denied based on the information that can be found in the packet headers. Although that approach does offer granular control over things such as source and destination addresses and Layers 3 and 4 protocols and port numbers, it still treats all types of traffic identically once the packets are permitted or denied.

A robust security appliance should also be able to identify specific traffic flows and apply the appropriate security policies to them. Fortunately, the ASA offers much more flexibility through its Modular Policy Framework (MPF). In a nutshell, the MPF provides an organized and scalable means of defining inspection policies for network traffic flows. With the MPF feature, you can define a set of policies that identifies traffic and then takes some specific actions on it. The MPF doesn't replace the use of ACLs—it simply augments ACLs with additional functionality.

Although the MPF syntax is similar to the Cisco Integrated Services Router (ISR) IOS Modular QoS CLI (MQC) syntax or the Cisco Common Classification Policy Language (C3PL) syntax, the configurable parameters differ. The ASA platform provides more configurable actions as compared to the Cisco IOS Zone-Based Policy Firewall (ZPF) on a Cisco ISR. The ASA supports Layer 5 to Layer 7 inspections using a richer set of criteria for application-specific parameters. For instance, the ASA MPF feature can be used to match HTTP URLs and request methods, prevent users from surfing to specific sites during specific times, or even prevent users from downloading music (MP3) and video files via HTTP/FTP or HTTPS/SFTP.

Cisco MPF consists of the following main components, which are similar to the three components for an IOS ZPF (covered on Day 9):

- **Class map:** A class map is a basic Cisco MPF object that is used to identify and group a set of particular traffic flows into a traffic class. A traffic flow is generally an OSI Layer 3 to Layer 7 network session between endpoints that is used by a specific application.

- **Policy map:** You use a policy map to associate one or more actions with a class of traffic for one or more classes. To associate an action with a specific traffic class, you would create a policy map, specify a traffic class in the policy map, and associate an action with this specific class of traffic. You can create policy maps for OSI Layers 3 to 7, which define actions that are applied to traffic classes for these layers.

- **Service policy:** You use a service policy to activate policies by specifying where policy maps should classify and apply actions to traffic. A service policy activates a policy map either on a specific Cisco ASA security appliance interface or globally on all appliance interfaces.

By default, the ASA configuration includes a policy that matches all default application inspection traffic and applies inspection to the traffic on all interfaces (a global policy). Default application inspection traffic includes traffic to the default ports for each protocol. Example 7-8 shows the default inspection policy on an ASA.

Example 7-8   ASA Default Inspection Policy

```
class-map inspection_default
 match default-inspection-traffic
policy-map global_policy
 class inspection_default
  inspect dns preset_dns_map
  inspect ftp
  inspect h323 h225 _default_h323_map
  inspect h323 ras _default_h323_map
  inspect ip-options _default_ip_options_map
  inspect netbios
  inspect rsh
  inspect rtsp
  inspect skinny
  inspect esmtp _default_esmtp_map
  inspect sqlnet
```

```
inspect sunrpc
inspect tftp
inspect sip
inspect xdmcp
service-policy global_policy global
```

The configuration includes a default traffic class that the ASA uses in the default global policy called Default Inspection Traffic; it matches the default inspection traffic. This class, which is used in the default global policy, is a special shortcut to match the default ports for all inspections. When used in a policy, this class ensures that the correct inspection is applied to each packet based on the destination port of the traffic. Policies can be applied per interface or globally. If defining a per-interface policy, classification and actions are applied in both directions. If defining a global policy, classification and actions are applied to all interfaces in the inbound direction.

To configure or view the Cisco MPF within ASDM, choose **Configuration > Firewall > Service Policy Rules**. Figure 7-15 shows the default global policy on the ASA.

Figure 7-15   ASA ASDM Service Policy Rules Window

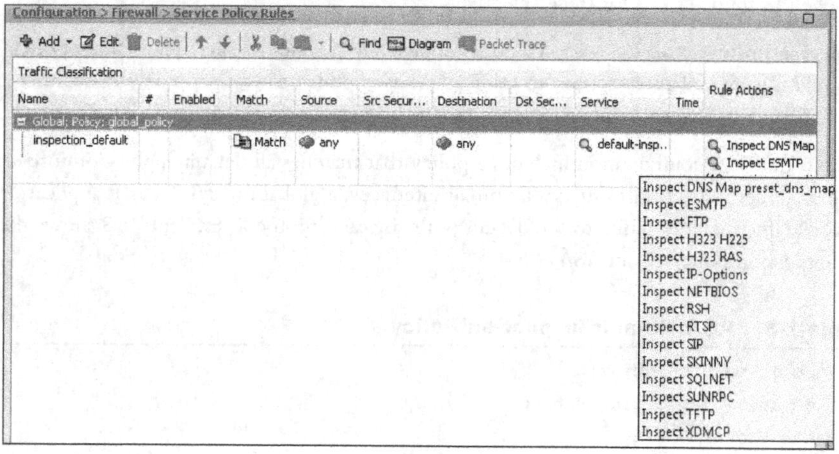

Notice in Figure 7-15 that the policy map is named global_policy and is applied globally. Also notice that the class map is called inspection_default and that the default-inspection-traffic service has been applied to the class map for any traffic. Finally, by hovering over the Rules Actions column, all 15 default inspections can be viewed.

Usually, to configure Cisco MPF, you must first configure a class map to classify traffic, then define an action to take on the matched traffic flow in a policy map, then apply the policy with a service policy. However, if you use the ASDM to configure Cisco MPF software-based policies, there are two details to keep in mind:

- MPF policies are called service policy rules in Cisco ASDM.

- The order in which the MPF components are created is different compared to when the configuration is done using the CLI.

To create a policy for Layers 3 and 4 using Cisco ASDM, the following tasks must be performed:

- Create a new service policy rule or edit an existing one.

- Identify which traffic to match (class map).

- Apply actions to the traffic (policy map).

From the Service Policy Rules window, clicking the Add button brings up a menu from which the Add Service Policy Rule option can be selected to create a new Cisco MPF policy on the ASA.

Another option is to edit the global policy to allow inspection of other protocols. For example, the default global policy does not inspect ICMP. Without inspection, the ASA does not track outbound ICMP requests in the state table, and hence it does not expect or allow an inbound ICMP echo reply. If an inside user pings an outside resource, the echo replies are dropped as they arrive at the outside interface. For this scenario, we will use ASDM to edit the default service policy rule to allow for ICMP inspection, which will resolve the ping issue for our inside users.

Select the **inspection_default** row in the Service Policy Rules window (see Figure 7-15) and click the **Edit** button. This opens the Edit Service Policy Rule window, shown in Figure 7-16. Notice that there are three tabs in the window. The window allows the definition of a class map and the actions that the policy map will take upon traffic that is matched by the class map. The Traffic Classification tab specifies the class map currently in use (inspection_default), the Default Inspections tab confirms which protocols and port numbers are associated with which applications by default, and the Rule Actions tab allows for further protocol inspection. Figure 7-16 shows that ICMP has been checked in the Protocol Inspection subtab of the Rule Actions tab in the Edit Service Policy Rule window.

Figure 7-16   ASA ASDM Rule Actions with ICMP Selected

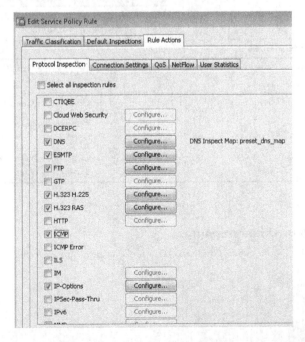

Clicking **OK** and then **Apply** sends the commands in Example 7-9 to the ASA.

Example 7-9   ASA CLI MPF Commands

```
policy-map global_policy
 class inspection_default
  inspect icmp
```

Activity: Match the ASA MPF Concept with Its Definitionv

Refer to the Digital Study Guide to complete this activity.

Video: Configuring ASA Modular Policy Framework

Refer to the Digital Study Guide to view this video.

Study Resources

For today's exam topics, refer to the following resources for more study.

Resource	Location	Topic
Primary Resources		
CCNA Security Official Cert Guide	16	Configuring Basic Firewall Policies on Cisco ASA
CCNA Security (Networking Academy Curriculum)	9	Implementing the Cisco Adaptive Security Appliance
	10	Advanced Cisco Adaptive Security Appliance
Supplemental Resources		
CCNA Security Complete Video Course	11	Configuring Basic Firewall Policies on Cisco ASA
CCNA Security Portable Command Guide	20	Configuring Cisco ASA Basic Settings
	21	Configuring Cisco ASA Advanced Settings
Cisco ASA (3rd ed.)	8	Controlling Network Access: The Traditional Way

Check Your Understanding

Refer to the Digital Study Guide to take a ten-question quiz covering the content of this day.

IDS/IPS Concepts

CCNA Security 210-260 IINS Exam Topics

- 6.1.a Network-based IPS vs. host-based IPS

- 6.1.b Modes of deployment (inline, promiscuous - SPAN, tap)

- 6.1.c Placement (positioning of the IPS within the network)

- 6.1.d False positives, false negatives, true positives, true negatives

Key Topics

Today we will review the concepts behind intrusion detection and protection. We will look at the difference between an intrusion detection system (IDS) and an intrusion prevention system (IPS), as well as compare a network-based IPS and a host-based IPS. We will also discuss the different network deployments options available for IPS sensors. Finally, we will define some of the common terminology related to IPS technologies.

IDS vs. IPS

Intrusion detection/prevention sensors are systems that detect activity that can compromise the confidentiality, integrity, and availability of information resources, processing, or systems. Intrusions can come in many forms. Various technologies have been developed to detect intrusions. The first technology that was developed, IDS, had sensing capabilities but little capability to take action upon what it detected. Traditionally, IDSs were implemented to passively monitor the traffic on a network. An IDS-enabled sensor receives copies of the traffic stream and analyzes this traffic rather than the actual forwarded packets. Working offline, it compares the captured traffic stream with known malicious signatures, similar to software that checks for viruses. Although the traffic is monitored and perhaps reported, no action is taken on packets by the IDS. This offline IDS implementation is referred to as *promiscuous* or *passive mode*.

An IPS works inline in the data stream to provide protection from malicious attacks in real time. This is called *inline mode*. Unlike an IDS, an IPS does not allow packets to enter the trusted side of the network if they are anomalous. An IPS has the ability to analyze traffic from the data link layer to the application layer. For example, an IPS can

- Analyze the traffic that controls Layer 2 to Layer 3 mappings, such as ARP and DHCP

- Verify that the rules of networking protocols such as IP, TCP, UDP, and ICMP are followed

- Analyze the payload of application traffic to identify things such as network attacks, the presence of malware, and server misconfigurations

Figure 6-1 shows a sensor deployed in IDS mode and a sensor deployed in IPS mode.

Figure 6-1   IDS and IPS Operational Differences

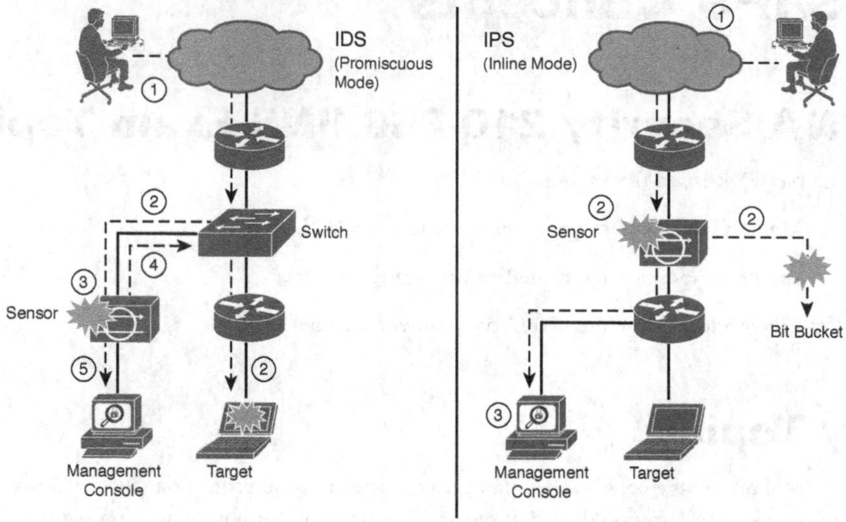

The following are the steps that occur when an attack is launched in an environment monitored by an IDS:

1. An attack is launched on a network that has a sensor deployed in IDS mode.

2. The switch sends copies of all packets to the IDS sensor (configured in promiscuous mode, which is explained later in this section) to analyze the packets. At the same time, the target machine experiences the malicious attack.

3. The IDS sensor, using a signature, matches the malicious traffic to the signature.

4. The IDS sensor sends to the switch a command to deny access to the malicious traffic.

5. The IDS sends an alarm to a management console for logging and other management purposes.

The following are the steps that occur when an attack is launched in an environment monitored by an IPS:

1. An attack is launched on a network that has a sensor deployed in IPS mode (configured in inline mode, which is explained later in this section).

2. The IPS sensor analyzes the packets as soon as they come into the IPS sensor interface. The IPS sensor, using signatures, matches the malicious traffic to the signature and the attack is stopped immediately. Traffic in violation of policy can be dropped by an IPS sensor.

3. The IPS sensor can send an alarm to a management console for logging and other management purposes.

NOTE: The term *management console*, as seen in Figure 6-1, refers to a separate workstation equipped with software to configure, monitor, and report on events. We will discuss this type of software on Day 5.

Figure 6-2 shows a common IPS deployment, in which the Cisco ASA controls access between the corporate network and the Internet, based on source and destination IP addresses and ports, while the FirePOWER IPS appliance controls access based on packet payload.

Figure 6-2   ASA and IPS Deployment

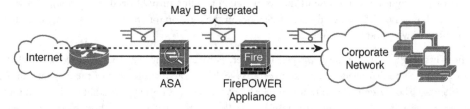

IPS technology is deployed in a sensor, which can be described as one of the following:

- An appliance that is specifically designed to provide dedicated IPS services (as seen in Figure 6-2).

- A module that is installed in another network device, such as an ASA, a switch, or a router. The ASA 5506-X with FirePOWER is an example of this type of deployment.

When intrusion detection technology was first conceived, two fundamentally different strategies were used:

- **Anomaly detection:** This type of technology generally learns patterns of normal network activity and, over time, produces a baseline profile for a given network. Sensors detect suspicious activity by evaluating patterns of activity that deviate from this baseline.

- **Rule-based detection:** Attackers use various techniques to invade and compromise systems. Many techniques are directed at known weaknesses in operating systems, applications, or protocols. Various remote surveillance techniques are also frequently used. Some surveillance and attack methods have known patterns by which the method can be identified. Malicious activity detectors typically analyze live network traffic using a database of rules to determine whether suspicious activity is occurring.

Modern IPS systems combine anomaly detection and rule-based detection, as well as other newer and sophisticated technologies such as reputation, context awareness, event correlation, and cloud-based services to ensure network protection.

Host-based vs. Network-based IPS

There are two types of IPS: network-based IPS and host-based IPS. Traditionally, a host-based IPS relied on agents that were placed on crucial systems in the enterprise. The agents monitored various aspects of the host operation for signs of suspicious activity. The agents would report detections to a central management console or write event activity to system logs.

A more modern approach is to position the IPS processing in the cloud and place a lightweight connector on the host to access the cloud-based protection. This architecture scales much more effectively, allowing the protection of all systems on the network.

A host-based IPS can detect intrusions that utilize encrypted communications. A network-based IPS does not normally have visibility into encrypted traffic streams, but a host-based IPS can analyze activities within the host operating system after traffic is received and decrypted and before traffic is sent and encrypted. A host-based IPS is well suited for detection of activity that does not generate network traffic. For example, a host-based IPS is likely to detect activity such as policy violations or physical compromise of the system, such as when unauthorized users attempt local access. A host-based IPS can easily detect changes in the integrity of crucial files by comparing file hashes to known-good hash profiles.

A host-based IPS has some disadvantages, however. For example, it requires agents to be installed on every machine that needs to be monitored. As such, remote management of these agents can be a challenge. Also, system administrators might be concerned with placing an additional processing burden on heavily utilized systems or simpler mobile devices. Finally, certain host-based IPS agents can present the user with pop-up messages, forcing the user to actively interact with the client software. This could detract from the overall user experience, resulting in users either disabling the agent (if they have the administrative rights) or calling technical support.

IPS Deployment Options

There are several options for deploying a network sensor in promiscuous or passive mode. One of the most common methods is to configure the Switched Port Analyzer (SPAN) feature on a Cisco Catalyst switch and connect the IPS sensor to the SPAN destination port. The IPS sensor will then see copies of all frames that match the SPAN capture configuration, as shown in the IDS scenario in Figure 6-1. One limitation of a SPAN solution is that the SPAN destination port may become oversubscribed. A solution is to use a network tap. A network tap is inserted directly between two devices. It provides full-duplex connectivity between the two devices, and allows the IDS to literally tap into the traffic flow. Figure 6-3 shows where a network tap would be deployed.

Figure 6-3   IDS with Network Tap

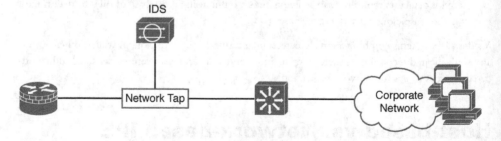

There are many different options for deploying sensors inline. If the traffic must traverse the sensor in the data forwarding path, the deployment is considered to be inline. For example, the sensor can be placed between a router and a switch, or between a pair of routers, or between a pair of switches. Traffic that travels between the two devices must traverse the sensor, as depicted in the IPS scenario in Figure 6-1.

The sensor can also be deployed as a software module in an ASA. Although the module is embedded within the ASA, the module is a separate entity with its own operating system and configuration. A policy can be configured to send traffic traversing the ASA to the FirePOWER module for deep IPS services. If the policy is configured with the monitor-only option, traffic is mirrored to the module for IPS services but the module is not in the forwarding path. On the other hand, if the monitor-only option is not specified, the module is in the forwarding path. The ASA forwards packets to the module, where the module may drop malicious traffic itself, preventing it from being forwarded by the ASA.

The policy on the ASA can also be configured to be fail-open or fail-closed. This setting determines what the ASA does with traffic that it is configured to send to the FirePOWER module when the module itself is down. With fail-open, the ASA continues to process the traffic itself and can still forward the traffic toward its destination. With fail-closed, the ASA drops the traffic that it is configured to send to the FirePOWER module. Fail-closed is configured in situations where network security is more important than network availability.

IPS Placement

An argument can be made for the use of IPS at any position in a network, but deploying IPS everywhere in the network is not feasible. Placement decisions must be made, and each scenario will have different requirements that influence the decisions. Figure 6-4 shows a network with three security zones: inside, outside, and DMZ. A sensor could be placed inline between the firewall and any of the zones.

Figure 6-4   IPS Placement

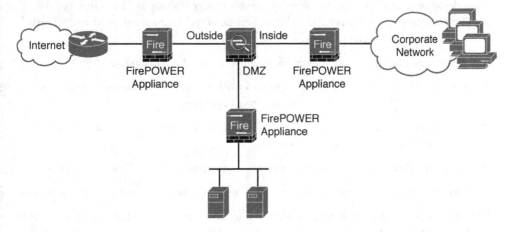

Consider the following information about this scenario to help determine where to place a sensor within your network:

- **Outside:** At first impression, the outside network may seem to be the best location for the sensor. The scariest threats are on the Internet, so it could seem reasonable to use the IPS to protect the network from the Internet. However, the ASA security appliance will provide substantial threat protection from the Internet. Furthermore, with the sensor on the outside network, the number of alarms will be high, and the alarms can be considered false positives if the ASA security appliance would have provided protection anyway.

- **DMZ:** DMZ servers have services that are exposed directly to the Internet. Any vulnerabilities in the service applications or configurations can be exploited. Certainly, IPS can play a security role on the DMZ. However, the data that is stored on DMZ systems is likely to be much less critical than data stored on internal servers. Because these systems are hardened by and managed by IT professionals, the likelihood of exposed vulnerabilities should be relatively low, and compromised systems should be recognized relatively quickly.

- **Inside:** The inside systems are best protected by the firewall, but they are typically run by users who lack experience in IT or information security. Users may unintentionally bring malware into the internal network, where the most critical and confidential data is stored. A compromised client PC is likely to have access to confidential information stored on internal servers. If you can place an IPS sensor in only one place, placing the sensor just inside the firewall may be the best option.

IPS Terminology

When deployed in real environments, security controls such as IPS may produce erroneous decisions, either because of their misconfiguration or because of the environment, in which legitimate activity may resemble malicious activity, and vice versa.

All decisions made by security controls can be classified as one of the following:

- **True positive:** The security control, such as an IPS sensor, acted as a consequence of malicious activity. This represents normal and optimal operation.

- **True negative:** The security control has not acted, because there was no malicious activity. This represents normal and optimal operation.

- **False positive:** The security control acted as a consequence of normal traffic or activity.

- **False negative:** The security control has not acted, even though there was malicious activity.

Positive or negative refers to whether the alarm was triggered. Positive designates an alarm has been triggered, and negative designates an alarm has not been triggered. True or false is more complex; this answers the question, "Was the result to trigger (or not trigger) the alarm the right decision?" If the action taken by the sensor was right, then the result is true, and if the sensor took the wrong decision, the result is false.

Video: IDS and IPS Concepts

Refer to the Digital Study Guide to view this video.

Activity: Match the IDS and IPS Terminology to Its Definition

Refer to the Digital Study Guide to complete this activity.

Study Resources

For today's exam topics, refer to the following resources for more study.

Resource	Location	Topic
Primary Resources		
CCNA Security Official Cert Guide	17	Cisco IDS/IPS Fundamentals
CCNA Security (Networking Academy Curriculum)	5	Implementing Intrusion Prevention
Supplemental Resources		
CCNA Security Complete Video Course	12	IPS Fundamentals
CCNA Security Portable Command Guide	13	Configuring Cisco IOS IPS
Cisco ASA (3rd ed.)	17	Implementing Cisco ASA Intrusion Prevention System (IPS)

Check Your Understanding

Refer to the Digital Study Guide to take a ten-question quiz covering the content of this day.

IDS/IPS Technologies

CCNA Security 210-260 IINS Exam Topics

- 6.2.a Rules/signatures

- 6.2.b Detection/signature engines

- 6.2.c Trigger actions/responses (drop, reset, block, alert, monitor/log, shun)

- 6.2.d Blacklist (static and dynamic)

Key Topics

Today we will review the important technological components behind IDS and IPS. We will look at how IDS and IPS sensors detect network threats using signatures, what actions sensors can take against malicious traffic, and how blacklisting can help protect corporate users against websites with a poor reputation rating. We will finish by discussing the advantages of Next-Generation IPS technology, in particular Cisco FirePOWER.

Detection Technologies

Multiple detection technologies are typically used to provide an effective intrusion detection or prevention architecture, including the following:

- **Signature-based IDS/IPS:** A signature-based approach is usually the starting point of an effective intrusion detection architecture. A signature is a set of rules that an IDS and an IPS use to detect typical intrusive activity, such as denial of service (DoS) attacks. Sensors allow you to modify existing signatures and define new ones. A signature-based IDS or IPS sensor looks for specific, predefined patterns (signatures) in network traffic. It compares the network traffic to a database of known attacks, and triggers an alarm or prevents communication if a match is found. The signature can be based on a single packet or a sequence of packets. New attacks that do not match a signature do not result in detection. For this reason, the signature database needs to be constantly updated.

- **Policy-based IDS/IPS:** In policy-based systems, the IDS or IPS sensor is configured based on the network security policy. You must create the policies used in a policy-based IDS or IPS. Any traffic detected outside the policy will generate an alarm or will be dropped. Creating a security policy requires detailed knowledge of the network traffic and is a time-consuming task.

- **Anomaly-based IDS/IPS:** Anomaly-based (or profile-based) signatures typically look for network traffic that deviates from what is seen "normally." The biggest issue with this methodology is that you first must define what normal is. If during the learning phase your network is the victim of an attack (or some other anomalous event takes place) and you fail to identify it, the anomaly-based IPS will interpret that malicious traffic as normal, and no alarm will be triggered the next time this same attack takes place. Some systems have hard-coded definitions of normal traffic patterns.

- **Reputation-based IPS:** A more recent approach to intrusion detection is through the use of reputation-based IPS. This technique uses reputation analysis for various traffic descriptors, such as IP addresses, URLs, Domain Name System (DNS) domains, and others. This typically translates into reputation filters, sometimes known as whitelists or blacklists, that round up a signature-based system by filtering known malicious sources, destinations, or application components. Blacklisting is discussed in more detail in the next section.

Signatures

As explained earlier, a signature is a set of rules that an IDS and an IPS use to detect typical intrusive activity, such as DoS attacks. IPS signatures are dynamically updated and posted to Cisco.com on a regular basis so that customers can access signatures that help protect their network from the latest known network attacks. The updates take the form of signature files, also known as signature packages or simply signature updates. Manual updates are also possible.

Cisco IPS devices use signature engines to load the signature files and scan signatures. Signatures that are contained within the signature packages are managed by various signature engines. The packages typically contain signature definitions for multiple engines.

Signature engines typically correspond to the protocol in which the signature occurs and look for malicious activity in that protocol. Each signature engine provides a common set of signature parameters that can be used to tune the sensitivity, scope, and actions of that particular signature engine, instead of making changes to individual signatures.

Table 5-1 summarizes the types of signature engines available.

Table 5-1   Summary of Types of Signatures

Signature Engine	Description
Atomic	Signatures that examine single packets, for ICMP, TCP, and UDP
Service	Signatures that examine the many services in use on networks and that can be attacked, such as the service HTTP engine
String/multistring	Signatures that use regular expression-based patterns to detect intrusions
Other	Internal engine to handle miscellaneous signatures

Trigger Actions

The distinction between IDS and IPS is based on whether the sensor interacts with traffic passively, limited to detective capabilities, or the sensor interacts with traffic actively, providing protective services. Regarding IDS and IPS, the terms "action" and "response" are used synonymously for the reactions a sensor can be configured to perform in response to suspicious events.

The following terms define passive actions or responses that are commonly available in IDS and IPS technology:

- **Alerts:** Generation of a loggable message upon detection of potentially malicious traffic flows. How alerts are used is dependent on the size and complexity of the deployment. Alerts should always be stored in a database so records can be reviewed later for forensic analysis. They are often sent to real-time event viewers that are monitored by IT staff in a Network Operations Center (NOC). Larger deployments will incorporate the alerts into a Security Information and Event Management (SIEM) system. The term "alarm" is often used interchangeably with "alert."

- **Monitor:** An IDS may react to suspicious events by concentrating more resources on traffic that is associated with a particular host or between a pair of hosts. For example, it may include a packet capture in the data that is logged.

The following terms define active actions or responses that are commonly available in IPS technology only:

- **Drop:** Packets that are determined to have suspicious payload may be dropped by the sensor, preventing the payload from reaching the destination.

- **Reset:** When a suspicious payload is detected with a TCP connection, the sensor may inject TCP resets to cause the offending TCP connection to be terminated.

- **Block:** A reset only functions with TCP. Attacks may be carried out using other protocols, such as UDP and ICMP. Also, it is possible for an attacking system and a compromised host to break the normal rules of TCP and ignore the TCP reset to counter the IPS reaction. Additional protection can be provided by blocking further traffic. A block may be implemented for a particular session, or between a particular pair of hosts, or for all traffic that is associated with a single host.

- **Shun:** Some IPSs have the ability to request that blocking be performed by other devices in the network. In some deployments, this dynamic blocking between security zones within a network is controlled by the SIEM. This action is often referred to as shunning. The term originates from the Cisco ASA security appliance command that is used to initiate the requested block.

Blacklisting

Some of the capabilities or features of an IPS sensor are intended to protect the network before an attack by controlling access to resources, enforcing policies, and generally hardening network devices.

Examples of features that play a role in protecting the network before an attack actually occurs include the following:

- **Blacklisting:** You can blacklist (deny traffic to and from) specific IP addresses that might pose a danger to your network. To help you build blacklists, the IPS can dynamically download, at configurable intervals, a collection of IP addresses that have been determined by the Cisco Collective Security Intelligence team (Talos, http://www.talosintel.com/) to have a poor reputation. Blacklisting will block matching traffic regardless of any other characteristics of the traffic. Entries on a blacklist can be manually defined, created dynamically as a response to a rule violation, and maintained dynamically based on a security intelligence service. The opposite of blacklisting is whitelisting. When whitelists are implemented, matching traffic is permitted, regardless of whether the IP address in question is blacklisted. Blacklisting and whitelisting can be used in various security solutions, including IPS, email security, web security, and firewall.

- **Cisco Advanced Malware Protection (AMP) for Networks:** This network-based component uses FirePOWER-based appliances to detect malware in transit over network connections. It, too, can communicate with the cloud to get instant access to the most current information that the cloud stores about file disposition and known malware. Network-based AMP allows the system to inspect network traffic for malware in several types of files.

Next-Generation IPS with FirePOWER

Cisco Next-Generation IPS (NGIPS) solutions build on typical IPS technologies by providing contextual awareness during an attack to promptly assess threats, and ensure a consistent and appropriate response. Not only does the IPS report the event, but it also provides information about network activity, systems, applications, locations, and people related to the attack.

NGIPS filtering analyzes network traffic in real time, comparing the traffic contents against known threats. Cisco Collective Security Intelligence (Talos) develops signatures that identify threats. Multiple signatures can map to a single threat. New threats and signature sets are updated by default every hour.

With NGIPS, threats are the focus instead of signatures. If a connection or traffic flow matches a threat, the NGIPS can drop the connection to block the threat.

The FirePOWER NGIPS solution also includes Cisco FireSIGHT Management Center, which centrally manages network security and operational functions for Cisco FirePOWER appliances, legacy non-FirePOWER appliances, and virtual appliances. The Cisco FireSIGHT Management Center, which aggregates and correlates the information that is gathered by managed devices, is a separate application that can be hosted on a separate FireSIGHT Management Center appliance or as a virtual appliance running on a VMware server.

Video: IDS and IPS Technologies

Refer to the Digital Study Guide to view this video.

Activity: Compare IPS Alarm Characteristics

Refer to the Digital Study Guide to complete this activity.

Study Resources

For today's exam topics, refer to the following resources for more study.

Resource	Location	Topic
Primary Resources		
CCNA Security Official Cert Guide	17	Cisco IDS/IPS Fundamentals
CCNA Security (Networking Academy Curriculum)	5	Implementing Intrusion Prevention
Supplemental Resources		
CCNA Security Complete Video Course	12	IPS Fundamentals
CCNA Security Portable Command Guide	13	Configuring Cisco IOS IPS
Cisco ASA (3rd ed.)	17	Implementing Cisco ASA Intrusion Prevention System (IPS)

Check Your Understanding

Refer to the Digital Study Guide to take a ten-question quiz covering the content of this day.

Email-based Threat Mitigation

CCNA Security 210-260 IINS Exam Topics

- 7.1.a SPAM filtering, anti-malware filtering, DLP, blacklisting, email encryption

Key Topics

Today we will review the Cisco email-based content security solution called Cisco Email Security Appliance (ESA). We will look at how the ESA is deployed, some of its features and benefits, and how it processes emails.

ESA Overview

Email is a medium through which spyware and viruses can be propagated. Email spam and malicious malware can reduce employee productivity. The Cisco ESA is a type of firewall and threat monitoring appliance for SMTP traffic (TCP port 25).

The Cisco ESA solution delivers the following:

- Fast, comprehensive email protection that can block spam and threats before they hit your network

- Flexible cloud, virtual, and physical deployment options to meet your ever-changing business needs

- Outbound message control through on-device data loss prevention (DLP) and email encryption

The Cisco ESA solution offers simple and fast deployment with few maintenance requirements, low latency, and low operating costs. The solution automatically forwards security updates to the Cisco cloud-based threat intelligence solution. This threat intelligence data is provided by the Cisco ESA every 3 to 5 minutes, providing timely threat defense.

These are the two major threats to your email system:

- A flood of unsolicited and unwanted email, called spam, that wastes your time due to high volume and uses valuable resources such as bandwidth and storage.

- Malicious email, which comes in two basic forms:

  - Embedded attacks, which include viruses and malware that perform actions on the end device when clicked.

  - Targeted or directed attacks, such as phishing attacks, which try to mislead you into releasing sensitive information such as credit card numbers, Social Security numbers, or intellectual property. Phishing attacks might direct you to browse malicious websites that distribute additional malware to computer endpoints.

Cisco ESA uses various mechanisms to filter spam and fight malicious attacks. The goal of the solution is to filter out positively identified spam and quarantine or discard email that has been sent from untrusted or potentially hostile locations. Antivirus scanning is applied to emails and attachments from all servers to remove known malware.

ESA Deployment

Cisco ESA protects the email infrastructure and email users by filtering unsolicited and malicious email before it actually reaches the end user. The ESA can be deployed as either a physical appliance or a virtual appliance. The ESA can also be deployed on-premises or as a cloud-based service. Alternatively, the ESA can be deployed using a hybrid approach and integrated into existing email infrastructures with a high degree of flexibility.

Logically speaking, the ESA acts as a mail transfer agent (MTA) within the email delivery chain. The MTA's job is to transfer the email messages from one computer to another. Since personal computers do not send email between themselves directly, they use a mail client application, such as Microsoft Outlook, that sends email to a mail server, such as a Microsoft Exchange server. The mail server accepts, forwards, delivers, and stores the email messages on behalf of the users. The mail server relays the user emails through the MTA and to the other mail domains.

Cisco generally recommends placing the ESA as close to the firewall as possible. There are two deployment approaches for the security appliance depending on the number of interfaces used:

- **Single physical interface:** The ESA may be deployed with a single physical interface to transfer emails to and from both the Internet and the internal mail servers. In this model, the ESA should be logically placed in the private DMZ network or inside network.

- **Two physical interfaces:** The ESA may be deployed with two physical interfaces, one for email transfer to and from the Internet, and another one for email communications to the internal servers. In this model, the ESA would have one interface connecting to the DMZ and the other interface connecting to the inside network. In this case, the DMZ-based interface would send and receive email to and from the Internet. The inside network interface would be used to deliver email to the internal mail server.

Figure 4-1 shows both deployment models.

Figure 4-1   Cisco ESA Deployment Models

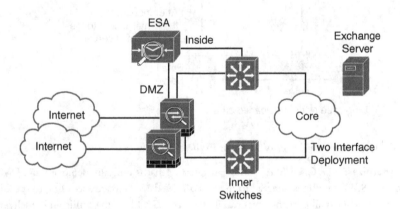

In our scenario, the typical firewall security policy should only allow SMTP traffic to the ESA. The ESA is allowed to send SMTP traffic, as well as HTTP and HTTPS connections, to the Cisco cloud. The Cisco cloud sends security intelligence updates to the ESA.

The ESA is also allowed to make inbound SMTP connections to the corporate mail server, as well as DNS requests to the corporate DNS server. In this deployment, the ESA handles the incoming and outgoing SMTP connections by relaying the outgoing connections to the external mail domains and also by restricting the incoming connections to the internal mail domain.

A normal email exchange in which an organization is using an MTA might look like the message flow that is shown in Figures 4-2 and 4-3.

Figure 4-2   Inbound Email Message Flow

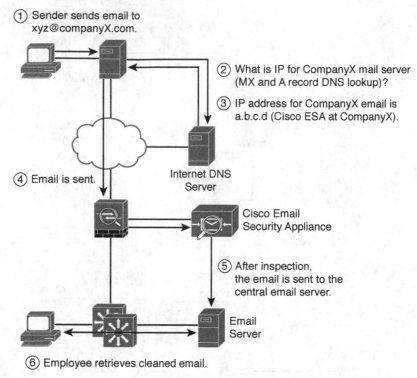

① Sender sends email to
   xyz@companyX.com.

② What is IP for CompanyX mail server
   (MX and A record DNS lookup)?

③ IP address for CompanyX email is
   a.b.c.d (Cisco ESA at CompanyX).

④ Email is sent.

Internet DNS
Server

Cisco Email
Security Appliance

⑤ After inspection,
   the email is sent to the
   central email server.

Email
Server

⑥ Employee retrieves cleaned email.

You can deploy Cisco email security solutions in these three ways:

- **On-premises:** The Cisco ESA is an email gateway that is typically deployed in a DMZ. Incoming SMTP traffic is directed to the Cisco ESA data interface according to specifications set by your mail exchange records. The Cisco ESA filters the traffic and redelivers it to your network mail server. Your mail server also directs outgoing mail to the Cisco ESA data interface, where it is filtered according to outgoing policies and then delivered to external destinations.

- **Virtual:** With Cisco UCS running in a small branch office, it is possible to host the Cisco ESAV with other Cisco products such as the Cisco Web Security Virtual Appliance (WSA). Together, they provide the same level of protection as their hardware equivalents, but save on money and space.

- **Hybrid:** Cloud-based email security for inbound mail, plus on-premises ESA for outbound mail.

Figure 4-3   Outbound Email Message Flow

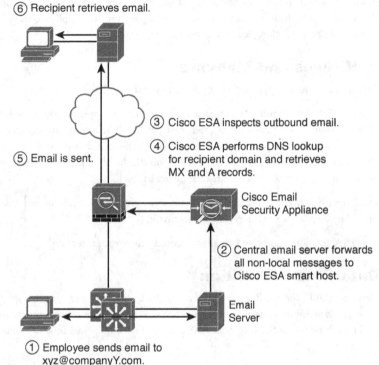

⑥ Recipient retrieves email.

③ Cisco ESA inspects outbound email.

④ Cisco ESA performs DNS lookup for recipient domain and retrieves MX and A records.

⑤ Email is sent.

Cisco Email Security Appliance

② Central email server forwards all non-local messages to Cisco ESA smart host.

Email Server

① Employee sends email to xyz@companyY.com.

ESA Features

The Cisco ESA provides features for all stages of accepting, filtering, and delivering email messages with SMTP. In a typical deployment, an ESA is deployed as the first mail server for email coming from the Internet, and the last mail server on the path out to the Internet. All models of appliance provide the following features.

Filtering Spam

There are two ways to filter spam and combat phishing attacks: (1) reputation-based filtering and (2) context-based filtering:

- **Reputation-Based Filtering:** This type of filtering relies on the likelihood that if a server is a known spam sender, it is more likely that email coming from that server is spam. Similar filters can be applied to emails carrying viruses and other threats. Reputation filters provide the first layer of defense by looking at the source IP address of the email server and comparing it to the reputation data downloaded from Cisco.

- **Context-Based Filtering:** These antispam filters in the appliance inspect the entire mail message, including attachments, analyzing details such as sender identity, message contents, embedded URLs, and email formatting. Using these algorithms, the appliance can identify spam messages without blocking legitimate email.

Fighting Viruses and Malware

The Cisco ESA uses a multilayer approach to fight viruses and malware:

1. The first layer of defense consists of outbreak filters, which the appliance downloads from Cisco. They contain a list of known malicious mail servers. These filters are generated by watching global email traffic patterns and looking for anomalies that are associated with an outbreak. When an email is received from a server on this list, it is kept in quarantine until the antivirus signatures are updated to counter the current threat.

2. The second layer of defense is the use of antivirus signatures to scan quarantined emails, to ensure that they do not carry viruses into the network.

3. The Cisco ESA also scans outbound emails to provide antivirus protection.

Email Data Loss Prevention

Data loss prevention (DLP) for email is content-level scanning of email messages and attachments to detect inappropriate transport of sensitive information. Examples of sensitive content are personal identifiers (credit cards or Social Security numbers) or corporate intellectual property (internal or confidential documents).

Regulatory compliance typically focuses on a few classes of information generally encompassed under the term personally identifiable information (PII): payment card numbers, bank routing numbers, other financial account information, government ID numbers, personal names, addresses, and telephone numbers, and healthcare records. The Cisco ESA DLP features provide rules for identifying these classes of data, or defining your own classes, and taking action on the messages as appropriate. A common policy is to encrypt content that contains sensitive information when that message would otherwise be sent to an external recipient in the clear. Encrypting email content satisfies the requirement that prohibits sending personal information in the clear.

Advanced Malware Protection

Cisco Advanced Malware Protection (AMP) provides malware detection and blocking, continuous analysis, and retrospective alerting to your Cisco email security solution license. AMP uses the vast cloud security intelligence networks of Cisco Talos to give users superior protection across the attack continuum: before, during, and after an attack. Cisco AMP uses a combination of file reputation, file sandboxing, and retrospective file analysis to identify and stop threats across the attack continuum. The features of Cisco AMP include the following:

- **File reputation:** File reputation captures a fingerprint of each file as it traverses the Cisco email security gateway and sends it to the AMP cloud-based intelligence network for a reputation verdict. With these results, you can automatically block malicious files and apply administrator-defined policies.

- **File sandboxing:** File sandboxing enables you to analyze unknown files that are traversing the Cisco email security gateway. A highly secure sandbox environment makes it possible for Cisco AMP to gather precise details about a file's behavior and to combine that data with detailed human and machine analysis to determine the file's threat level. This disposition is then fed into the Cisco Talos (http://www.talosintel.com/) intelligence network and used to dynamically update and expand the AMP cloud data set.

- **File retrospection:** File retrospection solves the problem of malicious files that pass through perimeter defenses but are later deemed a threat. Even the most advanced techniques may fail to identify malware at the perimeter because evasion techniques such as polymorphism, obfuscation, and sleep timers are highly effective at enabling malware to avoid detection. Malicious files simply wait until they are inside the network to do their dirty work.

ESA Mail Processing

SMTP connections and email messages that are handled by the Cisco ESA move from connection acceptance to SMTP conversation, to message acceptance, and then to filtering and delivery, in a step-by-step process that is known as the email security pipeline. The pipeline is important because the fixed order of certain steps dictates configuration and architecture, and the flexibility of other steps means that there is considerable leeway in designing and deploying an email environment that is based on Cisco ESA.

Incoming Mail Processing

Inbound security is provided by the incoming mail policy. Figure 4-4 provides a simplified depiction of the inbound mail pipeline.

Figure 4-4   Inbound Mail Pipeline

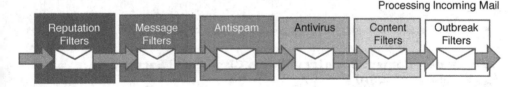

These are the major policies that are represented in Figure 4-4:

- **Threat prevention with reputation filters:** Reputation filtering is the first layer of spam protection, allowing you to control the messages that come through the email gateway that are based on sender trustworthiness as determined by the Cisco SenderBase Network.

- **Policy enforcement with message filters:** Message filters are special rules describing how to process messages and attachments as they are received.

- **Spam detection:** Uses contextual information to determine the email sender's reputation, the message content, the message structure, and the destination website's reputation.

- **Virus detection with Sophos or McAfee Antivirus:** Antivirus provides a virus detection engine that scans files for viruses, Trojan horses, and worms.

- **Content filters:** These filters can be used to filter specific file types or content. Some common reasons for using content filters include filtering attachments, adding disclaimers, and rerouting messages to other systems.

- **Outbreak filters:** Newly released viruses that do not have a published ID can be blocked by stopping files with the infected file's characteristics. This feature provides zero-day protections.

Outgoing Mail Processing

Outgoing email is defined as email sent from a company internal email server to outside receivers (through the Internet). Figure 4-5 shows a depiction of the outbound mail pipeline.

Figure 4-5   Outbound Mail Pipeline

Processing Outgoing Mail

Message Filters → Antispam → Antivirus → Content Filters → Outbreak Filters → RSA DLP Engine

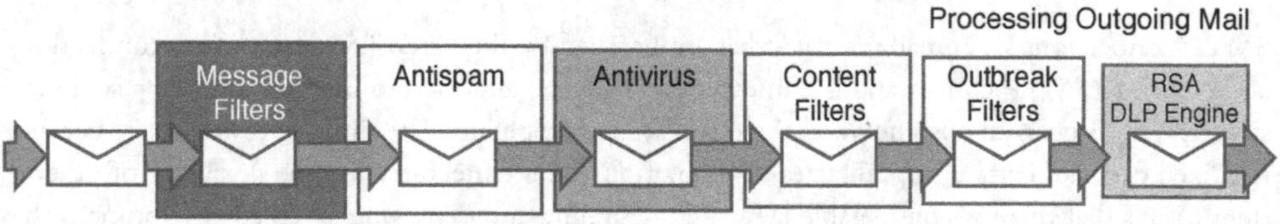

Outbound control is provided by the outgoing mail policy. It differs from the incoming mail processing in these ways:

- The default outgoing mail policy has antispam filters, content filters, and outbreak filters that are disabled by default.

- Provides an additional DLP function to the process to ensure that unsuitable or unauthorized information does not leak out of the company. DLP scanning can only be performed on outgoing messages.

- Reputation filtering is not used for outgoing mail, only for incoming mail.

Video: Content Security with the Cisco Email Security Appliance (ESA)

Refer to the Digital Study Guide to view this video.

Activity: Order the Steps in the ESA Incoming Email Process

Refer to the Digital Study Guide to complete this activity.

Study Resources

For today's exam topics, refer to the following resources for more study.

Resource	Location	Topic
Primary Resources		
CCNA Security Official Cert Guide	18	Mitigation Technology for Email-Based and Web-Based Threats
CCNA Security (Networking Academy Curriculum)	6	Endpoint Security
Supplemental Resources		
CCNA Security Complete Video Course	7	Mitigation Technologies for Email-based and Web-based Threats

Check Your Understanding

Refer to the Digital Study Guide to take a ten-question quiz covering the content of this day.

Web-based Threat Mitigation

CCNA Security 210-260 IINS Exam Topics

- 7.2.a Local and cloud-based web proxies

- 7.2.b Blacklisting, URL filtering, malware scanning, URL categorization, web application filtering, TLS/SSL decryption

Key Topics

Today we will review two web security solutions, the Cisco Web Security Appliance (WSA) and the Cisco Cloud Web Security (CWS) service. We will see how both operate to transparently offer corporate users a more secure web browsing experience.

Cisco WSA

The Cisco WSA is a web proxy that works with other network components to monitor and control outbound requests for web content and scrubs return traffic for unwanted or malicious content. The Cisco WSA is deployed on a network using one or more interfaces that are used to forward requests and responses. Traffic can be directed to the WSA either by using explicit proxies configured on the end host or by using a network protocol such as Web Cache Communication Protocol (WCCP) running on an inline device like the perimeter firewall or router.

Figure 3-1 shows the logical traffic flow using the Cisco WSA:

1. User initiates a web request.

2. The Cisco ASA firewall redirects the request to the Cisco WSA, which checks the request.

3. The Cisco WSA replies with denial if the request violates corporate policy.

4. The Cisco WSA initiates a new connection to the web if the request is acceptable.

5. The web server replies with content that is sent to the Cisco WSA.

6. The Cisco WSA checks content for malicious content and forwards the traffic to the originating user if no issues are found.

Figure 3-1   Cisco WSA Logical Traffic Flow

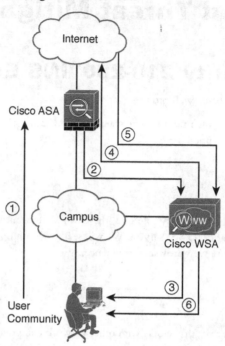

The Cisco WSA can be connected by one interface to the inside network of the Cisco Adaptive Security Appliance (ASA). In the Internet edge design, the Cisco WSA connects to the same LAN switch as the Cisco ASA appliance and on the same VLAN as the inside interface of the ASA appliance. Cisco ASA redirects HTTP and HTTPS connections to the Cisco WSA by using the Web Cache Communication Protocol (WCCP).

The Cisco WSA uses several mechanisms to apply web security and content control, such as the following:

- It begins with basic URL filtering with category-based Cisco web usage controls, which are based on an active database comprising the analysis of sites in 190 countries in over 50 languages. Key features of the Cisco WSA URL filters include the following: 79 predefined URL categories, custom URL categories, and dynamic content analysis.

- Content is also filtered by the reputation database. Cisco Talos updates the reputation database every 5 minutes. These updates contain threat information that is gathered from multiple Internet-based resources, and content reputation information that is obtained from Cisco security appliances of customers who choose to participate in the Cisco SenderBase network.

- If no details of the website or its content are known, the Cisco WSA applies dynamic content analysis to determine the nature of the content in real time and findings are fed back to the SenderBase repository, if the customer has elected to participate in it.

The Cisco WSA secures and controls web traffic by offering multiple layers of malware defense on a single, integrated appliance. These layers of defense include Cisco web reputation filters, multiple antimalware scanning engines, and the Layer 4 Traffic Monitor (L4TM) service, which detects non–port 80 malware activity. The Cisco WSA is also capable of intelligent HTTPS decryption, so that all associated security and access policies can be applied to encrypted traffic.

Key technology features of the Cisco WSA are as follows:

- Acceptable use policy (AUP) enforcement

  - The Cisco WSA URL filters offer the broadest reach and the highest accuracy rate in controlling web content. Cisco WSA URL filters provide coverage and accuracy against web traffic requests.

  - Policy, application, and protocol control are facilitated at a granular level, regardless of the protocol or application flowing through the network perimeter. The L4TM looks for "phone-home" malware activity, while intelligent HTTPS decryption inspects encrypted data for security or AUP violations.

- Multilayer, multivendor malware defense-in-depth

  - The L4TM service scans all 65,535 network ports, effectively stopping malware that attempts to bypass port 80. In addition, the L4TM is able to dynamically add IP addresses of known malware domains to its list of ports and IP addresses to detect and block.

  - The Cisco WSA web reputation filters examine every request that is made by the browser (from the initial HTML request to all subsequent data requests), including live data, which may be fed from different domains.

  - The Cisco WSA antimalware system offers multiple antimalware scanning engines on a single, integrated appliance. This system leverages the Dynamic Vectoring and Streaming (DVS) engine, and verdict engines from Webroot and McAfee, to provide protection against the widest variety of web-based threats.

- Data security enforcement

  - Data security and data loss prevention empower organizations to take quick, easy steps to enforce commonsense data security policies. Examples include preventing engineers from sending design files by webmail, blocking uploads by finance staff of Excel spreadsheets over 100 KB, or preventing posts of content to blogs or social networking sites. These simple data security policies can be created for outbound traffic on HTTP, HTTPS, and FTP.

  - Native FTP protection allows the Cisco WSA to provide complete visibility into FTP usage, enforcing acceptable use and data security policies, and preventing malware infections.

- Comprehensive management and reporting capabilities

  - The Cisco Web Security Manager provides a single, easy-to-understand view of all access and security policies that are configured on the appliance. Administrators manage all web access policies (including URL filtering, time-based policies, reputation filtering, and malware filtering) from a single location.

  - Enterprise-grade SNMP facilitates hands-off monitoring and alerting for key system metrics, including hardware, performance, and availability.

- Integrated authentication via standard directories (such as LDAP or Active Directory) and the ability to implement multiple authentication schemes enables enterprises to seamlessly deploy the Cisco WSA, while taking advantage of pre-existing authentication and access control policies within their networks.

- Extensive logging allows enterprises to keep track of all web traffic, benign and malware-related.

Cisco CWS

The Cisco CWS is a cloud-based method of implementing web security that is similar in function to the Cisco Web Security Appliance, which uses an on-premises appliance for web security. The Cisco CWS addresses the need for a corporate web security policy by offering a combination of web usage controls with category and reputation-based control, malware filtering, and data protection. The Cisco CWS is considered a Security as a Service (SaaS) product because no maintenance or upgrades are required. It provides real-time scanning and protection from malware, including previously unknown threats, called zero-day threats. The Cisco CWS is also known by its former name, ScanSafe.

The Cisco CWS data centers are located in the cloud and are geographically spread all over the world to provide this security service. These data centers are interconnected and redundant, so this network is characterized by the highest uptime and is very reliable. The Cisco CWS proxy servers in the worldwide data centers have visibility of various evolving network threats. This method provides the most effective defense against all types of malware.

Besides providing security services to onsite Internet users, the Cisco CWS also provides the same level of service to remote or mobile users who are using the Cisco AnyConnect Secure Mobility Client.

The Cisco CWS can be integrated with multiple Cisco network infrastructure elements to further enhance flexibility:

- **ASA connector:** The Cisco ASA integrates with the Cisco CWS to solve the combined problems of performance and breadth of security without affecting data center and network complexity.

- **ISR G2 connector:** You can save bandwidth, money, and resources by intelligently redirecting branch traffic to the cloud to enforce security and control policies away from the headquarters using a typical branch router such as the Integrated Services Router (ISR).

- **Cisco AnyConnect Secure Mobility Client with the Web Security Module:** Securely connects roaming users directly to the Internet through the nearest Cisco CWS proxy server. By eliminating the need to backhaul web traffic via VPN, Cisco CWS relieves web congestion at headquarters, reducing bandwidth usage while improving the end-user experience.

- **Web Security Appliance connector:** Processing is moved to the cloud, lifting the computing load from the on-premises Cisco WSA and centralizing management of access policy and reporting across the cloud.

Figure 3-2 shows the traffic flow when using an ASA in combination with Cisco CWS.

1. A user requests a URL via the web browser.

2. Traffic is sent to the Cisco ASA to go out to the Internet. The Cisco ASA performs the required NAT and, based on whether the protocol is HTTP or HTTPS, matches the traffic to the inside interface policy and gets redirected to the Cisco CWS.

3. The Cisco CWS analyzes the request based on the configuration done in the ScanCenter portal and, if the policy permits, forwards the request to approved sites.

4. The Cisco CWS inspects the returned traffic and redirects it to the Cisco ASA.

5. Based on the NAT session information, the Cisco ASA sends the traffic back to the users.

Figure 3-2   Cisco CWS Traffic Flow

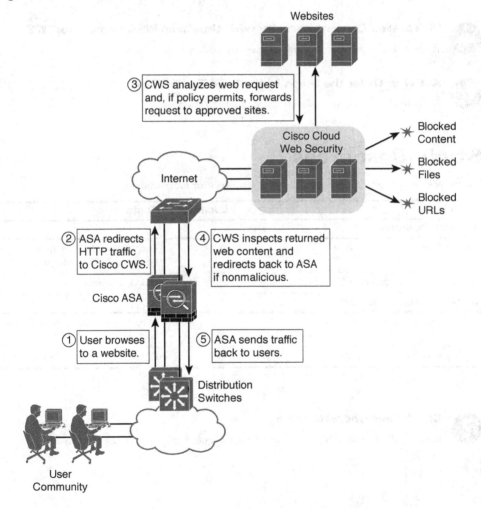

The Cisco CWS provides the following security features:

- **URL filtering:** Cloud Web Security uses URL filtering and Dynamic Content Analysis (DCA) to protect organizations from compliance, liability, and productivity risks by combining traditional URL filtering with real-time dynamic content analysis. The URL filtering database provides real-time coverage for known websites, while the Cisco DCA engine accurately identifies web content that URL filters would miss, using real-time dynamic categorization for unknown URLs.

- **Application Visibility and Control (AVC):** The Cisco CWS uses AVC to ensure acceptable use and security policy enforcement with deep application control for social networking, file sharing, games, IM, webmail, media, and more.

- **Reporting:** The Cisco CWS includes a business intelligence reporting tool to provide reporting from the cloud for analysis of web usage.

Video: Web Content Security with the Cisco WSA and Cisco CWS

Refer to the Digital Study Guide to view this video.

Activity: Order the Steps in the WSA Traffic Flow

Refer to the Digital Study Guide to complete this activity.

Study Resources

For today's exam topics, refer to the following resources for more study.

Resource	Location	Topic
Primary Resources		
CCNA Security Official Cert Guide	18	Mitigation Technology for Email-Based and Web-Based Threats
CCNA Security (Networking Academy Curriculum)	6	Endpoint Security
Supplemental Resources		
CCNA Security Complete Video Course	7	Mitigation Technologies for Email-based and Web-based Threats
CCNA Portable Command Guide	9	Endpoint and Content Protection

Check Your Understanding

Refer to the Digital Study Guide to take a ten-question quiz covering the content of this day.

Endpoint Protection

CCNA Security 210-260 IINS Exam Topics

- 7.3.a Anti-virus/anti-malware
- 7.3.b Personal firewall/HIPS
- 7.3.c Hardware/software encryption of local data

Key Topics

Today we will focus on the tools and methods used to protect the integrity of an endpoint. We will discuss personal firewalls and antivirus, antispyware, and antimalware solutions. Finally, we will look at using encryption to protect local data from theft.

Endpoint Security Overview

An important place to enforce security is at the endpoint, where data resides and the potential for damage is great. Endpoints can include devices such as laptops, mobile devices, and printers. Traditionally, endpoint security products such as the following have acted independently to provide endpoint protection:

- **Personal firewalls:** A personal firewall is typically a software program that is installed on an endpoint device to protect the device itself. Most modern operating systems have integrated personal firewalls.

- **Antivirus:** Antivirus is typically a software program that is installed on an endpoint device to prevent, detect, and remove the effects of malicious software on the endpoint. Antivirus software was originally developed to combat computer viruses. A virus is a type of malware that propagates by inserting a copy of itself into and becoming part of another program. It spreads from one computer to another, leaving infections as it travels. Viruses can range in severity from causing mildly annoying effects to damaging data or software and causing denial of service (DoS) conditions. To remain effective, antivirus software must be updated frequently.

- **Antispyware:** Antispyware is typically a software program that is installed on an endpoint to detect and remove spyware. Spyware is software that displays advertisements and tracks information on your endpoint device without your consent. Some types of spyware make changes to your endpoint device without your consent. These changes can be merely annoying or they can damage your device. To remain effective, antispyware must be updated frequently.

- **Malware analysis and protection:** Antivirus and antispyware tools certainly provide a line of defense, but their efficacy is declining. Today, it must be assumed that malware will penetrate an organization's network. Cisco Advanced Malware Protection (AMP) for

Endpoints offers protection against malware that has infiltrated an organization's network. It is an intelligent, enterprise-class advanced malware analysis and protection solution that uses big data, continuous analysis, and advanced analytics to detect, track, analyze, control, and block advanced malware outbreaks across all endpoints: PCs, Macs, mobile devices, and virtual systems.

Personal Firewalls

Personal firewalls protect a single host, in contrast to traditional firewalls. Traditional firewalls are installed at policy enforcement points between networks. Therefore, traditional firewalls control traffic arriving at and leaving networks, whereas personal firewalls control traffic arriving at and leaving individual hosts. Originally, personal firewalls were add-on systems for PC operating systems, but they have now been integrated into most modern operating systems. Pervasive use of personal firewalls can be used to implement a distributed firewall. A distributed firewall requires that the personal firewall policies are controlled by a centralized administration system. A distributed firewall can provide similar protection as a traditional firewall. If all the hosts on a network are configured to deny inbound HTTP, it is similar to a traditional firewall denying inbound HTTP to that network.

Personal firewalls can be important in the protection of systems that can be moved between networks. A laptop may be well protected by firewalls of an organization when it is within the campus network. But that laptop needs to protect itself when it is connected to an Internet service at an airport, hotel, coffee shop, or home of the user. Personal firewalls are an important tool when split tunneling is used for remote-access VPN. If the VPN client can access the Internet outside of the VPN tunnel, then likewise the Internet can access the client outside of the VPN tunnel. If there is a back door running on the VPN client, without a properly configured personal firewall, an attacker can access that back door and use the client VPN tunnel to access the internal network.

Personal firewalls have the ability to permit and deny traffic based on the application, regardless of the protocols and ports. Traffic is allowed to and from whitelisted applications and denied to and from blacklisted applications. When a new application attempts to use the network, the personal firewall may query the user whether the application should be whitelisted or blacklisted. This provides a level of protection against malware running as an executable program. Personal firewalls may also have the ability to define policies for different classes of networks, such as work, home, and public. When the personal firewall finds itself on a new network, it queries the user to identify the class of the network.

Antivirus

As the name suggests, antivirus software was originally developed to detect and remove computer viruses. But many other types of malware have emerged over the years, and antivirus software vendors have attempted to keep up. Examples of other types of malware that may be detected by antivirus software include keystroke loggers, back doors, root kits, browser hijackers, Trojan horses, and ransomware. The capabilities of antivirus software vary from vendor to vendor, as does the efficacy against any particular threat or class of threats. Unfortunately, the rate of malware proliferation is increasing and antivirus software efficacy is decreasing.

Most antivirus software uses signature-based detection. Antivirus software vendors analyze known malware, and catalog the characteristics that are used to recognize them in a signature database. Scanning files and memory for these signatures reveals the malware. The obvious shortcoming of this methodology is that it cannot protect against attacks that have not yet been recognized by the security industry, which are often called zero-day attacks.

Antivirus software may also use heuristics to detect malware. Heuristics allow for recognition on imprecise signature matches. Often malware will mutate over time into different variants. Sometimes, the intent of the mutation is simply to evade detection. Other times, the mutation is the result of the malware author adding new capabilities into the malware. The use of heuristics can help antivirus software to recognize entire classes or families of malware.

A third detection technique that may be used by antivirus software is behavioral-based detection. Instead of analyzing the code for signatures, the behavior of processes is monitored. If a process attempts to do something that is recognized as malicious, such as modifying another executable program or capturing keystroke information, behavioral-based analysis can detect the malware. This can provide a certain level of protection against zero-day threats.

Whatever combination of detection methods is employed by antivirus software, it is important to maintain the software databases. Most antivirus software has the ability to automatically check for and install updates on a regular basis.

Antispyware

As its name implies, spyware is software that attempts to gather information without raising awareness. Most people consider spyware to be undesirable, but not as malevolent as malware. The line between malware and spyware is blurred. For example, keystroke loggers gather information without raising awareness, so they may be considered spyware. But keystroke loggers are generally considered to be insidious enough to cross the line into malware. Adware is another related class of software. With adware, the user agrees to be exposed to advertisements in exchange for use of the software. Often adware tracks usage in different ways so that the advertisements are targeted to the user. When the behavior of the adware is clear and the user understands what they are trading for use of the software, then adware is not considered to be spyware or malware. However, if the adware is installed in such a way that the user is not aware that targeted advertisements will be displayed in their browser, then the software may be considered spyware. Also, if the adware covertly sends its tracking data to sites that will use the data to design phishing attacks against a particular target audience, then it has crossed the line into the territory of malware. Most commonly, spyware is implemented with tracking cookies in Internet browsers. Large retail sites may install tracking cookies, for example, and, based on what information they capture, show different content to the user with the intention of displaying merchandise that will interest the user and lead to increased sales.

The emerging prevalence of spyware led to the development of a whole new class of security applications known as antispyware. Just as the line is blurred between what is malware and what is spyware, the line between what antivirus software and antispyware software detect and mitigate is blurred. There is often a level of overlapping protection between the two types of systems.

Antimalware

Due to the nature of malware threats in current networking environments, even the best commercial products for malware detection can realistically achieve only about 40 percent success in detection. Most enterprises implement multiple layers of protection, so malware that makes it to an endpoint defeats all the safeguards. This means that to effectively deal with malware, you have to assume that at some point it will make its way into your networks and potentially persist for long periods of time before it is detected and acted upon.

With malware, endpoints must be protected before, during, and after attacks. Cisco Advanced Malware Protection (AMP) for Endpoints goes beyond point-in-time detection to provide the level of visibility and control you need to stop advanced threats that are missed by other security layers. It provides that protection across the attack continuum: before, during, and after an attack. Cisco AMP for Endpoints is an intelligent, enterprise-class advanced malware analysis and protection solution that

- Provides cloud-based detection of malware through the Cisco Collective Security Intelligence Cloud for rapid detection of known malware.

- Gives a historical perspective so that you can see, over time, the actions that files performed on a system. You can trace back an infection and identify the root cause by following the malware's file and device trajectory.

- Blocks malicious network connections based on IP reputation.

- Retrospectively alerts a system if a file that was previously seen changes disposition.

- Allows for the creation of custom signatures for malware detection.

Figure 2-1 shows the elements of Cisco AMP for Endpoints.

Figure 2-1   Cisco AMP for Endpoints

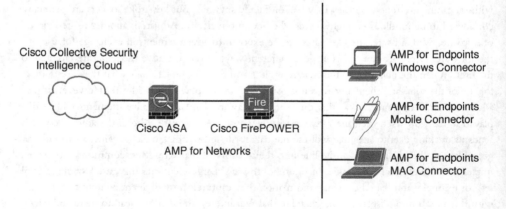

- **Cisco Collective Security Intelligence Cloud:** This is where the various detection and analytics engines reside.

- **Client Connector:** This is the component that runs on the endpoints. It communicates with the cloud to send information about files and to receive file disposition information.

- **Cisco AMP for Endpoints Windows:** Supports Windows XP through to Windows 10, as well as versions of Microsoft Windows Server.

- **Cisco AMP for Endpoints Mobile:** An application that you can install on a mobile device to communicate with the cloud for detection of mobile malware. Currently, only the Android operating system is supported. Cisco AMP for Endpoints Mobile is supported on Android 2.1 and higher.

- **Cisco AMP for Endpoints Mac Connector:** Supports Apple devices running OS X 10.7 or higher. This connector has a limited graphical interface that you can access from the menu bar, if you choose it as an installation option in the Mac policy.

- **Cisco AMP for Networks:** Gives FirePOWER devices the ability to query the cloud to obtain file disposition information on files that are detected by the FirePOWER device.

Data Encryption

Endpoints are also susceptible to data theft. For instance, if a corporate laptop is lost or stolen, a thief could scour the hard drive for sensitive information, contact information, personal information, and more.

The solution is to locally encrypt the disk drive with a strong encryption algorithm such as 256-bit AES encryption. The encryption protects the confidential data from unauthorized access. The encrypted disk volumes can only be mounted for normal read/write access with the authorized password.

Some operating systems, such as OS X, natively provide encryption options. The Windows operating system supports encryption software such as BitLocker, TrueCrypt, Credant, VeraCrypt, and others.

Video: Endpoint Security Technologies

Refer to the Digital Study Guide to view this video.

Activity: Identify Endpoint Security Technologies

Refer to the Digital Study Guide to complete this activity.

Study Resources

For today's exam topics, refer to the following resources for more study.

Resource	Location	Topic
Primary Resources		
CCNA Security Official Cert Guide	19	Mitigation Technology for Endpoint Threats
CCNA Security (Networking Academy Curriculum)	6	Endpoint Security
Supplemental Resources		
CCNA Security Complete Video Course	8	Mitigation Technology for Endpoint Threats
CCNA Portable Command Guide	9	Endpoint and Content Protection

Check Your Understanding

Refer to the Digital Study Guide to take a ten-question quiz covering the content of this day.

CCNA Security Skills Review and Practice

CCNA Security 210-260 IINS Exam Topics

- No exam topics

Key Topics

Tomorrow you take the CCNA Security exam. Therefore, today you should take the time to do some relaxed skimming of all the previous days' topics, focusing on areas where you are still weak. If you have access to a timed practice exam such as the one available in the *CCNA Security 210-260 Official Cert Guide*, use it to help isolate areas in which you might need a little further study.

Included as part of this book is a CCNA Security Skills Practice that covers most of the CCNA Security configuration skills in one topology. This scenario should help you quickly review many of the commands covered by the CCNA Security exam.

CCNA Security Skills Practice

This practice example includes most of the skills covered in the CCNA Security exam topics, but also assumes a good understanding of CCENT exam skill topics.

Introduction

In this comprehensive CCNA Security skills activity, the Groot Corporation uses a site-to-site IPsec VPN to connect its headquarters with a branch office, while teleworkers use an SSL clientless VPN to access an internal private HTTP server. A public HTTP server is also hosted in the headquarters' DMZ and is available for Internet-hosted devices. The branch router uses a Cisco IOS Zone-Based Policy Firewall (ZPF) to protect its local users. Both the headquarters and branch use PAT for address translation when accessing the Internet but use their private addresses when communicating directly with each other. Security best practices are also used on all Cisco devices.

You are responsible for configuring the HQ-ASA, R1_BRANCH, and HQ_SW.

Topology Diagram

Figure 1-1 shows the topology for the CCNA Security skills practice.

Figure 1-1   CCNA Security Skills Practice Topology

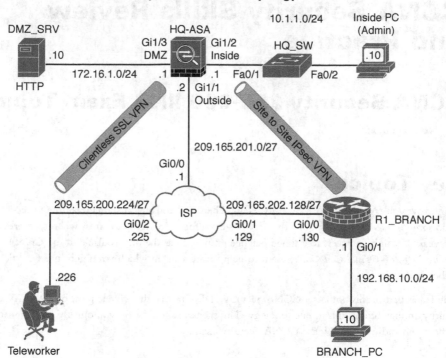

Addressing Table

Table 1-1 shows the addressing scheme for the network shown in Figure 1-1.

Table 1-1   CCNA Security Skills Practice Addressing Scheme

Device	Interface	IP Address	Subnet Mask
HQ-ASA	Gi0/1	209.165.201.2	255.255.255.224
	Gi0/2	10.1.1.1	255.255.255.0
	Gi0/3	172.16.1.1	255.255.255.0
R1_BRANCH	Gi0/0	209.165.202.130	255.255.255.224
	Gi0/1	192.168.10.1	255.255.255.0
HQ_SW	VLAN 1	10.1.1.2	255.255.255.0
Internet	Gi0/0	209.165.201.1	255.255.255.224
	Gi0/1	209.165.202.129	255.255.255.224
	Gi0/2	209.165.200.225	255.255.255.224

ISP Configuration

If you choose to configure this network on real equipment or a network simulator, use the script in Example 1-1 to configure the ISP. Use a router with at least three LAN interfaces or a multilayer switch to simulate the ISP. Start an HTTP daemon on the Inside PC and the DMZ_SRV for testing later in the lab.

Example 1-1   ISP Configuration

```
hostname INTERNET
!
interface GigabitEthernet0/0
 ip address 209.165.201.1 255.255.255.224
 no shutdown
!
interface GigabitEthernet0/1
 ip address 209.165.202.129 255.255.255.224
 no shutdown
!
interface GigabitEthernet0/2
 ip address 209.165.200.225 255.255.255.224
 no shutdown
```

Implementation

Implement the following requirements using the provided documentation.

Step 1: Cable the Network As Shown in the Topology

Attach the devices as shown in the topology diagram in Figure 1-1, and cable as necessary.

Step 2: Configure Initial Settings for R1_BRANCH

1. Configure a hostname of **R1_BRANCH**.

2. Configure the interface IP addresses, as shown in the IP addressing table (see Table 1-1).

3. Disable DNS lookup.

4. Configure a static default route that points to the 209.165.202.129 address.

5. Configure a minimum password length of ten characters.

6. Configure an enable secret password of **31daysenable** using the SCRYPT algorithm.

7. Encrypt plaintext passwords.

8. Configure the local user database with a user of **admin** and a SCRYPT secret password of **31daysadmin** with a privilege level of 15.

9. Enable AAA services globally.

10. Implement AAA services using the local database by configuring the default login authentication method list to use case-sensitive local authentication as the first option and the enable password as the backup option.

11. Configure a domain name of **31days.com**.

12. Configure the incoming vty lines to only accept SSH connections. Set the **exec-timeout** to log out after 15 minutes of inactivity. Prevent line messages from interrupting the command entry.

13. Configure the console line to set the **exec-timeout** to log out after 15 minutes of inactivity. Prevent console messages from interrupting the command entry.

14. Generate the RSA encryption key pair with 1024 as the number of modulus bits.

15. Configure the SSH version to only accept version 2 connections.

16. Configure enhanced login security. If a user fails two login attempts within a 30-second time span, then disable logins for 1 minute. Log all failed login attempts.

17. Configure a warning to unauthorized users with a message-of-the-day (MOTD) banner that says: Unauthorized access strictly prohibited and prosecuted to the full extent of the law!

18. Configure NAT Overload (PAT) on the Gi0/0 interface.

19. Ping from Branch PC to Teleworker PC to test connectivity.

20. SSH from Branch PC to R1_BRANCH router to test connectivity and authentication.

Step 3: Configure Initial Settings for HQ_SW

1. Configure a hostname of **HQ_SW**.

2. Configure an enable secret password of **31daysenable** using the SCRYPT algorithm.

3. Encrypt plaintext passwords.

4. Disable DNS lookup.

5. Configure the VLAN 1 management address, as shown in the IP addressing table (see Table 1-1), and enable the interface.

6. Configure the IP default gateway using the HQ-ASA's Gi0/2 address.

7. Configure a vty line password of **31dayslinevty** and enable login. Set the **exec-timeout** value to log out after 5 minutes of inactivity. Prevent line messages from interrupting the command entry.

8. Configure a console password of **31daysconsole** and enable login. Configure the console line to set the exec-timeout to log out after 5 minutes of inactivity. Prevent console messages from interrupting the command entry.

9. Disable HTTP and HTTPS access.

10. Configure port Fa0/1 on S1 as a trunk port. Disable DTP.

11. Configure port Fa0/2 as access mode only. Enable PortFast. Enable BPDU Guard. Enable Port Security with a maximum of two dynamically learned sticky MAC addresses.

12. Disable all unused ports.

13. Ping from HQ_SW to HQ Inside PC (10.1.1.10) to test connectivity.

14. Telnet from HQ Inside PC to HQ_SW to test connectivity and authentiction.

Step 4: Configure Initial Settings for HQ-ASA

1. Configure a hostname of **HQ-ASA**.

2. Configure an encrypted enable secret password of **31daysenable**.

3. Configure interface Gi1/1 as outside, with a security level of 0, and an IP address of 209.165.201.2/27.

4. Configure interface Gi1/2 as inside, with a security level of 100, and an IP address of 10.1.1.1/24.

5. Configure interface Gi1/3 as dmz, with a security level of 50, and an IP address of 172.16.1.1/24.

6. Configure the ASA as a DHCP server for the inside network with a range of addresses from 10.1.1.100 to 10.1.1.150.

7. Enable HTTPS access from the inside network.

8. Configure PAT using the IP address of the outside interface for any source.

9. Configure a static default route for the outside interface with a next hop of 209.165.201.1.

10. Generate the RSA encryption key pair with 1024 as the number of modulus bits.

11. Configure SSH access from the inside network.

12. Configure the local user database with a user of **admin** and a secret password of **31daysadmin** with a privilege level of 15.

13. Implement AAA services using the local database by configuring the default login authentication method list to use local authentication for HTTPS and SSH access.

14. Configure static NAT from outside devices to the DMZ server using a public address of 209.165.201.10.

15. Modify the Modular Policy Framework firewall default inspection policy to include ICMP.

16. Modify the default firewall access rules to allow HTTP access from any outside source to the DMZ server.

Step 5: Configure Clientless SSL VPN

Using the ASDM wizard, configure HQ-ASA to allow the Teleworker PC to establish a clientless SSL VPN connection and access the Inside PC via HTTP. Use the following parameters in your configuration:

1. Use a connection profile name of **HQ_teleworkers**.

2. Use the **outside** interface for terminating the SSL VPNs.

3. Create a connection group alias of **HQ**.

4. Create a local user of **teleworker** with a password of **31daystele**.

5. Create a new group policy of **HQ_teleworkers**.

6. Create a new bookmark list called **HQ_bookmarks** with a URL named **HQ_webserver** for the Inside PC at http://10.1.1.10.

After sending the configuration to the ASA, use the Teleworker PC to connect to https://209.165.201.2/HQ. After accepting the certificate and authenticating with the **teleworker/31daystele** credentials, click the **HQ_webserver** bookmark to access the 10.1.1.10 web server. The landing page of the HTTP daemon should display.

Step 6: Configure Site-to-Site IPsec VPN

Using the ASDM wizard on the ASA, and the CLI on R1_BRANCH, configure a site-to-site IPsec VPN between HQ-ASA and R1_BRANCH. The VPN will be used to encrypt data when devices on the ASA's inside network and the Branch Gi0/1 LAN communicate with each other.

For the ASA, use the following parameters in your ASDM configuration:

1. Use a peer IP address of 209.165.202.130.

2. Use the outside interface to terminate the VPN.

3. Encrypt traffic from the local network of 10.1.1.0/24 to the remote network of 192.168.10.0/24.

4. Using the Simple Configuration option, enter a pre-shared key of **VPNpass**.

5. Enable NAT exempt for the inside interface. This will bypass NAT when the 10.1.1.0/24 network is communicating with the 192.168.10.0/24 network.

For the R1_BRANCH router, use the following parameters in your configuration:

1. Define an ISAKMP policy using AES-256, DH group 5, pre-shared password authentication.

2. Use a password of **VPNpass** when authenticating the VPN peer at 209.165.201.2.

3. Define an IPsec transform set using ESP-AES-256 and ESP-SHA-HMAC in tunnel mode.

4. Create a crypto ACL to match the source network (192.168.10.0/24) and the destination network (10.1.1.0/24) for all IP traffic.

5. Create and apply a crypto map to the Gi0/0 interface, setting the peer at 209.165.201.2 and assigning the newly created transform set and the crypto ACL.

6. One last important detail needs to be configured on the router. Since PAT was implemented earlier, the PAT ACL needs to be modified to deny translation when the 192.168.10.0/24 network is communicating with the 10.1.1.0/24 network, while still allowing PAT when the 192.168.10.0/24 network is communicating with the Internet. This step is similar to the NAT Exempt step accomplished on the ASA.

Pings between the BRANCH_PC and the Inside PC should trigger the VPN and travel encrypted across the Internet. Confirm this by using the **show crypto isakmp sa** and **show crypto ipsec sa** commands on R1_BRANCH, as shown in Example 1-2.

Example 1-2   Site-to-Site IPsec VPN Verification

```
R1_BRANCH# sh crypto isakmp sa
IPv4 Crypto ISAKMP SA
dst               src             state          conn-id status
209.165.201.2    209.165.202.130 QM_IDLE           1007 ACTIVE


R1_BRANCH# show crypto ipsec sa

interface: GigabitEthernet0/0
    Crypto map tag: BRANCHMAP, local addr 209.165.202.130

   protected vrf: (none)
   local  ident (addr/mask/prot/port): (192.168.10.0/255.255.255.0/0/0)
   remote ident (addr/mask/prot/port): (10.1.1.0/255.255.255.0/0/0)
   current_peer 209.165.201.2 port 500
     PERMIT, flags={origin_is_acl,}
    #pkts encaps: 16, #pkts encrypt: 16, #pkts digest: 16
    #pkts decaps: 16, #pkts decrypt: 16, #pkts verify: 16
    #pkts compressed: 0, #pkts decompressed: 0
    #pkts not compressed: 0, #pkts compr. failed: 0
    #pkts not decompressed: 0, #pkts decompress failed: 0
    #send errors 0, #recv errors 0

     local crypto endpt.: 209.165.202.130, remote crypto endpt.: 209.165.201.2
     plaintext mtu 1438, path mtu 1500, ip mtu 1500, ip mtu idb GigabitEthernet0/0
     current outbound spi: 0x713ACC25(1899678757)
     PFS (Y/N): N, DH group: none

     inbound esp sas:
      spi: 0xFB9C325A(4221317722)
        transform: esp-256-aes esp-sha-hmac ,
        in use settings ={Tunnel, }
```

```
          conn id: 2009, flow_id: Onboard VPN:9, sibling_flags 80004040, crypto map:
             BRANCHMAP
          sa timing: remaining key lifetime (k/sec): (4373423/3475)
          IV size: 16 bytes
          replay detection support: Y
          Status: ACTIVE(ACTIVE)

        outbound esp sas:
         spi: 0x713ACC25(1899678757)
            transform: esp-256-aes esp-sha-hmac ,
            in use settings ={Tunnel, }
            conn id: 2010, flow_id: Onboard VPN:10, sibling_flags 80004040, crypto map:
               BRANCHMAP
            sa timing: remaining key lifetime (k/sec): (4373423/3475)
            IV size: 16 bytes
            replay detection support: Y
            Status: ACTIVE(ACTIVE)
```

Step 7: Configure a Zone-Based Policy Firewall

Using the CLI, configure a ZPF on the R1_BRANCH router. Many steps are required to maintain network functionality while still protecting the Branch LAN. Use the following parameters in your configuration:

1. Define an inside zone and an outside zone.

2. Create an extended ACL for ICMP traffic (echo, echo-reply, traceroute) from any source to any destination.

3. Create an extended ACL for SSH access from any source to any destination. This will be used to maintain SSH accessibility from outside devices to the router.

4. Create an extended ACL for ISAKMP/IPsec traffic from any source to any destination.

5. Define an Internet protocols inspect class map matching any of the following Internet protocols: ICMP, TCP, UDP, HTTP, HTTPS, POP3, POP3S, SMTP.

6. Define an ICMP inspect class map matching the ICMP access list.

7. Define an ISAKMP/IPsec inspect class map matching the ISAKMP/IPsec access list.

8. Define an inspect class map matching the SSH access list.

9. Create an inspect policy map for inside to outside traffic that will inspect the Internet protocols class map and the ICMP class map but drop the default class map.

10. Create an inspect policy map for outside to router traffic that will inspect the SSH class map, the ICMP class map, and the ISAKMP/IPsec class map but drop the default class map.

11. Create an inspect policy map for outside to inside traffic that will inspect the ICMP class map but drop the default class map.

12. Create an inside to outside zone pair and assign the inside to outside policy map as its service policy.

13. Create an outside to self zone pair and assign the outside to router policy map as its service policy.

14. Create an outside to inside zone pair and assign the outside to inside policy map as its service policy.

15. Assign Gi0/0 as a member of the outside zone.

16. Assign Gi0/1 as a member of the inside zone.

Verify that the BRANCH_PC can still establish a secure VPN connection with the Inside PC.

Verify that the Teleworker PC can establish an SSH connection with the Branch router.

Verify that ICMP traffic is still allowed through the Branch router.

Verify that the BRANCH_PC can still access the web server hosted in the DMZ off of HQ-ASA.

Answers to CCNA Security Skills Practice

The following are the scripts you would enter for each of the configuration steps described in the preceding skills practice.

Step 1: Cable the Network As Shown in the Topology

No script is required.

Step 2: Configure Initial Settings for R1_BRANCH

```
!-----------
! R1_BRANCH
!-----------
hostname R1_BRANCH
!
service password-encryption
!
security passwords min-length 10
enable secret 9 $9$qjtRkSeB56rxLU$MyznvwOiYJpq5oopTzUbaIj9IkinG785PVn6ubPZ00s
!
aaa new-model
!
aaa authentication login default local-case enable
!
no ip domain lookup
ip domain name 31days.com
login block-for 60 attempts 2 within 30
```

```
login on-failure log
!
username admin privilege 15 secret 9 $9$Dyk3vJ02FJ.Wg.$dvjhsdzHvMGzCgj6VnVwhAbzqoxy
   t78CI3KxDPNmQgg
!
crypto key generate rsa general-keys modulus 1024
ip ssh version 2
!
interface GigabitEthernet0/0
 ip address 209.165.202.130 255.255.255.224
 ip nat outside
 ip virtual-reassembly in
!
interface GigabitEthernet0/1
 ip address 192.168.10.1 255.255.255.0
 ip nat inside
 ip virtual-reassembly in
!
ip nat inside source list 102 interface GigabitEthernet0/0 overload
ip route 0.0.0.0 0.0.0.0 209.165.202.129
!
access-list 102 permit ip 192.168.10.0 0.0.0.255 any
!
banner motd ^CUnauthorized access strictly prohibited and prosecuted to the full
   extent of the law!^C
!
line con 0
 exec-timeout 15 0
 password 7 101D581D040E0108030A3924282D
 logging synchronous
line vty 0 4
 exec-timeout 15 0
 password 7 115A4801160B18000D242E323C2A
 logging synchronous
 transport input ssh
!
```

Step 3: Configure Initial Settings for HQ_SW

```
!-----------
! HQ_SW
!-----------
hostname HQ_SW
!
service password-encryption
!
```

```
enable secret 9 $9$y1VZ0p6XgOOZeb$CjykddM2fZzQFLJfEbUsJE7TKcWrg/m9hF4aAsrT4ps
!
interface FastEthernet0/1
 switchport mode trunk
 switchport nonegotiate
!
interface FastEthernet0/2
 switchport mode access
 switchport port-security maximum 2
 switchport port-security
 switchport port-security mac-address sticky
 spanning-tree portfast
 spanning-tree bpduguard enable
!
interface range Fa0/3-24
 shutdown
!
interface Vlan1
 ip address 10.1.1.2 255.255.255.0
!
ip default-gateway 10.1.1.1
no ip http server
no ip http secure-server
!
banner motd ^CUnauthorized access strictly prohibited and prosecuted to the full
  extent of the law!^C
!
line con 0
 exec-timeout 5 0
 password 7 15415A0805333827273D262D1F02
 logging synchronous
 login
line vty 0 4
 exec-timeout 5 0
 password 7 06555E254D571A150C19171D181D
 logging synchronous
 login
```

Step 4: Configure Initial Settings for HQ-ASA

```
!----------
! HQ-ASA
!----------
hostname HQ-ASA
enable password AZ9LkA7H6paEqCfW encrypted
interface GigabitEthernet1/1
```

```
 nameif outside
 security-level 0
 ip address 209.165.201.2 255.255.255.224
!
interface GigabitEthernet1/2
 nameif inside
 security-level 100
 ip address 10.1.1.1 255.255.255.0
!
interface GigabitEthernet1/3
 nameif dmz
 security-level 50
 ip address 172.16.1.1 255.255.255.0
!
object network obj_any
 subnet 0.0.0.0 0.0.0.0
object network NETWORK_OBJ_10.1.1.0_24
 subnet 10.1.1.0 255.255.255.0
object network dmz-server
 host 172.16.1.10
!
access-list outside_access_in extended permit tcp any object dmz-server eq www
!
object network obj_any
 nat (any,outside) dynamic interface
object network dmz-server
 nat (dmz,outside) static 209.165.201.10
access-group outside_access_in in interface outside
route outside 0.0.0.0 0.0.0.0 209.165.201.1 1
!
aaa authentication http console LOCAL
aaa authentication ssh console LOCAL
username admin password 895MGhX7fmySfp4W encrypted privilege 15
http server enable
http 10.1.1.0 255.255.255.0 inside
!
ssh 10.1.1.0 255.255.255.0 inside
ssh timeout 5
ssh key-exchange group dh-group1-sha1
!
dhcpd address 10.1.1.100-10.1.1.150 inside
dhcpd enable inside
!
class-map inspection_default
 match default-inspection-traffic
```

```
!
!
policy-map global_policy
 class inspection_default
  inspect dns preset_dns_map
  inspect ftp
  inspect h323 h225
  inspect h323 ras
  inspect rsh
  inspect rtsp
  inspect esmtp
  inspect sqlnet
  inspect skinny
  inspect sunrpc
  inspect xdmcp
  inspect sip
  inspect netbios
  inspect tftp
  inspect ip-options
  inspect icmp
!
service-policy global_policy global
```

Step 5: Configure Clientless SSL VPN

```
!-----------
! HQ-ASA
!-----------
webvpn
 enable outside
 error-recovery disable
group-policy DfltGrpPolicy attributes
 vpn-tunnel-protocol ikev1 l2tp-ipsec ssl-clientless
!
group-policy HQ_teleworkers internal
group-policy HQ_teleworkers attributes
 vpn-tunnel-protocol ssl-clientless
 webvpn
  url-list value HQ_bookmarks
dynamic-access-policy-record DfltAccessPolicy
username teleworker password 9bUt4WTKYdXU7/J8 encrypted privilege 0
username teleworker attributes
 vpn-group-policy HQ_teleworkers
tunnel-group 31days_teleworker type remote-access
tunnel-group 31days_teleworker general-attributes
```

```
default-group-policy HQ_teleworkers
tunnel-group 31days_teleworker webvpn-attributes
 group-alias HQ enable
 group-url https://209.165.201.2/HQ enable
```

Step 6: Configure Site-to-Site IPsec VPN

```
!-----------
! HQ-ASA
!-----------
object network Branch_net
 subnet 192.168.10.0 255.255.255.0
access-list outside_cryptomap extended permit ip 10.1.1.0 255.255.255.0 object
  Branch_net
access-list outside_cryptomap_1 extended permit ip 10.1.1.0 255.255.255.0 object
  Branch_net
nat (inside,outside) source static NETWORK_OBJ_10.1.1.0_24 NETWORK_OBJ_10.1.1.0_24
  destination static Branch_net Branch_net no-proxy-arp route-lookup
!
crypto ipsec ikev1 transform-set ESP-AES-256-SHA esp-aes-256 esp-sha-hmac
crypto ipsec security-association pmtu-aging infinite
crypto map outside_map 1 match address outside_cryptomap
crypto map outside_map 1 set peer 209.165.202.130
crypto map outside_map 1 set ikev1 transform-set ESP-AES-256-SHA
crypto map outside_map 2 match address outside_cryptomap_1
crypto map outside_map 2 set peer 209.165.202.130
crypto map outside_map 2 set ikev1 transform-set ESP-AES-128-SHA ESP-AES-128-MD5
ESP-AES-192-SHA ESP-AES-192-MD5 ESP-AES-256-SHA ESP-AES-256-MD5 ESP-3DES-SHA ESP-
3DES-MD5 ESP-DES-SHA ESP-DES-MD5
crypto map outside_map interface outside
crypto ca trustpool policy
crypto ikev1 enable outside
crypto ikev1 policy 1
 authentication pre-share
 encryption aes-256
 hash sha
 group 5
group-policy GroupPolicy_209.165.202.130 internal
group-policy GroupPolicy_209.165.202.130 attributes
 vpn-tunnel-protocol ikev1
tunnel-group 209.165.202.130 type ipsec-l2l
tunnel-group 209.165.202.130 general-attributes
 default-group-policy GroupPolicy_209.165.202.130
tunnel-group 209.165.202.130 ipsec-attributes
 ikev1 pre-shared-key VPNpass
```

```
!-----------
| R1_BRANCH
!-----------
crypto isakmp policy 10
 encr aes 256
 authentication pre-share
 group 5
 lifetime 3600
crypto isakmp key VPNpass address 209.165.201.2
!
crypto ipsec transform-set BR_to_HQ esp-aes 256 esp-sha-hmac
 mode tunnel
!
crypto map BRANCHMAP 10 ipsec-isakmp
 set peer 209.165.201.2
 set transform-set BR_to_HQ
 match address 101
!
interface GigabitEthernet0/0
 crypto map BRANCHMAP
!
access-list 101 permit ip 192.168.10.0 0.0.0.255 10.1.1.0 0.0.0.255
!
! ***** Delete access-list 102 before creating this new version
! ***** This allows PAT to work with split tunneling
access-list 102 deny    ip 192.168.10.0 0.0.0.255 10.1.1.0 0.0.0.255
access-list 102 permit ip 192.168.10.0 0.0.0.255 any
```

Step 7: Configure a Zone-Based Policy Firewall

```
!-----------
| R1_BRANCH
!-----------
class-map type inspect match-any Internet-cmap
 match protocol icmp
 match protocol tcp
 match protocol udp
 match protocol http
 match protocol https
 match protocol pop3
 match protocol pop3s
 match protocol smtp
class-map type inspect match-all ICMP-cmap
 match access-group name ICMP
```

```
class-map type inspect match-all IPSEC-cmap
 match access-group name ISAKMP_IPSEC
class-map type inspect match-all SSHaccess-cmap
 match access-group name SSHaccess
!
policy-map type inspect inside-outside-pmap
 class type inspect Internet-cmap
  inspect
 class type inspect ICMP-cmap
  inspect
 class class-default
  drop
policy-map type inspect Outside-Router-pmap
 class type inspect SSHaccess-cmap
  inspect
 class type inspect ICMP-cmap
  inspect
 class type inspect IPSEC-cmap
  pass
 class class-default
  drop
policy-map type inspect outside-inside-pmap
 class type inspect ICMP-cmap
  inspect
 class class-default
  drop
!
zone security inside
zone security outside
zone-pair security inside-to-outside source inside destination outside
 service-policy type inspect inside-outside-pmap
zone-pair security outside-to-router source outside destination self
 service-policy type inspect Outside-Router-pmap
zone-pair security outside-to-inside source outside destination inside
 service-policy type inspect outside-inside-pmap
!
interface GigabitEthernet0/0
 zone-member security outside
!
interface GigabitEthernet0/1
 zone-member security inside
!
ip access-list extended ICMP
 permit icmp any any echo
 permit icmp any any echo-reply
```

```
 permit icmp any any traceroute
ip access-list extended ISAKMP_IPSEC
 permit udp any any eq isakmp
 permit ahp any any
 permit esp any any
 permit udp any any eq non500-isakmp
ip access-list extended SSHaccess
 permit tcp any any eq 22
```

Exam Day

Today is your opportunity to prove that you have what it takes to develop a secure network infrastructure, recognize threats and vulnerabilities to networks, and mitigate those threats. Just 90 minutes and up to 60 to 70 questions stand between you and your CCNA Security certification. Use the following information to focus on the process details for the day of your CCNA Security exam.

What You Need for the Exam

Remember the following items on exam day:

- Write down the exam location, date, exam time, exam center phone number, and the proctor's name on a piece of paper and take it with you to the exam center.

- You must have two forms of ID that include a photo and signature such as a driver's license, passport, or military identification. In addition, the test center admission process requires the capture of a digital photo and digital signature.

- The test proctor will take you through the agreement and set up your testing station after you have signed the agreement.

- The test proctor will give you a sheet of scratch paper or a dry erase pad. Do not take these out of the room.

- The testing center will store any personal items while you take the exam. It is best to bring only what you will need.

- You will be monitored during the entire exam.

What You Should Receive After Completion

When you complete the exam, you will see an immediate electronic response as to whether you passed or failed. The proctor will give you a certified score report with the following important information:

- Your score report including the minimum passing score and your score on the exam. The report will also include a breakout displaying your percentage for each general exam topic.

- Identification information that you will need to track your certification. *Do not lose your certified examination score report.*

Summary

Your state of mind is a key factor in your success on the CCNA Security exam. If you know the details of the exam topics and the details of the exam process you can begin the exam with confidence and focus. Arrive early to the exam. Bring earplugs in the off chance that a testing neighbor has a bad cough or any loud nervous habits. Do not let an extremely difficult or specific question impede your progress. Answer each question confidently and move on.

Post-Exam Information

The accomplishment of signing up for and actually taking the CCNA Security exam is no small feat. Many network engineers have avoided certification exams for years. The following sections discuss your options after exam day.

Receiving Your Certificate

If you passed the exam, you will receive your official Cisco certificate in about six weeks (eight weeks internationally) after exam day. Your certificate will be mailed to the address you provided when you registered for the exam.

You need your examination score report to access the certification tracking system and set up a login to check your certification status. If you do not receive your certificate, open a case in the certificate online support located at the following web address:

https://ciscocert.secure.force.com/english/MainPage

When you receive your certificate, you may want to frame it and put it on a wall. A certificate hanging on a wall is much harder to lose than a certificate in a filing cabinet or random folder. You never know when an employer or academic institution could request a copy. It is also possible to electronically publish your credentials, to prove the status of your certifications. You do this by logging into https://cisco.pearsoncred.com with your Cisco.com ID.

Your CCNA Security certification is valid for three years. To keep your certificate valid after three years, you must either pass the CCNA Security exam again or pass a more advanced Cisco certification before the end of the three-year period.

U.S. Government Recognition

Recently, the U.S. National Security Agency (NSA) and the Committee on National Security Systems (CNSS) recognized that the Cisco CCNA Security certification courseware meets the CNSS 4011 training standard. This standard is intended for Information Security professionals who are responsible for identifying system vulnerabilities, investigating and documenting system security technologies and policies, and analyzing and evaluating system security technologies. As such, candidates who meet the standard are issued a letter of recognition acknowledging their completion of the recommended training requirements. This letter of recognition can be used as confirmation of having met the CNSS 4011 requirements and is sent along with the certificate.

Furthermore, the U.S. Department of Defense has certified the Cisco CCNA Security certification as DoD 8570.01-M compliant and has approved it for DoD Information Assurance Technician Levels I and II. The CCNA Security certification also meets the ISO 17024 standard accredited by ANSI.

Examining Certification Options

After passing the CCNA Security exam, you may wish to pursue a higher-level Cisco security certification. The hierarchy of Cisco security certifications, from low to high, is as follows:

1. Cisco Certified Entry Networking Technician (CCENT)

2. Cisco Certified Network Associate Security (CCNA Security)

3. Cisco Certified Network Professional Security (CCNP Security)

4. Cisco Certified Internetwork Expert Security (CCIE Security)

Although passing one of the many CCNA exams is not an easy task, it is the starting point for more advanced Cisco certifications such as the Cisco Certified Network Professional exams. To learn more about Cisco certifications, visit The Cisco Learning Network at https://learningnetwork.cisco.com/community/certifications.

If You Failed the Exam

If you fail your first attempt at the CCNA Security certification, you must wait at least 5 calendar days after the day of the exam to retest. Stay motivated and sign up to take the exam again within a 30-day period of your first attempt. The score report outlines your weaknesses. Find a study group and use The Cisco Learning Network (http://learningnetwork.cisco.com) online community to help you with those difficult topics.

If you are familiar with the general concepts, focus on taking practice exams and memorizing the small details that make the exam so difficult. If you are a Cisco Networking Academy alumnus, you have access to the curriculum and the Packet Tracer network simulator. Consider your first attempt as a formal practice exam and excellent preparation to pass the second attempt.

Summary

Whether you display your certificate and update your resume or prepare to conquer the exam on your second attempt, remember to marvel at the innovation and creativity behind each concept you learn. The ability of our society to continually improve and secure communication will keep you learning, discovering, and employed for a lifetime.

Index

E

X - Y

X.509 standard, 25

Z

zone-based policy firewall
  configuration skills practice, 288-289,
  295-297

ZPF (Zone-Based Policy Firewalls)
  benefits of, 210
  C3PL and ZPF configuration, 210-211,
    216-218
      class maps, 214-215
      policy maps, 215
  C3PL and ZPL configuration, 216-218
      class maps, 212-215
      policy maps, 212-215
      service policies, 213
  DMZ-private policies, 210
  private-DMZ policies, 210
  private-public policies, 210
  public-DMZ policies, 209
  self zones, 211
  traffic flows, 209, 213-214
  verifying, 217-218
  zone pairs, 211, 214
  zones, 211-214